An American Cardinal

An American Cardinal

The Biography of Cardinal Timothy Dolan

Christina Boyle

ST. MARTIN'S PRESS ❧ NEW YORK

AN AMERICAN CARDINAL. Copyright © 2014 by Christina Boyle. All rights reserved. Printed in the United States of America. For information, address St. Martin's Press, 175 Fifth Avenue, New York, N.Y. 10010.

www.stmartins.com

Design by Omar Chapa

Library of Congress Cataloging-in-Publication Data

Boyle, Christina.
 An American Cardinal : the biography of Cardinal Timothy Dolan / Christina Boyle. — First Edition.
  pages cm
  ISBN 978-1-250-03287-4 (hardcover)
  ISBN 978-1-250-03288-1 (e-book)
  1. Dolan, Timothy Michael.   2. Cardinals—United States—Biography.   I. Title.
  BX4705.D57B69 2014
  282.092—dc23
  [B]

2014028470

St. Martin's Press books may be purchased for educational, business, or promotional use. For information on bulk purchases, please contact Macmillan Corporate and Premium Sales Department at 1-800-221-7945, extension 5442, or write specialmarkets@macmillan.com.

First Edition: November 2014

10   9   8   7   6   5   4   3   2   1

For my mother: for her selfless love, support, and encouragement.
And for my father: whose wise words still guide me.

TABLE OF CONTENTS

PREFACE

Cardinal Timothy Dolan came bounding down the stairs of his Madison Avenue residence wearing black pants with suspenders and a gray polo shirt. "So, what's this project you're working on?" he asked, settling into the seat opposite me. This was our first one-on-one meeting after I had been commissioned to write his biography, so I started to explain how it all came about, going over phrases I'd rehearsed vaguely in my head. "Do you want anything to drink? Coffee? Water?" he interrupted. "Water would be great, thanks." His director of communications, Joseph Zwilling, motioned he would get it. "Your Eminence, do you want anything?" he asked politely. Dolan looked up and without hesitation replied, "I'll have a Coors Light."

About an hour and a half earlier I'd been seated in a pew inside St. Patrick's Cathedral listening to Cardinal Dolan's Sunday morning homily. He was holding the attention of maybe two thousand people as he spoke about not being afraid to stand up and defend your faith. He was skillfully making an earlier Bible reading relevant to his audience. First he recounted meeting some New York University students at a dedication ceremony for the new Cardinal Egan Catholic Center the night before. They "radiate the faith" on the campus, he said, and aren't afraid to defend their views. Then he told a tale that struck closer to home. As a teen, his father worked as a part-time barman in Missouri to bring in some extra cash. One evening, his dad had just served a beer to an African American man when he overheard two white regulars talking. "There was a great day when that man would not have been welcome here," they said. "And the reason our country is changing is because of those G.D. knee-bending Catholics." (Dolan abbreviated the word *goddamn* to *G.D.*)

"My dad was a very religious man, but you wouldn't call him a Shi-ite Catholic," Dolan told the rapt congregation. "He was kind of very humble and behind the scenes in his faith. He kind of rose up and he went down to them and he said, 'Fellas, I happen to be one of those G.D. knee-bending Catholics, and I happen to be very proud of the teaching of my church that all men and women are created equal. And I happen to be rather proud of the posture of my church in the Civil Rights movement, and his business is highly appreciated here. Yours isn't. Get out of here." It was a simple story, told in simple terms, but the point had been made. His blue-collar dad had defended his beliefs and all the Catholics sitting in the pews should not be afraid to, either.

As Mass ended I was led toward the back of the cathedral, where streams of well-wishers lined up to meet the cardinal. There was a tour group from Rockland County who erupted into loud laughter as Dolan cracked a joke while posing for a photograph with them. Then an Irish woman approached and started sobbing as they spoke in close, hushed tones. The cardinal's priest-secretary, Father Jim Cruz, was prompted to bring over holy water, and Dolan blessed her. Next came the young man on the brink of getting married who had attended Mass with three friends. He was eager to hear a quick, reassuring word from New York's Catholic leader. Dolan moved from situation to situation with patience and ease, resting his big heavy hand on one person's shoulder before putting his arm around another. Eventually his staff signaled it was time for him to leave and attempted to steer him away, to limited success because Dolan was in constant demand. Clearly long accustomed to assuming the role of killjoys, they persevered and eventually got their way.

An inconspicuous door at the back of St. Patrick's Cathedral leads to a narrow staircase and directly into Dolan's private residence. The cardinal was carrying his big gold crosier, wearing long green vestments, and had a pointed green miter on his head. He is a large man in both height and girth and, as I was invited to pass through the entrance ahead of him, I glanced back. I was struck by how imposing and regal he looked. "Wait down here a moment while I go and get changed," he said as soon as we stepped into his home. While we waited, Zwilling gave me a tour of the reception rooms. The white papal chair Pope Benedict XVI used during his 2008 visit was displayed prominently against one wall. The carpeted staircase leading to Dolan's study and living quarters was lined with large commissioned portraits of all his predecessors at the New York archdiocese, and there were icons and relics all over the walls. Just to the left of the front door, which opens onto Madison Avenue, hung the framed edict declaring Timothy Dolan a cardinal, signed with Pope Benedict's small, neat scrawl. On a table directly beneath it three red hats had been placed in a triangle. Front and center was the three-pointed cardinal's biretta Dolan had received in Saint Peter's Basilica in Vatican City seven months prior. To the right and left were souvenirs linked to Dolan's second passion in life: baseball caps. One for the New York Yankees and the other for his childhood team, the St. Louis Cardinals. In the living room I spotted another personal sporting keepsake: a baseball signed by the St. Louis Cardinals legend Stan Musial, inscribed: "One cardinal to another." It was impressive and imposing until Cardinal Dolan came striding back down the stairs to sit opposite me and swig his cold beer. "Do you want a glass?" Zwilling asked his boss. "No, you know me," Dolan replied, sipping straight from the bottle. It was impossible not to find this man fascinating.

"So, how can we help?" Dolan continued. "You should get a trip out of this when I go to Ireland or Rome. You want to follow me around for the day?" I managed to get a word in that yes, I would like to do all of the above. "Sure," he said. "I'm flattered." He apologized and explained that he couldn't chat for very long, as he had family in town waiting on the veranda for him. "In fact," he said after a second's hesitation, "you should come and meet them because you'll want to speak to them at some stage." We rose, and Dolan led me onto the terrace, his arm around my shoulder, and introduced me to his sister-in-law, his niece Caitlin, and the other family friends. "She's writing a book about me," he told them as we all shook hands. "For the record, I don't drink Manhattans," he told me. "That's been written about me before. I drink whiskey, but I never drink Manhattans. Make sure you don't put that."

Minutes later I was standing outside the main doors to the cardinal's residence on a bustling Madison Avenue with people and cars whizzing past. The whirlwind introduction was over. I pulled my phone from my bag and called my mother, explaining that the meeting was certainly unlike anything I had prepared myself for, but I thought the cardinal was on board and I had a feeling this project was going to be a lot of fun.

I have interviewed more than one hundred people in the course of researching and writing this book and sat down with Dolan multiple times. He is an incredibly busy man but made himself far more accessible and open to my endless lines of questioning than I ever could have hoped he would be. Anyone I reached out to was given the green light to speak to me, if they so desired. And Dolan gave me lists of people from various stages in his life who might be useful to speak to. We chatted in his twentieth-floor office in the Archdiocese of New York Catholic

Center while he devoured a bowlful of popcorn. We toured his private living quarters, where baseball caps are dotted around and photos of his family and mentors cover every spare inch of wall. He showed me his chapel, where he sits quietly every morning, flicking through index cards scribbled with the names of people he's been asked to pray for. We walked through his study, where a large plate, piled high with signed baseballs, adorns a small table at the end of his desk. He also showed me his makeshift exercise room with an elliptical machine and bicycle, where he listens to Spanish tapes while trying to keep his weight in check.

True to his word, Dolan allowed me to follow him around for a couple of days to get a sense for his daily routine as head of the Archdiocese of New York. We started at the seven A.M. Mass in St. Patrick's Cathedral one Wednesday in January before heading to the Catholic Center on First Avenue, the administrative hub of the archdiocese. His boardroom meetings typically began with an off-the-cuff one-liner, which put the room at ease, followed by a short prayer, reminiscent of a family saying grace before diving into a meal. During one meeting with department heads, Dolan listened attentively to the reports by each person present while reluctantly ingesting spoonfuls of a cottage cheese concoction his dietician had instructed him to eat. He has long had a habit of doling out nicknames and jokingly referred to her as the "fat lady"—a reference to his size, not hers. Then he turned to his chief financial officer, William Whiston: "Dollar Bill, what have you got for me?" It was no coincidence this was also the nickname for Missouri-born NBA player Bill Bradley. Sporting references rarely, if ever, pass Dolan by.

Dolan's day was consumed by myriad back-to-back discussions around a conference table or in the more private confines of his office, with his one-hour weekly live radio show on SiriusXM's The Catholic Channel squeezed in between. His long afternoon drew to an end with a presentation by the Pro-Life Commission, where he stared each speaker in the eye and leaned forward attentively in his leather office chair as they spoke, unconsciously playing with the large gold crucifix around his neck.

It was abundantly clear that Dolan liked to keep things moving. When a meeting dragged on too long, he would fidget restlessly and playfully poke the person seated next to him or whisper in their ear. He grasped concepts swiftly and could impressively summarize complex issues in a matter of sentences, cutting to the core of the issue at hand. Still, there remained a boyish playfulness about Cardinal Dolan's persona, an informality despite his title. He seemed genuinely baffled to discover I found the day interesting when he clearly would far have preferred to have been anywhere other than a boardroom table.

Late in my first day watching Dolan in work mode, he wrapped up his responsibilities at the Catholic Center and turned to his evening agenda: attending a fund-raiser. Dolan skillfully worked his way from top to bottom of the long, narrow room, talking to one guest while placing his hand on the next person's shoulder to draw them into the conversation, enabling himself to keep moving on. Despite the throngs gravitating in his direction to grab a quick word, and with his closest aides looking on and chuckling, Dolan got his hands on a bottle of beer within minutes of arriving. He only had time for a couple of sips before giving a brief off-the-cuff speech, weaving in a personal anecdote from a conversation he'd had only moments earlier, and then he politely took his leave to attend a wake.

Early the next morning, Dolan was on the road again, charming children and adults alike as he walked the corridor of St. Joseph's School of Yorkville on East Eighty-seventh Street before pausing for an interview with a local TV reporter while chewing a mouthful of cookies. In the car ride there he had planned a celebration for a nun who had been in the same parish for sixty years and had coordinated his schedule for upcoming trips to Dallas and Washington, D.C. On the journey back to the Catholic Center, he dictated an op-ed for *The Wall Street Jour-*

nal, laying out the archdiocese's reasoning behind recent school closures while his director of communications took notes and his superintendent of schools weighed in with any pertinent points. Dolan was the consummate multitasker.

Toward the end of the two days at the Archdiocese of New York, I hadn't had a huge amount of one-on-one time with the cardinal, and as he headed to his barbershop, he asked if I wanted to jump in for the ride. Of course, I said yes. As his driver navigated us through the busy Manhattan streets, I asked him about his childhood, about the tape recordings his father sent to him in Rome when he was studying for the priesthood and painfully homesick. As I mentioned the multitude of people I had spoken to who had memorable stories about him, Dolan said, "Well, I hope you interview people that don't like me, there's a couple of those." I told him I'd been trying. "Heck, I'll tell you the weak points. That's why critics never bother me: because I'm a tougher critic of myself than they are."

As we pulled up to the tiny Kips Bay barbershop tucked away between Madison and Park Avenues and run by a family from Uzbekistan, Dolan slid back the side door of his vehicle and waved into the store. "Are you ready?" he bellowed. They enthusiastically beckoned him inside. I sat and made casual banter as Dolan had the hair on his head and inside his nostrils trimmed. He explained how he first stumbled across the barbershop during his regular Saturday morning walk, when he covers eighty blocks before swinging past the Church of Saint Francis of Assisi to line up for confession. It's been a regular fixture ever since. By the time he gets home at about 9:30 A.M.: "I'm on top of the world. I'm a new man."

If there is one phrase about Cardinal Dolan I have heard more than any other during the course of my research, it is "what you see is what you get." Time and again, people explained how when they first met him they had doubts about his sincerity. Wary priests in Milwaukee referred to him as the "smiling steamroller" when he first arrived as archbishop. He exudes such energy and joy in public it naturally leads people to question if he maintains that demeanor in private. They wondered if this was somehow simply a well-rehearsed act. Those close to him eventually came to realize it is his natural disposition; he really is that optimistic and he really is that jovial. However, when the situation dictates, he won't shy away from a fight to defend his values, yet he has a gift for making the disagreement about principles rather than personality. I also heard people say repeatedly that had he not entered the priesthood, he could have been a successful politician. He has the brains, he has the people skills, and he has the deep-seated convictions and ideology. Cardinal Dolan has clearly learned to cultivate those skills over the years. He knows that by cracking a joke he can disarm people or steer an uncomfortable line of questioning in a different direction, and by staying true to his humble beginnings, he becomes accessible and approachable to ordinary people. By reaching out and hugging those he meets, laughing with them and crying with them, he strips away the pomp and circumstance usually associated with his position, and he has the ability to make people excited to be Catholic once again—no small feat, given the tumult the church has been through in recent decades. There are some critics who feel that his insistence on doggedly fighting about so-called "pelvic issues"— gay marriage, abortion, and contraception—is a distraction from the issues real Catholics should be focusing their energies toward: eradicating poverty and homelessness, and ending war.

I visited Maryhouse, in Manhattan's East Village, the home of the Catholic Worker's movement, which was established in 1933 by social activist Dorothy Day. Dolan is championing efforts to have Day named a saint, and while they are hugely appreciative of his support, the staff feels the world he occupies remains far removed from their daily struggle. Of course, there are also those on the other end of the spectrum. Many lay Catholics think he panders too much to people, especially

Catholic politicians who pursue legislation that runs counter to their core values. And inevitably, there are people who come from outside his faith and disagree with him entirely.

Regardless of which side of the fence you fall on with Cardinal Dolan, it is indisputable that he is a man who has rewritten the rule book frequently through his career. He became rector of the North American College in 1994 despite having served as vice-rector at Kenrick-Glennon Seminary in St. Louis for only two years. He returned from seven years in Rome to become the youngest auxiliary bishop in St. Louis in 2001. Less than a year later, he was made the youngest archbishop in the country and put in charge of the Archdiocese of Milwaukee, one of the most challenging nationwide. Soon after his appointment to New York in 2009, he was elected president of the United States Conference of Catholic Bishops, marking the first time the vice president had stood for the position and not been appointed. Three months later he was elevated to cardinal several months before his predecessor in New York, Cardinal Edward Egan, turned eighty and thereby became too old to vote in a papal conclave. It's typically unheard of for an archdiocese to have two cardinals under eighty at any one time since if the papacy was to become vacant unexpectedly, that archdiocese would be represented twice during the vote inside the Sistine Chapel. At the time of his elevation in 2012, Dolan was handpicked by Pope Benedict to deliver a speech to the College of Cardinals on New Evangelization, a clear sign the ailing pontiff saw him as a bright hope for the future. And, during the 2013 conclave, Vatican experts seriously wondered if he could become the first American pope.

This is the story about how a young boy from a small rural Missouri town grew up to become one of the most prominent Catholics in the world.

An American Cardinal

PRELUDE: CONCLAVE

THURSDAY, FEBRUARY 28, 2013

The blades of the white helicopter started to rotate with Pope Benedict XVI settled comfortably inside the cabin. In just three hours, his eight-year reign as leader of the world's 1.2 billion Catholics would officially end. The frail eighty-five-year-old had just left his papal apartment and said farewell to his staff, many of whom bowed to kiss his gold fisherman's ring in one last show of deference. The day before, Benedict had said farewell to the public in Saint Peter's Square, Vatican City. Earlier that morning, he had a final audience with the College of Cardinals inside Clementine Hall, a reception room where the pope's body usually lies in state. He had thanked his brother cardinals for their service and pledged obedience to his successor. Now, as five P.M. rolled around, Benedict was taking flight from Vatican City and would soon assume the title of Pope Emeritus Benedict XVI. His ring would be destroyed, along with his papal seal, and he would set aside his red leather shoes. Many of the staff on the helipad were visibly moved by the solemnity of the occasion and all were swept up in the unprecedented nature of the event. For the first time in nearly six hundred years, here was a pontiff stepping aside as leader of the Catholic world instead of dying in the position. It was both poignant and surreal.

The bells of Saint Peter's Basilica were chiming loudly by the time the rotating helicopter blades gathered enough pace to make the aircraft lift. A couple thousand people had gathered in the square, and their eyes were glued to the two large screens broadcasting all the action on the helipad. The crowd was a mixture of the devout and the curious. Dozens of nuns and priests stood alone or in small groups quietly murmuring prayers and running rosary beads through their fingers. Tourists from all parts of the world stood solemnly among them, soaking up the atmosphere and lifting cameras into the air to capture a keepsake. It seemed like the Italian locals had come out to bear witness also. One chicly dressed elderly couple stood arm in arm toward the back of the crowd. The woman's eyes were full of tears and she was too choked up to speak.

There was still time for one last lap of honor. As Benedict's helicopter took flight, the pilot directed it on a path over Saint Peter's Square. All eyes looked up for the brief flyby. Many waved, others cheered, one handwritten sign pointed to the sky simply read: DANKE!!! Then a pensive silence fell over the crowd as people turned back to the screens to watch the remainder of the unprecedented journey.

Benedict was en route to Castel Gandolfo, the stunning papal summer residence fifteen miles southeast of Rome. The sprawling villa with high walls and manicured lawns is set within a beautiful little town full of narrow, winding cobbled streets overlooking a lake. It was here that Benedict planned to begin dedicating the rest of his days to prayer, well out of the public eye. The small plaza in front of the main gates was at capacity by the time the helicopter touched down fifteen minutes later. People had been gathering all day, waiting for the world's very last glimpse of Benedict as pope. He emerged onto the balcony with arms outstretched to address the crowd. "You know this day is different for me than the preceding ones: I am no longer the Supreme Pontiff of the Catholic Church, or I will be until eight o'clock this evening and then no more," he said. "I am simply a pilgrim beginning the last leg of his pilgrimage on this Earth." After the short address he turned and stepped slowly out of view.

On the roof of the Pontifical North American College, the elite seminary school for men from the United States, situated a short walk up the hill from Saint Peter's Square, a group had also gathered to wave Benedict good-bye. Among them was Cardinal Timothy Dolan, New York's larger-than-life Catholic leader. At eight the previous morning, his eight-and-a-half-hour Alitalia flight direct from JFK had touched down at Leonardo da Vinci Airport in Rome. Wearing his black flat cap and a long black coat, he stepped through the arrivals terminal and was back in the city he had lived in for more than a decade throughout the course of his life. He was in the Holy See to say good-bye to the man who gave him his red three-pointed biretta and the opportunity to vote in his first conclave. Long before he arrived in Europe, Dolan had been touted as a *papabile*—the local term for a papal contender—but he continued to laugh off the notion with a big, hearty laugh and his characteristic wit. "I'd say those [suggestions] are only from people smoking marijuana," he'd told a reporter after his last Sunday Mass in St. Patrick's Cathedral before heading to the Italian capital.

Dolan had been as surprised as any by Benedict's announcement on February 11, which was delivered in Latin to an audience of cardinals who had gathered to discuss an entirely different matter of church business. After getting confirmation that the news was in fact true, Dolan had walked over to the *Today* show studios at Rockefeller Center, across Fifth Avenue from St. Patrick's Cathedral, to talk on air with cohost Matt Lauer. Shortly after, he met with a gaggle of press who looked to him for answers when he had none. "I'm not kidding, I was very startled, and I don't know what to say," he told the media. "I myself am waiting for information, for instructions, as to what we would do now as the College of Cardinals and boy, as soon as I find out I'll let you know." When they asked him about his chances of taking the top job he said it was "highly improbable," then glanced down at a reporter crouching at his feet in the scrum. "Is that why you're kneeling?" he joked, and that line of questioning dissipated with the laughter. Now he was finally in Rome and, as Benedict's helicopter passed by, Dolan cheered and waved with the rest of the crowd, who spontaneously started singing "Ad Multos Annos," meaning, "To Many Years."

At eight P.M., the bells of Saint Peter's Basilica chimed and the Catholic world was officially without a pope. Small clusters of people were holding vigils around the square. Among them was a group of students from Minnesota who had congregated near the central obelisk, where they had been reading from the Gospel, reciting the rosary, and singing hymns until shortly before the top of the hour, when they dropped to their knees and fell silent. A large crowd had gathered around them and the air was cool and still. The only movement came from the flames of the candles gently flickering in their hands. As the Catholic world mourned the untimely loss of one leader, thoughts quickly turned to the future and the upcoming conclave. "We are praying for the cardinals right now that they listen to the Holy Spirit," a twenty-one-year-old among the group said. "And [for them to] make a wise decision for the future pope." The notion of an American pontiff did seem far-fetched, but there were some who started to wonder: "What if?"

SUNDAY, MARCH 3, 2013

Dolan walked into Saint Peter's Basilica as the first rays of sunlight cast a red-tinged hue across the façade. Despite the early hour, several of the altars inside the vast church were already occupied. At some, small groups knelt in solemn prayer; at others priests said Mass all alone. The basilica was tranquil and void of the usual hum of visitors at this time of day, allowing it to feel like a place of worship, not a stop on the tourist map. Dolan and his small entourage headed to a chapel in the grottoes beneath the ground floor of the basilica dedicated to Our Lady, Queen of the Hungarians. It is located next to the tomb of Pope Paul VI and, as he would soon tell the congregation, plucking a phrase from his vast repertoire of sporting analogies, "just a nine-iron shot from the tomb of Saint Peter."

Saying Mass inside Saint Peter's is on the cardinal's "to do" list every time he visits Rome, but this intimate service was a far cry from the one he had given one week before. The previous Sunday, Dolan had said his usual 10:15 A.M. Mass at the altar of St. Patrick's Cathedral on Manhattan's Fifth Avenue in front of a few thousand worshippers. Today there were about twenty invited guests in the pews, including some members of the media who had flown to Rome to report on the conclave and follow Dolan's every move closely. He urged those present to realize they were there because of Benedict's resignation but never to forget that the practice of celebrating Mass transcended that. "The life of the church goes on," he said with a calm and reassuring sense of authority. "The life of the church centers around what we're doing right now."

As a man accustomed to making use of all his time, Dolan was keen to get things moving. This was his fifth day in Vatican City and he had already taken care of many formalities. He had said farewell to Benedict both en masse during his final general audience in Saint Peter's Square and in private during the pontiff's meeting with the College of Cardinals on the morning of his last day in power. The cardinals had all lined up for a brief one-on-one chat inside Clementine Hall, and Dolan had used his turn to ask Benedict if he would "please still try and write." Benedict was a master church theologian who spent decades in academia before donning his white papal vestments. "He didn't say yes or no," Dolan later confessed. "At least he heard me say it." Dolan had also sat down with the press, who were clamoring for interviews; visited a friend in the hospital; and was treating the New York seminarians and priests from the North American College to lunch that afternoon at one of his favorite haunts, Restaurant Abruzzi, near the national monument to Victor Emmanuel II, Altare della Patria, in downtown Rome. He had even made time to phone back to New York to check in, leaving a voice mail for the head of the Priests' Council inquiring: "How are things, priest-wise?" His concern for his flock and his responsibilities as leader of the New York Archdiocese were never far from his mind. But now the enormity of the task ahead was finally starting to dawn on him. "To think that this boy from Ballwin is going to be participating in it—wow," he said. "I kind of waver from high-intensity interest to awe and intimidation." The time had arrived to shift focus to the real reason they were all in Rome: setting a date for the conclave and electing a new pope. "I'm eager to get started," he said. "Let's go. Let's get home."

MONDAY, MARCH 4, 2013

A man with graying hair and a purposeful stride headed toward the Paul VI gate to the side of Saint Peter's Basilica. It was a crisp, clear morning in early spring, and he wore a black fedora on his head and a long black overcoat. The rosary beads dangling from his right hand and the red trim of the cassock visible at his ankles were the only giveaways. Here was a cardinal on his way to the first of the pre-conclave meetings, known as General Congregations. As soon as the throngs of media clocked him, they surged forward to pepper him with questions. He kept his head down and marched on quietly without comment. Moments later, another cardinal came into view, and the journalists swiftly directed their attention to him instead, hoping for better luck. Within seconds the man had disappeared from view amid a sea of cameras and microphones as questions were fired in an array of European languages.

This frenzied scene played out for more than half an hour as the princes of the church arrived at New Synod Hall for the first of the General Congregations. Dolan and the other American cardinals successfully avoided the scrum by being shuttled in a minibus from the North American College, while many others arrived by car. Those who arrived on foot, however, continued to be mobbed. A few stopped to share their thoughts. "This is not about party alliance," Parisian cardinal André Vingt-Trois explained. "It's about finding the person that has the personality most adaptable to the position." Personally he wanted someone "pastoral, spiritual, capable," he said. Could it be an American? "Everything is possible," came the response. "There is someone in there who does not know he is going to be pope in a few days—he will find out."

By nine A.M. the cardinals were in their seats inside the hall, which resembled a large lecture theater, and were invited to the stage one by one to take an oath of secrecy on the Bible. They would meet every morning and some afternoons throughout the week, and each man had an opportunity to address the entire group, even those cardinals over the age of eighty who were no longer eligible to vote in a conclave but were present to impart their wisdom to the younger generation. Views were aired on a multitude of topics, including the Vatican bureaucracy, known as the Curia, and the scandal surrounding leaked Vatican documents that exposed widespread corruption and rivalry in its highest ranks. Of course, the main priority was determining the qualities needed in the next pope. Finding a pontiff to promote New Evangelization was also an oft-repeated phrase, as the cardinals were looking for someone who could attract lapsed Catholics back to the faith. Of the 115 cardinal-electors, twenty-eight had been elevated to cardinal in the past twelve months, and some barely knew each other's names. These General Congregations were therefore a vital opportunity for the men to get to know one another. However, it was during the more intimate chats during the coffee breaks with espressos and biscotti, as well as the lunches and dinners behind closed doors, that the real maneuvering and opinion making took place.

Having been elevated into the exclusive club of cardinals only the previous February, Dolan considered himself something of a rookie. He had little time to really consider whom he would vote for before arriving in Rome, and he eagerly took on board advice from the elders among the American camp like Cardinal Edward Egan, his predecessor in New York. "Listen a lot, and meet as many cardinals as you can," they told him, and, "speak candidly to the cardinals you trust." He took their pearls of wisdom to heart. The American cardinals, eleven of whom were eligible to vote, were a tight-knit group and second only to the Italians in terms of numbers. As such, they wielded significant power. They already knew each other well and would meet nearly every night in the North American College, where they were all staying. Inside the red room, reserved for faculty and guests, they met to have frank discussions about what had transpired during that day's General Congregation. "Who are you really leaning toward? Who really impresses or inspires you?" they would ask each other. "We were very blunt with one another and helpful to one another, enlightening," Dolan said. During the week they also invited cardinals from other nations to join them at their dinner table, or accepted a request to dine at another residence. These afforded more opportunities to make inquiries, take in different viewpoints, and discuss the strengths and weaknesses of various emerging frontrunners. "People would go around," Dolan would later explain. "Are there caucuses at any of these meetings? No. But is there a lot of conversation, and just good fraternal conversation? Yup."

This was the first conclave in a world of rampant social media, where the demand for fresh information was relentless. Already, at least five thousand journalists representing more than a thousand news organizations from sixty-five countries had arrived in Rome. As the conclave drew nearer and the grip of secrecy tightened on the proceedings, journalists turned their attention with increased fervor to speculating who would emerge on the balcony dressed in white. Unlike the previous conclave, when then-cardinal Ratzinger was the clear favorite going in, the field of possible *papabili* this time was vast. Italian cardinal Angelo Sodano was seen as one to watch, though perhaps too akin to the old guard at a time many felt serious reform was needed. Cardinal Peter Turkson of Ghana was being touted as a contender to become the first black pope, and Cardinal Odilo Pedro Scherer of Brazil was a leading name from the developing world. Then there was Canadian cardinal Marc Ouellet, who had the intellect, experience, and language skills, but perhaps was too cerebral to bring about the necessary tough reforms. The list went on.

Dolan's name had been continuously floated around among the American press. He had long been nicknamed "America's Pope," but the idea of electing a pontiff from a superpower had never gained much traction. However, toward the end of the week, an attitude shift started to take effect as the Italian media began paying increasing attention to Dolan also. Italy's fourth-largest daily, *Il Messaggero,* said the Holy See might be warming up to the idea: "If the church's New Evangelization will come through a smile, not a frown, maybe Dolan is the best candidate of all," the paper wrote. Veteran Vatican reporter Sandro Magister called Dolan the "consummate candidate." "For the first time in the bimillennial history of the church, the successor of Peter could come from the Americas. Or to hazard a more targeted prediction: from the Big Apple," he wrote. Italy's *La Repubblica* said Cardinal Tarcisio Bertone, an influential player, was working hard behind the scenes to advance Dolan's chances. And Cardinal Camillo Ruini, another big hitter who was too old to vote in the conclave, was reportedly making moves to drum up support for team Dolan.

There were questions about whether Dolan's language skills were adequate for such a global role as his Italian was not completely fluent, and he spoke only halting Spanish and no French or Latin. Others said he lacked sufficient Vatican experience, and for some he seemed too brash and, quite simply, too American. "If Dolan is elected, the other five thousand bishops of the world might as well take the next fifteen years off, because they'll never be seen or heard from again," one church-watcher said. But Dolan had clearly won the popular vote. People were also impressed with the informal style of the American camp as well as their attempts at transparency, so with no clear front-runner, it left open the possibility that a big surprise could be around the corner. "It would represent the overcoming of the ineligibility of a 'Yankee' cardinal," *Corriere della Sera* reporter Massimo Franco wrote about Dolan's chances. "It would mean the radical reform of the Curia. And the adoption of a skilled and extroverted communicator: even too much, according to the critics."

There certainly were those critics vehemently against the idea of a pope from New York. Representatives of the Survivors Network of those Abused by Priests (SNAP) had flown from the United States and walked around Saint Peter's Square, handing out business cards to reporters. They held near-daily press briefings highlighting their concerns about various cardinals and released a "dirty dozen" list of candidates they felt should be disqualified. Dolan was on it, along with fellow American cardinals Seán O'Malley of Boston and Donald Wuerl of Washington, D.C. The group criticized Dolan's handling of the fallout from the sex abuse crisis while he was archbishop of Milwaukee (his post before New York), especially his payment of up to $20,000 to expedite the removal of priests from ministry. "It isn't really up to SNAP to determine who should participate or not in the conclave," responded Vatican spokesman Father Federico Lombardi, but the group's presence did put the issue of a prelate's track record into the minds of many. It was something Dolan had dealt with in his two prior assignments, Milwaukee and St. Louis, and it continued to follow him. One week before he boarded the plane to Rome, he had spent three hours giving a legal deposition in New York about his decision to publicly name priests who had molested children in Milwaukee. It was part of ongoing bankruptcy hearings involving the archdiocese, as two years after Dolan left in 2009, his successor filed for Chapter 11, saying financial claims by victims far outstripped the church's funds.

Despite the critics, there was still no denying Dolan was attracting attention and positive media wherever he went. Many saw him as a breath of fresh air, a formidable communicator, and one of the biggest proponents of New Evangelization. "One dynamic in this conclave would be the Vatican old guard versus those who want a shake-up of established ways," respected church analyst John Allen said. "Dolan is emerging as one of the candidates in the second camp." He would be "breaking a mold," Allen continued. "All options are on the table." By the end of the week, Dolan's name had started to flash up on every news outlet's shortlist of candidates. Bookmakers had him as a long shot at 33/1 or 50/1, while hundreds of TV stations, magazines, blogs, and newspapers from Asia, Australia, Japan, and throughout Europe were requesting a few minutes of his time. During Dolan's four years at the Archdiocese of New York, his press team had never had to cope with interest of this intensity. Cardinal Egan had voted in the previous conclave and there had been interest from the American media, but his appeal had never gone global. This felt like something different.

SUNDAY, MARCH 10, 2013

Cardinal Dolan contemplated not visiting Our Lady of Guadalupe in the Monte Mario section of Rome for Sunday morning Mass to spare parishioners the inevitable media circus that would ensue. With one week of General Congregations over, every cardinal-elector was now in Rome, and it had been decided the conclave would begin Tuesday, so every media outlet in the world was trying to get a few last glimpses of the *papabili*. Dolan was still a long shot but undeniably a name on many people's watch list. Despite his concerns about overwhelming the local parishioners, the Vatican press office announced that every cardinal in Rome would be visiting their titular church, the local parish each is assigned upon receiving their red hat. Dolan obediently followed suit. Bemused locals gathered in the sleepy square outside the modest church as reporters, photographers, cameramen, and well-wishers started to arrive a couple of hours before the service. They were unaccustomed to this level of activity on a Sunday morning and wanted to know which celebrity was coming to town. The American cardinal from New York, they were told. The one who smiles a lot.

The one-room church with its earthy-colored façade and yellow and white stained-glass windows shaped into a simple cross is located in a working-class community with a large Mexican population. Dolan pulled up in a black SUV and was set upon the moment he stepped out of his car, but he navigated the crowd effortlessly. "Where are my St. Louis people?" he asked at the sight of a cameraman from his hometown. The parishioners were excited to have Dolan in their church, and he came down the aisle with typical exuberance at the end of a long procession of Italian and American priests. He had been holed up in meetings all week and seemed relieved to be back with the ordinary folk again. He wore pink vestments, waved at everyone he saw, and blessed every child he could lay his hands on. Despite the honor of having the cardinal in their midst, the church retained its humble feel. The altar boys walking in line ahead of Dolan wore crisp long white cassock shirts but their scuffed sneakers poked out at the bottom. "I hope he becomes pope," one parishioner remarked to the woman seated beside her in the wooden pew. "Wouldn't that be beautiful."

"Thank you for coming," Dolan told the standing-room-only crowd in Italian before taking up position at the altar, where he beamed and gave an occasional wink. He explained to the audience of more than three hundred that he wasn't there that morning as a cardinal but as a regular parish priest. "What I wanted to be since my first Holy Communion," at age seven, he told them. As the service neared its end, Dolan teased the locals by saying they were only happy to see him because his homilies are shorter than those of their regular pastor. Then he joked he planned to take the candy brought to the altar as an offering into the conclave with him because "I've heard the food is no good." The crowd laughed loudly. Throughout the service he spoke in Italian with a strong American accent. There was no mistaking him for a local, but it was clear he had won them over.

After Mass, the media waited for a few words, and Dolan did not want to disappoint. The journalists were ushered down a narrow pathway into a courtyard beside the rectory, where the jostling for a spot was intense. A couple of neighborhood boys scaled a chain-link fence to get a better look at the excitement and to find out what this gaggle of foreigners with cameras, recorders, and notepads was waiting for. Dolan arrived and situated himself in the middle of the scrum as microphones were shoved in his face from every direction. He towered calmly over the pack with his bulky frame. "The only feeling I have is one of immense serenity," he said, grasping the heavy gold crucifix hanging around his neck as he spoke. "The last week has been just filled with apostolic fraternity and good prayer and solid conversation. [There's] a real sense of trust and confidence." He masterfully sidestepped any questions about the likelihood he would become pope by changing the topic entirely. "Boy, it's good to see you all," he said, looking around, laughing heartily, and then moving on to a question he preferred to address.

"A week ago we would have said, 'Wow, we've got a lot of work to do,'" he added. "But now you see a sense of resignation and trust and faith." When asked how he was able to make a decision on whom to vote for, his answer was simple: "You get to know them, you listen to them, you say a lot of prayers, and it works. Just like you learn to marry somebody." Dolan added, "The Italians have a beautiful saying: You can only make gnocchi with the dough you've got. We want to be good dough for the Holy Spirit to work with." He then worked his way through the scrum to a waiting car, clambered inside, and was off as a small group of American pilgrims who had come to catch a glimpse chanted, "Do-lan, Do-lan."

In the next morning's edition of Italy's *La Repubblica,* the New York cardinal was now being tipped as a "shadow candidate" to succeed Benedict.

TUESDAY, MARCH 13, 2013

The North American College was already a flurry of activity when the silver minibus pulled up at seven A.M. to take the cardinals to Casa Santa Marta, where they would live during the conclave. Seminary students were starting to form a line on either side of the driveway, media were staking out their spots, and the cardinals' assistants were checking that their bosses had everything they needed for the next few days, shut off from all contact with the outside world. The American cardinal-electors posed for a final picture indoors and then walked through the drizzle to the vehicle. Dolan kept up the rear, waving at everyone and hoisting up his long black cassock to show the press that his socks were black, not cardinal red, this morning. He stepped into the bus and took a seat near a window on the front right-hand side. His face and demeanor exuded a serene sense of joy and calm. As the bus pulled out of the driveway, the bells of the chapel tolled and the seminarians applauded and waved as though saying good-bye to heroes going off to war. Dolan smiled through the window, tapping his gold signet ring on the glass and giving a quick salute. The time for talking was finally over. The time for voting was about to begin.

Dolan's youngest brother, Patrick, had been watching from the sidelines with knots of anxiety in his stomach. He had flown in from St. Louis two days earlier, after a local TV channel offered to pick up the tab. When Benedict first resigned there had been a brief discussion among the family about their all coming out, but Dolan had quickly shot that down. As the hype around him had intensified, Patrick phoned to say he had been offered a free trip to Rome, and would Dolan like him there. Patrick explained he had made no guarantee he could provide the journalists any exclusive access, but they were happy to pay for his trip all the same. Dolan said to come. For Patrick, it was a relief to be near his big brother instead of watching him on TV from a distance spanning several time zones and thousands of miles; Dolan was equally thrilled to see a familiar face. He is prone to bear-hugging his family members every time he greets them. When he saw Patrick that Saturday, he almost squeezed the life out of him. Patrick couldn't help wondering if this was a sign his brother was as apprehensive about the outcome of the upcoming conclave as the rest of the Dolan family.

At Casa Santa Marta, the 115 cardinal-electors settled into their rooms, which had been allocated by lot. Roughly ninety staff, all under oath of secrecy, were on hand to cater to their every need, but there was neither access to phones, the Internet, newspapers, or televisions, nor any means of getting a message to, or from, the outside world. The windows of their rooms were nailed shut. They adjusted to their new surroundings and prepared for the Mass for the Election of the Pontiff.

At ten A.M., the solemn procession of cardinals entered Saint Peter's Basilica wearing regal red and gold robes and filed down the center aisle in order of seniority. They held their palms together in prayer and most looked down or straight ahead despite the hundreds of cameras trained in their direction. There were thousands of worshippers inside the basilica, crammed into row after row of plastic seats, and the anticipation was palpable. As Dolan processed down the aisle he looked around and absorbed the scene, as if struggling to take it all in. He cast a quick glance out at the crowd and gave a wink to the congregation before pointing the index fingers of his clasped hands toward the sky and smiling.

Cardinal Sodano, as dean of the College of Cardinals, led the Mass and gave a fifteen-minute homily calling for the church to pull together. "Saint Paul teaches that each of us must work to build up the unity of the Church," he said in a seeming reference to the sex scandals and financial corruption that had marred much of Benedict's papacy. He stressed the importance of evangelization, charity, and working for greater justice and peace. "Let us pray that the Lord will grant us a pontiff who will embrace this noble mission with a generous heart," he said.

At 4:30 P.M., the wait was almost over. The cardinals formed a procession that led from the Pauline Chapel, in the Apostolic Palace, about fifty yards through Regia Hall to the Sistine Chapel, where the voting would take place beneath Michelangelo's *The Last Judgment*. Dressed in red choir dress, the cardinal-electors chanted the hypnotic Litany of the Saints as they reached the chapel and then, as they stepped inside, their melodic chant became "Veni, Creator Spiritus," to evoke the Holy Spirit's assistance in the task ahead. They filtered into the chapel past two Swiss Guards who stood stoically at either side of the doorway and up a wooden ramp into the main chamber. The Sistine Chapel had been closed to the public for one week as workmen made it conclave-ready. The floor was elevated to eliminate any unevenness, as the average age of the cardinals was nearly seventy-two, and not all were as steady on their feet as they had once been. Four rows of desks, two running the length of the room on either side, had been built specially and laid with burgundy tablecloths. They were set with 115 places. Each had a red blotter, two white voting cards inscribed with the words *I vote* in Latin, a pen, a Bible, and an instruction book in Latin that laid out the rules for the conclave. The Sistine Chapel was also spy proof, as a blocker had been installed to ensure no messages could be transmitted out and no one on the outside could get a message in.

Once seated, the cardinal-electors made a vow of secrecy in unison before rising one by one to place the palm of their right hand on the open Book of Gospels and say their name aloud and seal the oath. Dolan waited his turn behind Italy's cardinal Giuseppe Betori and ahead of German cardinal Rainer Maria Woelki. His lips pursed, he gazed off to the right and up at the beautiful frescoes adorning the walls in wonder. Here he was, inside the Sistine Chapel, about to choose the Catholic world's future pope. There was no higher honor. When his turn arrived he said his name and repeated in Latin: "So help me God and these holy Gospels that I touch with my hand." His left hand instinctively reached for the gold crucifix hanging around his neck.

All that remained was for Monsignor Guido Marini, master of papal liturgical ceremonies, to declare the two all-important words: *"Extra omnes"*—everyone out. At 5:34 P.M. everyone not involved in the conclave left the chamber. Marini approached the heavy wooden doors and swung them shut slowly. He and the eighty-seven-year-old Maltese cardinal Prosper Grech had the privilege of remaining inside the historic chamber for a few extra moments. Grech had been chosen to give a meditation on the problems facing the church and the need for careful discernment in choosing the new pope. They were the final words of guidance the cardinal-electors heard before starting to cast their ballots. Then they, too, took their leave and the outside world was left to wait.

1

BALLWIN, MISSOURI

Dinner is bubbling away on the stove, and Shirley Dolan, a soft-spoken Missouri native, pops her head into the living room, where her husband is jovially chatting to friends on the sofa, beer in hand. The children can be heard playing games in a bedroom at the end of the short hallway. Their meal is almost ready and soon the family will gather around the table to say grace, as they do together every night. Their home, 229 Victor Court in Ballwin, Missouri, does not look like much from the outside, but inside this one-story house at the end of a quiet cul-de-sac, an extraordinary person was being shaped: Timothy Michael Dolan. One day he would leave this close-knit community epitomizing 1950s small-town America and become the most prominent Catholic in the United States.

The future cardinal was born to Shirley Jean (née Radcliffe) and Robert Matthew Dolan on February 6, 1950. Named after his paternal grandfather, he was the first child for the young Catholic couple who had met less than two years earlier on a blind date. Dolan's parents were both born and raised in Maplewood, a suburban town on the border of St. Louis's city limits. His father had enlisted in the U.S. Navy in 1943, immediately after graduating high school, and served as a radioman on the cruiser USS *Cleveland* in the Pacific Ocean. Robert Dolan, who was known as Bob, was the middle of three children, and his older brother, Bill, also served his country in the U.S. Army. When the young men returned home at the end of World War II, Bob was deaf in his left ear and reluctant to talk about his experiences, but he and his brother were otherwise unscathed. Their younger sister, Frances, doted on her popular and protective older sibling, who loved baseball, fishing, and hunting excursions.

Like many of the young men who had gone to war at the time, the experience made Bob realize life was short and instilled in him a new sense of purpose. So, when Frances gave her brother a nudge about a pretty young girl in the neighborhood she remembered from grade school, and whom she regularly saw walking to church with her sister, he took note. Coincidentally, Shirley's pals also had ambitions for her to meet this local boy named Bob Dolan. Her older sister's best friend was dating one of Bob's pals, and the friend invited Shirley along to a group picnic by a lake. It was July 4, 1948, and the attraction was instant. Shirley was drawn to the twenty-one-year-old's sense of humor, and he was equally taken with this cute eighteen-year-old. "Life was so simple in those days," Shirley would later recall. "That's all we wanted. That was it."

Although Bob and Shirley had been raised in the same community, their paths had not crossed prior to that first meeting. Shirley and her older sister had been raised in a home on Saint James Square by their single mother, Lucille Radcliffe, who was originally from Arkansas. Lucille had started working as a switchboard operator when Shirley was in third grade and was also a seamstress who made all her children's clothes and coats. Their wayward father, Thomas Radcliffe, was of English heritage and an abusive alcoholic who walked out on his wife and was not present in his daughters' lives. He was born Catholic, and Lucille had converted because of him after their daughters were born. She became an exemplary churchgoer and very proud of her adopted faith. Bob's ancestry and home life was more typical of the local families in Maplewood at that time. His parents were both born and raised in Missouri, and his great-grandparents traveled over from Ireland in a wave of immigration in the 1800s. Bob's father, William Timothy Dolan, worked as a delivery-truck dispatcher at the Shell Oil Company's refinery. He left for work at four A.M. and walked at least a mile to catch a streetcar the rest of the way, typically not returning home until at least three P.M. Bob's mother, Martha Troy Dolan, stayed home to raise the kids in their Anna Avenue house, situated across from the school where Frances first came to recognize Shirley, even though they were in separate grades.

From the moment Bob and Shirley met on Independence Day, 1948, they were inseparable. Shortly before Christmas, Bob turned to his girlfriend after an evening at the bowling alley and asked, "Do you think it's about time we set a date?" There was not a flicker of doubt in her mind, and she instantly said "yes." Being a wife and a mother was every young girl's dream, and this was the man she loved. The couple married in May at their parish church, Immaculate Conception, in Maplewood just eleven months after they first set eyes on each other. Both families were thrilled at the union. Shirley wore a floor-length white lace dress for the ceremony and chose three women as bridesmaids: her best friend; her sister, Lois; and Bob's sister. Bob's brother, Bill, served as best man. The newlyweds headed straight for their honeymoon at Pere Marquett, a beautiful lodge in a state park overlooking the Illinois River. They spent three romantic nights in a bungalow and happily returned to Maplewood as Mr. and Mrs. Dolan.

The 1950s was a decade of rapid change in St. Louis, as in other cities around the United States. Streetcars and commuter railroads grew in efficiency, which started to eliminate the need for employees to live close to their place of work. New highways were being constructed at a brisk pace, and increasing numbers of people began to own cars. These developments, coupled with the postwar baby boom, led many young couples to make a beeline for suburbia. Previously the countryside had been predominantly the domain of the rich, but now small urban hubs were springing up, offering more space for expanding families and cheaper, affordable homes.

Eager to have a place of their own, but still contemplating where to lay down roots, the newlyweds rented two rooms in a private family house in Maplewood. This was where their first two children, Timothy Michael and Deborah Ann, were brought home as newborns, and they were baptized at the same local parish church where the young parents had exchanged vows.

Timothy Dolan was four years old when Shirley's father mentioned a new subdivision in a place called Ballwin, about thirteen miles farther west. The couple was just starting their lives together and didn't have enough money to buy a property on their own, but Bob was eligible for a G.I. loan, which enabled them to get a low-interest mortgage with zero down payment. Full of anticipation, they drove out to Ballwin to take a look at this new community in the countryside. At the end of a cul-de-sac they spotted a plot of land laid out with only the foundations of a new home. It felt ideal. They would have a huge yard and neighbors on just one side, and Shirley was able to pick out all the colors just to her liking. The property cost $11,500. All of a sudden, 229 Victor Court was theirs.

Today, Ballwin has a population of thirty thousand and the city is divided by the four-lane Manchester Road, which stretches west from St. Louis. The busy thoroughfare is lined with car dealerships, fast-food restaurants, and strip malls housing chain superstores like Lowe's, Target, and Walgreens. Hundreds of vehicles speed past every minute, and vast new housing developments and mansion-style homes account for the majority of the residential subdivisions. When the Dolans moved to the neighborhood in 1954 with two toddlers and a car full of suitcases, it was a very different scene. Ballwin was barely on the map, having been incorporated only four years prior with a grand total of 750 residents. Manchester Road was a two-lane route with no streetlights, and beyond the perimeters of the city were rolling hills as far as the eye could see. The city was about as far west as anyone migrating from the St. Louis area was likely to go. It felt very provincial but it was a city on the cusp of big change, and a place that held much promise. Fields had been cleared to make way for the new homes, which were arranged in neat gridlike patterns on large lots. Short, private driveways led to newly paved streets with pretty-sounding names like Nancy Place and Dennison Drive. As for the buildings themselves, they were all strikingly similar: small, simple, wood-framed structures with clapboard siding and a shingle roof.

The home the Dolans chose for themselves was 925 square feet. The front door opened directly into an L-shaped dining room and living room. A little kitchen was around a small corner with an exit into the backyard. A short corridor to the left of the living room led to three bedrooms and a bathroom. There was also a basement used for storage and to house a washing machine where Shirley did the laundry once a week before hanging the clothes on a line outside to dry. The home's biggest selling point was the yard, which measured nearly half an acre and wrapped around from front to back. It was packed with midsized oak and hickory trees that grew to soar over the house in later years. The family also planted three beautiful pine trees, and a creek with a small bridge ran along the southern perimeter of the property.

Although Bob and Shirley had left behind their families in Maplewood, it was not long before they spotted some familiar faces. Unbeknownst to them, three couples moving into properties on their road had been to high school with Bob, and they soon began forming friendships with these neighbors, and others, that would span a lifetime. There was an instant feeling of camaraderie among the new residents who had fled the city with their hopes and dreams. People were excited about their future and shared core similarities, too: the majority were young blue-collar families of Irish Catholic heritage. The shared history and spiritual outlook made bonding that much easier.

Jobs were hard to come by in the postwar era, and the men, mostly war veterans, took what they could find while the wives stayed home to raise the kids. Back in Maplewood, Bob had worked for a friend who ran a business rebuilding car generators, earning $50 a week. Once they moved to Ballwin, he wanted something that paid a little more and found work as a foreman at McQuay-Norris and later Emerson Electric. He lost both those jobs over the years and finally found another job at McDonnell Douglas Corporation, an aerospace manufacturer and defense contractor that built commercial and military aircraft. It involved long hours and the money was far from rolling in, but living paycheck to paycheck was the norm for most families in the community and was even considered lucky by some. Bob was a diligent employee and wore a suit and tie to work every day. His hour-long drive to the office began shortly after 4:30 A.M., when his bedside alarm clock rang. He liked to be the first person at his desk but never failed to leave a note for Shirley on the table before heading out the door and always phoned to check in on her during his coffee break. He always took a brown-bag lunch from the cool box, and when he returned home around five P.M., the couple stole an hour of precious time together, just the two of them. It was a chance for Bob to offload some of the frustrations of his day and shift focus back to what was really important in his life: his wife and kids. As the children got older, they knew better than to intrude on these private moments and left Mom and Dad alone before bounding into the kitchen for dinner.

•　　•　　•

The women in the community were responsible for keeping the family affairs and children in order. On days Shirley needed the car for errands, she woke up early and drove her husband to work. Bob taught her how to drive, and she piled the youngsters in the back. There were no car seats in those days, and she quickly developed a reputation for being heavy-footed on the brake. "Mom, please don't throw us on the floor," the children often pleaded before clambering into the vehicle. When they first moved to Ballwin, Shirley had only Timothy and Deborah to manage, but it was not long before more babies arrived—first Robert Matthew in 1960, followed by Lisa Marie in 1962. The youngest of the five, Michael Patrick, who goes by his middle name, was not born until 1964, when the future cardinal was already fourteen. The home should have felt like it was bursting at the seams by this stage, but the family found a way to make space for the latest arrival to the Dolan clan. Bob and Shirley shared the master bedroom, the girls shared one room, and the three boys had bunk beds in the third. In a neighborhood where families with ten or eleven kids was common, having five children failed to raise any eyebrows.

Dolan's section of the room was always immaculate, and he urged his brothers to keep their belongings just as orderly. Fights among the siblings were infrequent, though the kids took great pleasure in playing pranks on one another and evenings were often consumed with games. Bob used the hallway as his private bowling alley; Deborah and Lisa whipped out jacks or played dress-up. The boys crawled around in the yard and hid in the bushes playing war or Cowboys and Indians. The family had a black-and-white television set and one phone hooked on the wall in the kitchen, but they placed great importance on all sitting down to eat together without distraction. If the phone rang during dinner it was left to ring off the hook. When the entire family sat together outside mealtimes, board games were one of their favorite pastimes, especially Battleship, Risk, or Monopoly.

On weekends Bob frequently drove back to the Maplewood area to bring his mother-in-law, Lucille, to the house for the day, and drove her home again in the evening. She was a gritty, strong, and independent woman who doted especially on Dolan, her first grandson. Every few weeks, other relatives also made the trip out to Ballwin to visit. Fish was on the menu on Fridays, and on Sundays there was always a roast. The leftovers were made to stretch the rest of week. On Saturday, Bob often picked up a shift bartending to bring in a few extra dollars, or helped a friend with an odd job for cash. He sometimes had to work a "7/12," which meant heading to the office seven days in a row for twelve hours at a time, but despite his conscientious attitude the bills kept piling up, along with the repairs. The basement typically leaked during a heavy downpour, or sometimes when the shower was running, and despite Bob's attempts at basic car maintenance and mechanics, the family's vehicle was prone to breaking down. There simply wasn't the money to fix these things.

For the most part, the kids were blissfully unaware of the financial pressure their father was under and never heard him complain about his long hours or inevitable fatigue. Occasionally, they'd spot a pile of bills on his desk or hear their parents quietly discussing: "We better pay this one next" or "Put this one at the top of the list." When the bill collector phoned, Bob would blame the delay on the slow mail or buy more time saying he was *just* about to write that check. Every household in the community was in similar financial difficulties, so the only time the Dolan children got a glimpse that others might have more than they did was during visits to their aunts and uncle. They lived in much bigger homes in nicer, more affluent neighborhoods, and the families typically got together on Christmas Day or Easter for a few hours. Young Dolan and his older sister, Deb, looked in awe at their cousins' new skis or the bicycle they had received as a gift. The Dolans' presents tended to be coloring books or Hardy Boys books, which were the cardinal-to-be's personal favorite. Maybe in a big year he received a new baseball glove, and there were always the customary slippers and socks or some item of clothing the children had to pretend to like but secretly hated. Looking back, the Dolan kids never remember the wealth disparity between cousins ever making them feel jealous or deprived, but being poor was a daily reality they could not ignore. Growing up without money became an important lesson as they matured. "It taught us to be appreciative and humble later in life," Bob, Dolan's middle brother, explained. "And to place very little emphasis and importance on material things."

Part of the allure of moving to Ballwin was the promise of a new Catholic parish with a young congregation and a good Catholic school. The idea of living in a community that revolved around church life and religious education was inherently familiar to Bob and Shirley, and, around the exact time they relocated, the parish of the Church of the Holy Infant was established. The Reverend Robert J. Schwegel, a dashing and athletic priest who loved outdoor activities like hunting and fishing, was appointed founding pastor. The newcomers and parish priest were eager to have a permanent place of worship to serve as a focal point for their community, so he immediately began searching for a plot of land on which to build. However, these things took time and, spiritually speaking, it was a disjointed period. In the interim, the congregation started celebrating Mass inside the Ellisville Athletic Building on nearby Clarkson Road, and Schwegel spent a year commuting back and forth between his room at the rectory at St. Joseph Parish, about two miles farther east, until he could live among the parishioners he served. A six-acre plot of land on New Ballwin Road was eventually selected as the site of what would become Holy Infant School and Church, and a group of parishioners gathered there for a small groundbreaking ceremony in July 1955. It was about a half mile south of Manchester Road and, as luck would have it, a five-minute walk from the Dolan family's front door.

Construction came together quickly, but building work could still not keep pace with the ever-expanding numbers of new parishioners who kept arriving from the city. As the congregation outgrew the athletic building, Mass moved to a big old white farmhouse down the road from where the school was taking shape, but soon this also became standing room only. As soon as the school's basement was completed, it was turned into a temporary church and Mass was relocated yet again until the remainder of the building became habitable. Some of the older children in the neighborhood celebrated their First Communion in what would later become their cafeteria. Finally, on Mother's Day 1956, the wait was over and Holy Infant hosted a symbolic cornerstone-laying ceremony. The first students were accepted in September of that year.

Six-year-old Timothy Dolan was enrolled in first grade and his class was the first to go through all eight years at Holy Infant. Initially, Shirley accompanied him to school. In later years the kids walked themselves, with the older siblings watching out for the younger ones. It was an easy stroll, across the bridge that traversed the creek bordering their property and up a short hill to a tranquil country road, which led a few hundred yards to the entrance. The weekly meager contributions of the Catholic families had been used to help cover the building costs, and everyone pitched in however they could. The women gave a hand with cleaning, cooked treats for bake sales, or supervised recess, while the men ushered at Mass and coached soccer teams. However, there was still one thing missing: nuns.

No Catholic school in that era could operate without the presence of sisters, and a hunt was already well under way to find some. The plans were initially set in motion by the then-archbishop of St. Louis, Joseph Ritter, who realized the Catholic Church needed to adapt and expand to meet the religious needs of parishioners leaving in droves for the sub-urbs. When he dispatched Rev. Schwegel to Ballwin to establish the new parish, part of his remit was to find nuns who could serve as teach-ers. As Schwegel scouted for land and set about getting to know his parishioners, he spoke to his good friend and former classmate, Father Glennon Flavin, who was auxiliary bishop of St. Louis. Flavin had previously worked as secretary to Ritter's predecessor, Cardinal John Glennon, who had been born in Kinnegad, Ireland, in the Diocese of Meath. As a result of his work, Flavin had established good contacts in that part of Ireland and Schwegel asked him to put in a request: "Please send us sisters."

As the sisters would later remember the chain of events, Flavin eventually made a personal trip to the Diocese of Meath with another former classmate, Father Jack Freiberger, to seal the deal. The pair went to see the mother superior at the convent in Drogheda, but she did not think they could afford to part with so many sisters when their own community needed teachers also. She consulted with the bishop of Meath, John Kyne, who pondered the issue and finally gave the de-finitive answer: "The sisters shall go to St. Louis." In their absence, lay teachers had been brought in to teach the Holy Infant children, but the buzz was all about four nuns from Ireland soon crossing the Atlantic to take up posts.

With the school doors flung open and a permanent parish church in which to worship, Bob and Shirley Dolan felt like the community they had dreamed about was finally becoming a reality. Ballwin was slowly establishing its own identity, and the population continued to expand at pace. By 1960 the city had swelled to five thousand residents; by 1970 it had doubled again and Manchester Road was now a bustling four-lane highway. Despite its growth spurt, Ballwin retained a country-town feel—one of its most appealing characteristics. A couple of family-run businesses became the destination for the weekly groceries, and Schroeders drugstore was a favorite for the kids. It was walking or cycling distance from Victor Court, and a food counter at the back of the premises sold coveted cheeseburgers and chocolate malts, which the youngsters in the neighborhood devoured.

Society was on the cusp of big change. Women were entering the workforce in droves and a series of federal laws introduced equal pay and penalties for gender discrimination. Industry was thriving in the post–World War II economic boom, aiding an urban sprawl and massive suburban development. The 1960s also introduced ideas about social justice, sexual liberation, and civil rights, which beckoned radical political change. Pope John XXIII was elected in 1958 and convened the Second Vatican Council four years later, which would bring its own dramatic changes to the way the Catholic hierarchy interacted with their flocks. These societal shifts were slower to take effect in places like rural Missouri, so there continued to be a reassuring predictability to daily life and, for the moment, one of the strongest things that pulled the community together remained the church. Social events revolved around the religious calendar. It dictated what people ate, what they wore, how they spent their Sundays and occasionally their evenings. On Tuesday nights there were devotions to honor Our Mother of Perpetual Health at the church, which was always packed with familiar faces. As an added incentive, attendance got students out of their evening homework assignments. During Lent there were fish fries, where the men knocked back a couple of beers while standing over a huge vat of boiling oil, and the women made coleslaw. Advent and feast days were opportunities for people to get together, and civic clubs emerged as a place where the young Catholics could meet in a casual way and get to know one another. The Men's Club and Women's Sodality Club convened monthly. The women played cards, planned events, or sat and talked. Given the community's strong Irish roots, soon to be strengthened by the arrival of Irish nuns, Saint Patrick's Day became one of the biggest celebrations of the year. The school closed for the day and residents gathered for Irish dancing and a meal of corned beef and cabbage. Around Thanksgiving, the person with the best shot on a target could win a turkey, and the parish organized a big jamboree with skits and dancing as a fund-raiser one year where Bob Dolan reluctantly agreed to be master of ceremonies. The Dolan family was not overly pious or devout, but they were intrinsically culturally Catholic, and far from being a burden on their daily routine, it was comforting and liberating to have the church guide them in this way.

Bob and Shirley were an affable couple who found it easy to make friends and, outside of the church, their Victor Court residence became a center of activity for many social gatherings. Bob was an unassuming man who did not thrive on being the center of attention. He was not loud or boisterous in a large crowd, but when he was in the comfort of his own home, he was the ultimate host. Any visitor that stepped over the threshold received the red-carpet treatment, which included making sure they had a beer in their hand at all times and a full belly when they headed home for the night. It also went without saying that no one would ever leave the Dolan home without having had plenty of laughs. The grill was always being fired up in the backyard for an impromptu cookout and loaded with hamburgers, pork steaks, and chicken. The radio was tuned in to the ball games as the men played horseshoes and croquet, or sat around smoking cigarettes. The women, meanwhile, prepared more food in the kitchen and gathered around the table or on lawn chairs outside to talk, occasionally calling upon the children to help with chores. Neighbors helped each other with yard work and knew each other's names. Doors were left unlocked, sometimes even when families were on vacation.

During the long, hot summer months, the entire neighborhood

became a playground for the youngsters. The cul-de-sac at the end of Victor Court provided a perfect car-free play area where the boys set up games of dodgeball, kickball, soccer, and Wiffle ball. Balls flew in all directions. The girls sat in small huddles on the curb, chatting. Groups cycled with packed lunches to nearby Castlewood State Park, where they spent the entire day swimming and hiking through the woods. When autumn arrived the children raked the fallen leaves in the yard into a huge pile for a bonfire. The aromatic smell of the burning leaves wafted across the neighborhood at night. In the winter, the kids had their favorite haunts to go sledding, or occasionally one local family with a huge pond on their land opened it up for ice skating. Going on a real vacation beyond the confines of Ballwin was a rarity. A trip out of state was uncommon, and heading overseas was out of the question financially, but when the weather was warm, Bob Dolan took time off work and drove the family a couple of hours to Lake of the Ozarks or Kentucky Lake for the day. They piled into the car early in the morning with a packed lunch and arrived back home late at night exhausted but happy from the day spent jumping in freshwater lakes and running through the state park. A couple of times, when there was enough money to spare, the trip spanned an entire week. It was on one of these excursions that a teenage Tim Dolan cannonballed into the water and landed on top of his middle brother, breaking his toe.

Dolan's parents had few hobbies outside the family. His father occasionally went to a friend's for a Friday poker night, but it was the exception as opposed to the rule. On his way home from work Bob rarely stopped for a drink, unlike many other men in the community, preferring to come home and have a beer in his own living room surrounded by his wife and children. When he entered the bowling league, Shirley accompanied Bob to the alley to cheer him on with the other wives and, if the couple ever had enough to spare to go out for dinner, the kids tagged along, too. Bob Dolan worked in order to live, not vice versa, and everything came secondary to his family.

Life felt simple and easy for the Dolan kids, who look back fondly on their *Leave It to Beaver* upbringing, but there were simmering problems behind the closed doors of many other families within the community. Money was perennially tight for nearly everyone, and alcohol often served as an escape. It became an issue among many of the adults. Bob loved his beer and Shirley was partial to a Manhattan cocktail, but never to the point where the kids saw them drunk. The same could not be said for many others in the area. However, the heavy-drinking culture was ingrained within parish life, and it often went unaddressed.

Still, as far as the Dolans were concerned, Ballwin was home and everything Bob and Shirley had hoped it would be. A neighbor who knocked on the door one evening remembers seeing Bob Dolan sitting on the sofa with a group of men having beers and lively conversation. The smell of Shirley's cooking wafted through the room as she occasionally peered around the corner to join in the banter before returning to the stove. The kids were playing in a bedroom. They were a united family, and the siblings were involved in all aspects of family life. "It was a generation that didn't have much," Shirley Dolan later recalled. "But we had it all."

2

HOLY INFANT

On August 23, 1957, a group of Ballwin parishioners stood in an excited huddle at St. Louis Airport. The wait was finally over: A plane carrying Holy Infant School's new Catholic teachers had just landed on the tarmac. Among the group of jubilant locals was seven-year-old Timothy Dolan, just a few weeks shy of entering second grade. Although he was too young to realize it then, the women he was about to meet would have a life-altering impact on him.

As the four Irish nuns stepped into view, the welcoming committee could no longer contain its excitement and jubilantly waved a colorful array of American and Irish flags in the air. Loud cheers rang out, flashbulbs went off, and they burst into a rendition of "When Irish Eyes Are Smiling." The nuns had spent the better part of two days traveling to Missouri, first driving from their convent about thirty miles north of Dublin to Shannon Airport in Limerick, then boarding a plane to St. Louis, which stopped first in Detroit, then Chicago. They stepped off the plane tired, disorientated, and jet-lagged, and were initially overwhelmed by the scene that greeted them. Timothy Dolan and his younger sister Deborah stood among the crowd a short distance from their parents. He was instantly entranced by the sight of these devout women in full-length black habits with broad, beaming smiles. They looked and sounded unlike anything he had ever seen before, and the day made an indelible impression on his young mind.

Father Schwegel, Holy Infant's founding pastor, was among the happy group who warmly welcomed the sisters, and they were driven back to Ballwin in a convoy of vehicles. Their first stop was the newly built parish church, where they said the benediction of the Blessed Sacrament. The newcomers were then shown around the elementary school where they were to teach and given their first introduction to the neighborhood where they would live. It was not what they were expecting. The nuns' best insight into American life had, until that moment, come from Hollywood. They had seen stars like Bing Crosby ambling through vibrant cities full of dazzling buildings and envisioned a country where everyone was wealthy and lived in huge homes. "We thought America was nothing but skyscrapers," the youngest in the group, Sister Bosco Daly, would recall. Yet here they were in Ballwin, a half-built country town in its first few years of existence; it could not have been more different. Ballwin appeared to have little in common with this dynamic young country everyone was touting as the land of opportunity. They could not help feeling disappointed. "It was quite a shock," Bosco confessed.

When the announcement had first been made that the Sisters of Mercy were sending nuns on a mission to St. Louis, everyone at the convent in Drogheda was invited to put their names forward for consideration. The mother superior selected just four nuns to go, though others would be sent to bolster numbers and replace any who returned home in future years. They were carefully chosen based on their skills and ability, and they felt honored to be picked for the task. They varied in age from sixty-two-year-old Mother Xavier O'Donnell, who was to be Holy Infant's new principal, to Sisters Gertrude Duffy and Berchmans Digan, who were in their fifties and forties respectively, and Sister Bosco, who was just thirty. The sense of adventure was not lost on them, but as soon as they arrived there was much to lament about what they had left behind. The women had come from a beautiful, sprawling forty-eight-bedroom convent with a big reception room and an abundance of activity. Now they were to share a tiny three-bedroom wood-framed bungalow. It was situated in a concrete parking lot across from the school building, and their living room had one solitary table surrounded by four chairs. They had been given four plates, four cups, four saucers, and four knives and forks. Plus, it wasn't even ready for them to move into yet. The women spent the first ten days living with a group of sisters about half an hour away from Ballwin before they could finally attempt to get settled.

Their belongings had also not arrived. The four had packed their possessions into a tea chest and sent it ahead by ship, thinking America was a country of superefficiency and modernity so the package was bound to beat them to their destination. Their shipment would not arrive for three more months, and they were left with just the contents of their individual carry-on hold-alls, containing basics like a toothbrush and toothpaste and a change of underwear. The nuns considered themselves missionaries, and religious teaching placed great emphasis on having minimal material possessions, but even this was a stretch. None of them had a second habit to change into, and each had only the one veil. They tried to keep their surprise and dismay to themselves. When they saw their home with its blue shutters, Mother Xavier attempted to look on the bright side and exclaimed, "Oh, blue for Our Lady." Yet on the inside her heart sank and her hopes of getting into their new home and pulling up the rugs to make the place exactly to her liking failed to materialize, as the floors were bare.

Holy Infant School had been open just one year before the sisters arrived and, to tide them over, Father Schwegel had enlisted the help of a group of women who were qualified to work as lay teachers. Eileen Quinlan Shannan, who lived in Ballwin with her husband, was among them and taught Dolan in first grade. He came across as a quiet and diligent little boy who was more introspective than some of the other pranksters, but he was also incredibly sharp and never gave a wrong answer if called upon in class. However, with only one room for each grade, most classes had in excess of sixty students, and teaching often felt more like being the ringmaster in a circus rather than an educator. The nuns' arrival changed the atmosphere instantly. When Dolan arrived for his first day of second grade just after Labor Day 1957, he walked into his new class to find Sister Bosco at the helm. She was standing, ready to learn the names of her new students and instruct them in how to behave. Dolan would have nuns as teachers for six of his eight elementary school grades, and Bosco for three of those. As the youngest of the four nuns, she had the biggest sparkle in her eye. Her calm demeanor, sense of joy at her vocation, and thoughtful way of teaching instantly captured Dolan's imagination, and he thrived under her instruction. The beginnings of a lifelong respect and friendship began to form, and he would come to consider her his "spiritual mother."

The nuns instantly recognized the monumental task ahead of them to turn Holy Infant into a school they could be proud of. The sisters were all qualified teachers working in schools in Ireland before arriving in Missouri, and the first thing that struck them was the lack of law and order. When the bell rang to mark the end of the day, the students dashed out of the school gates in disarray, prompting one local resident to comment the children looked like they "were coming out of a factory." That was enough of a dent to the sisters' pride and they wasted not a moment longer putting their stamp on the place. "We started our discipline that day," Bosco explained. Shortly after, kids were released class by class in an orderly fashion. No rushing, no running. Students also had to stand up if an adult entered the room, no one could leave the class without permission, and there was no talking while getting in line for recess. Their rules were unequivocal; they were serious about learning and they did not tolerate anyone pulling pranks in class.

Corporal punishment is now socially unacceptable and is no longer condoned in schools. At the time, however, the nuns saw no issue with doling out a harsh physical reprimand for disobedience. They were strict disciplinarians unafraid to give a student a brisk shake by the collar to instill order or to bring out the ruler and smack the child on the palm of the hand, knuckles, or legs. Occasionally their instrument of choice was a chalkboard pointer with a black tip. One boy reprimanded by Sister Mary Gemma, who arrived with a later wave of nuns, had to be taken to the hospital when her brisk swing of the ruler missed his palm and broke his wrist. There were many children who inevitably feared the nuns even if with hindsight some appreciated that each punishment came with a lesson. "The Sisters of Mercy was a big misnomer—there was no mercy," one student in the grade above Dolan's recalled. "I got beat every day, but it was a good experience. They beat some sense into me." When one sister caught Dolan's class fooling around in Mass one morning, they were marched back to the classroom and reprimanded. "Which one of you was talking?" the nun asked sternly. A solitary girl raised her hand. The sister excused that student from the class to enjoy recess outside and lined up the others to receive the ruler. The children never forgot the importance of owning up to their actions and not trying to lie their way out of trouble.

The school building itself was tiny, and conditions were cramped. There were only two hallways, joined together in an L shape, which led to the classrooms along one length and the church along the other. There was only one room for each grade, and every student had their own chair and attached wooden writing desk with a small storage space beneath the seat for books. Resources were limited, and there were no blinds on the windows, so classrooms became as hot as a sauna when the sun beat through the glass. The church, used by the school and the wider community, was functional rather than ornate but had a beautiful stained-glass window, which cast a calming pastel-colored hue over the interior in bright weather. Father Schwegel, a talented carpenter, built the Communion rail and carved the redwood crucifix for the altar as well as the Stations of the Cross and the candleholders. The church was never supposed to be permanent, however. The original plans envisioned the space becoming a gymnasium once a larger and more affordable plot was found for a separate place of worship, but as with many things in the community, the money simply wasn't there, and that vision did not materialize for thirty-five more years.

Dolan thrived at school, and his Holy Infant days remain some of the happiest of his life. Putting on his uniform never felt like a chore, and in all eight years, he was marked late only once. The day began at 8:30 A.M., and specific grades would congregate for Mass each morning with the entire school getting together on Fridays. After Mass, the students filtered down the corridor to class in unison, the boys decked out in navy blue pants and white shirts, and the girls in plaid skirts. Recess was outside in the playground and there was an hour for lunch. Mothers were hired as cooks in the cafeteria, including Shirley Dolan in later years, but the kids who lived within walking distance typically headed home. Timothy and Deborah, the first two Dolan kids to attend Holy Infant, often walked to Victor Court together at lunchtime to find their middle sibling, Bob, ready to play. When he wasn't yet old enough to attend Holy Infant, he lined up all his toys in anticipation of their arrival home, but his older siblings were eager to gobble down their food and rush back to the school to run around with their friends.

The future cardinal was occasionally made fun of by his peers for being slightly different and for reading his prayer books in the playground, but he never retaliated with insults of his own. "He was probably the nicest guy you could ever imagine," one classmate said. "Unfortunately, kids being kids, they would kind of tease him and stuff. Kids can be mean but Tim never had anything bad to say." It was during recess in the playground that things were liable to get the scrappiest. The nuns kept an eye on the students, and the boys and girls were segregated, but fights broke out frequently. Dolan found himself on the receiving end of a flying fist on at least one occasion when a troublesome boy and habitual fighter in the grade above sparked a fight. Other kids gathered around as the two squabbled, and although Dolan was a large child physically, he managed to muster only a few weak punches in his defense. "I remember it was probably the only time that I beat somebody and then I felt bad afterwards," his aggressor recalled. "Because it was like you beat up a holy man or a saint. He wasn't aggressive, he didn't seem to know how to fight very well." He was always a kind soul and, as a result, it seemed the nuns often took care to watch out for him while never hesitating to beat some sense into the more wayward students under their rule.

Religious values and teachings were incorporated seamlessly into Holy Infant's lessons so devotion became an inherent and implied part of the school day. The sisters also told the students they should never pass a church door without going in for a prayer. Before each of Sister Bosco's classes, regardless of the subject, she made her students pause briefly and put their heads down and hands together in a calm little prayer: "Sacred heart of Jesus, I place my trust in you. Sacred heart of Jesus, I believe in your love for me. Sacred heart of Jesus, may your Kingdom come." It is a prayer Dolan would use throughout his life.

The students were taught about the Bible and Jesus in a way that made religion come to life. Sister Bosco showed her young students a painting of Christ knocking on a door and asked if they could see anything unusual about the image. One girl spotted it: There was no knob to let someone in. Exactly, Bosco explained, because you have to let Jesus into your hearts by opening up from the inside, not from the outside. Dolan absorbed these teachings like a sponge and never forgot them. Five decades later, during the vespers ceremony the night before he was to be formally installed as archbishop in New York City, with Sister Bosco watching on from the front pews, her former student would tell the exact same story to a packed St. Patrick's Cathedral. It nearly took her breath away that he still remembered it.

Aside from the subtle emphasis on religion, subjects followed a typical elementary school curriculum, with students learning math, English, history, geography, and science. Timothy Dolan stood out as one of the brightest students in the class from day one. The nuns submitted annual report cards where they ranked the children on a scale from exceptional to unsatisfactory. E for exceptionally high achievement was reserved for students with average marks of 97 to 100 percent, followed by H for high average achievement (90 to 96 percent), G for good or average achievement (80 to 89 percent), L for low average achievement (70 to 79 percent), and U for unsatisfactory (69 percent or lower). In his first three years, he received an E in every subject on his report card. And throughout his entire eight-year stint, he never received anything less than a G—and that only on a handful of occasions. He was always given top marks for his respect of authority, his courteousness, and for completing homework on time and keeping his notes neat. In short, Dolan was a model student who thrived on the discipline the Sisters of Mercy instilled and looked forward to attending school each day.

Despite their emphasis on discipline and order, the nuns had a fun-loving side, too. It did not take long for them to introduce Irish music and dancing, which quickly became a hit, to the curriculum or to jump into soccer games with the boys occasionally. The nuns also learned to embrace American celebrations like Halloween and Valentine's Day—anomalies in Ireland at the time. On October 31, they made barnbrack, an Irish fruit loaf, for the kids as treats, and on February 14, every child's name was placed on a card in a box to ensure they all got a special note. Mothers brought in baked goods for them all to enjoy. The sisters saw the amusing side of instances when their attempts at teaching students a lesson in religion did not quite go as planned. "Ask your mom and dad tonight what's the name of the saint you were named after," Sister Bosco once said to her second-grade class. Young Timothy headed home and, as instructed, posed the question to his parents. When he came back to school the next day and his classmates were relaying their findings, Dolan relayed the unconventional reply his mother had told him: "You were named after your grandfather, and let me tell you, he was no saint!"

Outside of Holy Infant the nuns became involved in every aspect of Ballwin's Catholic life. The Irish arrivals were immediately fond of the community of hardworking religious families, yet as hard as they worked at getting to know people and settling in, they could not shake the fact that they were painfully homesick and lonely. Sundays were especially tough. The sound of the early morning church bells reminded them of their friends back home at the convent in Drogheda, and the days felt devoid of activity. Families attended morning Mass, and the parish priest performed baptisms, but people then disappeared on personal errands or to visit relatives. In Ireland, there was always an abundance of people to spend Sundays with. The nuns sometimes spent time alone poring over old photographs and playing Irish records, feeling heartbroken. They also missed, and were deeply missed by, the sisters they had left behind. The letters they exchanged could take at least a week to cross the Atlantic, but Ballwin's newest residents tended to keep their correspondence brief with regard to the specific details of their assignment and surroundings. They didn't want to sound like they were complaining or ungrateful. "They didn't want to tell us how bad it was," one nun who stayed in Ireland recalled.

American culture was unusual in surprising ways, food being one of the most obvious. Pizza, meatballs, lasagna, and chili were dishes that their Irish taste buds had never encountered before but were staples for the locals. They couldn't get a decent cup of tea and thought the bread tasted like cotton wool, so started to make their own. In an effort to make the women feel at home, families often invited them out to a restaurant for dinner. But as much as they appreciated the gestures, the nuns sometimes couldn't even decipher the different dishes on the menu and preferred their home-cooked meals of meat or fish, with potatoes and vegetables on the side. The culture shock cut both ways. The community was fascinated by these pious women wearing full-length habits who talked in a thick brogue. Some children's overactive imaginations led them to believe the nuns had no legs, because their religious garments always ran all the way to the floor. During a trip to a shopping center one day, one nun overheard a child remark, "Mom, are they witches?" The sisters always drank copious pots of tea, and when special guests stopped by they were presented with sandwiches made with sliced bread, cut diagonally into triangles, with the crusts cut off. Their daily meals of meat or fish, potatoes, and vegetables were also an oddity to this barbecue-loving bunch. There were language barriers, too. The sisters used the word *fortnight* instead of saying "two weeks," and instead of asking if someone needed to go to the bathroom, they would inquire, "Do you need to wash your hands?" More colloquial slang left people dumbfounded. After attending a concert, Sister Bosco turned to a parishioner and said sarcastically, "A big crowd how are you?" meaning she thought the audience was pitifully small. The somewhat baffled woman replied, "Very well, thank you."

The nuns were initially dependent on the community for even the most basic requirements. They had to ask people to buy groceries for them for the first two years until they were taught how to drive by mothers in the community and then acquired a car of their own. The weather also felt extreme compared to Ireland. Winters were brutally cold and summers were hot and intensely humid. One of the conditions of their mission was that they could not return home at all in their first five years. After they had completed this first stint, they could return home again after three more years, then two, and finally annually. This was mostly because the parish in Ballwin was so poor it could not afford to send the sisters home more frequently, but it also helped ensure they gave settling in their best shot. When some of them did finally get a chance to go home, they were barely recognizable to their old friends. The climate had made their skin much paler, they had lost weight, and they looked gaunt. Amid all this, there remained one massive misconception that took many years, even decades, to set straight. The community had somehow come to believe these women had come from much more meager backgrounds than they were confronted with in Ballwin. There was a widespread assumption that life in Missouri was a step up, and therefore few, if any, residents fully appreciated the sacrifices these women had made and how disorientated they sometimes felt. When one parishioner many years later visited the Drogheda convent, where Bosco had returned to live, he was dumbfounded to realize this stunning residence was where they had come from. "I don't know how you left it," he told them.

It was at Holy Infant that Timothy Dolan's intrigue and dedication to the church was really able to blossom, but his first religious calling happened long before the sisters arrived in Ballwin. One Sunday, when he was seven years old, his maternal grandmother—whom he affectionately nicknamed Nonnie Lu after her first name, Lucille—had taken him to Sunday Mass. She asked her grandson where he wanted to sit, and he motioned to the second pew. "I want to sit up front so I can watch Father," he explained. As his family likes to tell it, that was it, and it soon became a given he would devote his life to God.

Dolan was always very close to his two grandmothers, who had a profound influence on his life from an early age. They took him to Mass, where he watched them follow the Latin service using their missals, a book containing all the prayers and texts. When Dolan became old enough they taught him how to use it, and Nonnie Lu passed hers on to him as a gift. The women both encouraged his devotion to Catholicism and were proud of his young desires to enter the priesthood. His paternal grandmother, Martha, whom he called Nonnie Marie, took him to First Friday devotions, and when he stayed with her they always stopped by the Church of the Immaculate Conception in Maplewood during their day walking or shopping around town. It was where she had wed her husband, William, where Bob and Shirley had tied the knot, and where Dolan and his older sister, Deborah, were baptized, so it held great significance for the family. The two women were formative examples of women of faith to their young grandson.

At school, Dolan developed a reputation for being a good student with an avid curiosity in the priesthood. The nuns frequently asked the students who among them wanted to be a priest or nun when they grew up. When the children were younger, all hands shot enthusiastically into the air, but as they got older, fewer hands were held aloft each time the same question was posed. Dolan's arm never wavered. It always reached for the sky. When one of the sisters asked her class to say a message into a tape recorder, a new device that had just hit the market, Dolan's personal message was definitive: "My name is Timothy Michael James Dolan and I'm in fourth grade and when I grow up I'm going to be a priest." James was the confirmation name he had been given in first grade.

Dolan's first real taste of being active in the priesthood came when he served as an apprentice altar boy. Two older boys were assigned to train him how to assist a priest at Mass, and he followed them around proudly, kneeling where told and watching from a short distance. He absorbed the lessons and never passed up the chance to try himself, honing skills that would become second nature later in life. One day after Mass the nuns handed young Dolan some wafers that had been blessed but were all broken and discarded. He gladly took them and started distributing them among his classmates as if he were a priest giving Communion. At lunchtime, kids took turns to read Bible or saint stories in front of the school cafeteria, and when it was his turn, Dolan held many of the students spellbound. He rarely needed a microphone and his clear, booming voice carried over the noisy din of the students all diving into their food and held their interest, an impressive feat in a room full of hungry and animated youngsters.

At home, little signs began to emerge of Dolan's devotion to the church. He transformed the living room card table into his personal "altar" using a white tablecloth and held court over his congregation of siblings, offering Communion with Welch's Grape Juice and torn-off chunks of Wonderbread. On occasion, his older sister, Deborah, donned a towel on her head to imitate a nun while Dolan recited Mass, thankfully sparing his family the homily or collection. It made Shirley and Bob proud to think a life of devotion and service might be in store for their firstborn, but they never pushed it. Their attitude was "It would be great if you do, but it's great if you don't," Shirley later recalled. "We never talked about it that much because we didn't want to be like we were trying to influence him. It wouldn't be a good life if it wasn't you. It's him."

Aside from the nuns, the local pastors also became a powerful guiding influence in Dolan's spiritual life in these early years. Although Father Schwegel was Holy Infant's first pastor, he left the parish one year after the sisters arrived, when Dolan was eight, so the first parish priest the future cardinal really came to know and adore was Father Jeremiah Callahan. Callahan arrived in August 1958 and was a towering figure with a boisterous personality. Raised by Irish parents, he was very much a man of the people who liked to drink, smoke, entertain, and, most important, laugh. He had served as a chaplain to American troops during World War II along with his brother John, who was killed, and was also chaplain of the Ballwin fire department. Callahan greeted parishioners with a hearty slap on the back and occasionally treated the sisters to dinner out. It was something they had never been exposed to in Ireland and an excursion they came to adore. He piled them into his car, scaring the wits out of them in the winter as he navigated his vehicle through the snow, and took them to Schneithorst's, the local German *bierkeller* in west St. Louis. He invited them to order anything they wanted from the menu, and the toasted ravioli became the firm favorite.

Callahan was something of a hero to the schoolkids, and Timothy Dolan adored him as much as anyone. When the priest walked through the playground, students stopped what they were doing to race in his direction, clambering all over him. He patiently trained them to be servers at Mass, popped his head into the classrooms to check how lessons were going every couple of weeks, and was always at morning Mass. His associate pastor was Father Norman Schrodi, who arrived at Holy Infant in May 1960 as a newly ordained priest and instantly slotted right in. He was a fun-loving character and together he and Callahan coached the seventh- and eighth-grade students soccer and sometimes dove into spontaneous ball games with them. Callahan invited some of the older children in the parish for dinner from time to time, and the kids spotted the priests driving around the neighborhood, likely delivering Communion to someone who was sick.

Callahan was a kind man, but his zest for life came at a price. Like others in the community, he battled alcoholism, and it was not uncommon for parishioners to see his car parked on the lawn instead of the driveway the morning after a particularly heavy night. Still, he helped to create a joyful atmosphere in the community and brought people to-gether. He also presided over the construction of a permanent home for the sisters adjacent to the main school building. It was a significant im-provement from the three-bedroom bungalow in the middle of a park-ing lot that they had first lived in and that was later demolished. They now had eight bedrooms—each with a single bed—a couple of bathrooms, one large living room with sofas, and a dining room with a large table adjacent to the kitchen. It was under Callahan's tenure that the school was also expanded to include eight new classrooms, which became func-tional in 1962. One year later three more nuns were brought over from the convent in Drogheda to teach. Mother Xavier stepped aside as prin-cipal to return home, and Sister Gertrude—now Mother Gertrude—took the helm. After a rocky few years full of change, adjustments, and construction, Holy Infant was making the sisters proud. Amid all this, young Timothy Dolan was soaking it all up like a sponge and thriving.

3

STUDENT DAYS

When it came time for their firstborn to graduate from Holy Infant and enter high school, Bob and Shirley sat young Timothy Dolan down to discuss his options. The teenager looked at his parents somewhat incredulously and replied, "I thought you always knew that I wanted to be a priest? So, that means I have to go into Prep." Shortly after, Dolan was enrolled at St. Louis Preparatory Seminary South. It was 1964 and he was fourteen years old.

The redbrick building had been constructed in 1957 so was still relatively new when Dolan arrived for his first day of class. The school was located in Shrewsbury, a quiet suburb just southwest of St. Louis, and about a forty-minute drive east of Ballwin. It was a significant step up in size from Holy Infant. Classes spanned two floors and there was a large chapel, cafeteria, and gym on the ground floor. The west side of the building looked out onto a grassy bank that sloped down toward numerous sports fields. This was a boom era in terms of enrollment into the priesthood, and there were 520 students in the four high school years from freshman through senior. Each student was assigned a locker to share, where they kept the clip-on ties they were required to wear during the day. Dolan's entering class numbered 167, and they were split into five classes, labeled A through E, with roughly thirty people in each.

The young men had all enrolled in the school hoping to become priests—or were at least open to exploring the idea—but they had yet to fully grasp what that reality entailed. Luckily, they had plenty of time ahead to work that out. The path from high school to ordination was twelve years. They would spend four years at St. Louis Preparatory Seminary South, followed by another four at Cardinal Glennon College majoring in philosophy. At the conclusion of that, the men would undergo an additional four years at Kenrick Seminary studying theology before they would finally be ordained priests. The high school, college, and seminary were all situated on one large parcel of archdiocese-owned land with the different buildings joined by walkways that cut through woodland. Even though the three institutions were largely separate, especially the younger grades, it gave the feel of being on a giant campus.

St. Louis Preparatory Seminary South was much like any other Catholic high school in the 1960s. Many of the faculty were priests and the focus was on providing a rigorous, first-rate education in all core subjects while instilling solid values and religious principles. This made for an easy transition for Dolan. Growing up in Ballwin, he already viewed Catholicism as a way of life and Prep South, as it was nicknamed, provided the perfect environment for him to build on these spiritual foundations and explore the vocation he first set his sights on as a seven-year-old. The students he met in class and passed in the corridors were mostly from blue-collar two-parent Catholic families similar to his own, but if he felt like he stood out as one of the brightest students at Holy Infant, here at Prep South he soon discovered his peers were equally intelligent and driven. They were unmistakably typical teenagers, too. Many felt like they had just joined a large fraternity instead of a school gearing them up for a life of devotion, and as much as they were prepared to work hard, they were also determined to have plenty of fun.

The first formal initiation into Prep South was Frosh Night. It was an annual rite of passage for the freshmen, who were pitted against senior classes and faculty in games of skill and agility. The event involved a tug of war, an obstacle race, and a watermelon-eating contest, and concluded with the newcomers putting on a talent show with performances and comic skits. The activities were an opportunity for the incoming students to get to know their peers, elders, and teachers in an informal setting, and as soon as it was over, they started plotting ways to put the following year's crop of freshmen through their paces.

There were many other key events on the academic calendar, Las Vegas Night being one of the favorites. The cafeteria was transformed into the "Gold Nugget Café" for the evening with plentiful dice and board games, and the classrooms became dens for cardsharps. At Halloween, the young men carved quotes from religious scriptures into pumpkins, and on German Irish Day they sat in class wearing handmade green or red three-pointed birettas, depending on their national affiliation of choice, and competed in basketball, baseball, or football contests at the end of the day.

There was no shortage of clubs, societies, and committees to get involved with, and Dolan quickly found his niche. In his junior year, he was a member of speech club, which entered archdiocese-wide contests. Prep South won a slew of first- and second-place awards. In his senior year, Dolan worked on the school newspaper, *The Spectrum,* and he was also a member of the Pep Committee, which organized rallies to cheer the sporting teams on to victory. Sports were a dominant feature of life at Prep South. There were intramural contests and obligatory gym classes, as well as extracurricular basketball, baseball, football, soccer, and even golf. Dolan was never hugely athletic. He had always been a big child physically and he wasn't the fastest runner or the most skilled pitcher, but he was a fanatical supporter of his local baseball team, the St. Louis Cardinals, and could more than hold his own talking strategy with the jocks, even if he wasn't considered one himself.

Dolan's all-encompassing love of baseball had been cultivated since childhood. His father was a huge fan who took his kids to watch a game at Sportsman's Park about once a year. Stan Musial became Dolan's personal hero, and watching him hit a double in a game against the Cubs in 1958, snagging his three thousandth hit, became a memory forever etched into Dolan's mind. Although he was only six years old at the time, he would later describe it as "a defining moment" in his life. As he grew older, Dolan's knowledge of the sport and team statistics, garnered largely by checking the baseball standings and box scores in the *St. Louis Globe-Democrat* every morning throughout the season, became enviable. During the balmy summer months in Missouri, the voices of sportscasters Jack Buck and Harry Caray gently coaxed him to sleep.

Dolan and Musial crossed paths multiple times in future decades, as the baseball great was a devout Catholic, but one of the standout moments for Dolan was the very first. He and his younger brother Bob were waiting to pick up their grandmother from the airport one day in 1960. She was on her way back from a visit to New York, and as they stood at the gate, Musial walked toward them. Their father gently nudged his boys forward to introduce themselves. "Hi, Stan," a ten-year-old Dolan said. Musial looked down, ruffled his hair, and replied, "How are you, slugger?" Dolan never forgot it. By the time he arrived at Prep South, his knowledge of the game was hard to beat.

The teachers at St. Louis Preparatory South did their best to keep the students busy with a demanding set of curricular and extracurricular activities. It was a highly academic school, but there was an extra incentive for keeping the teenagers preoccupied: It prevented them from getting too distracted by girls. At least that was the hope. Classes were fifty-five minutes long, with eight periods a day, including one for lunch. From just before 8:00 A.M. until 3:30 P.M., the teenagers barely had a second to themselves, and they returned home at night with plenty of homework. They were constantly reminded of the importance of celibacy in the priesthood and were urged not to attend dances, but it was impossible for many of the young men to resist the allure of the opposite sex as puberty kicked in. Dolan never went to prom, but others could not pass up the chance to experience this childhood rite of passage if an opportunity presented itself. When one of Dolan's classmates was asked to accompany a female friend to her dance, he agreed, despite the consequences of getting caught. The relationship was purely platonic, but it would still have been grounds for immediate dismissal had any faculty found out. The event was held on the top floor of the Chase building in downtown St. Louis with sweeping vistas out over the city. As the teenager stepped into the room he scanned the crowd. Across the room his eyes locked on a couple of other high school seminarians who were with their own dates. They all gave one another knowing looks and their lips were collectively sealed.

As if there wasn't already enough to occupy Dolan's time, his day was made longer by his commute to Prep South. In his first three years he would make the seventeen-mile journey by bus or jump in the car with another Ballwin resident who worked or studied nearby. As a senior, he was allowed to borrow the family 1964 Plymouth station wagon, and five other seminarian friends would regularly hop in, joking they were "Rollin' with Dolan." Even with the long commute and his academic obligations, Dolan continued to make space for his first spiritual home, Holy Infant. On weekends, he still crossed the little creek and climbed the grassy bank that led from Victor Court to the small church and school building to help serve seven A.M. Mass. He and other seminarians from the area also helped with chores around the building like cutting the grass and scrubbing the floors.

It had been ten years since the plane carrying four wide-eyed Irish nuns had landed on the St. Louis tarmac, and the women were now well settled in the community and over their initial longing for home. Some had returned to the convent in Drogheda, and new arrivals had been sent to replace them. Among the new recruits was Sister Rosario Delaney. She had arrived in Ballwin to teach first grade the year before Dolan had graduated the elementary school, so their interactions had been minimal while he was still a student there, but they began to spend time together during his frequent visits back to the church and school. Sister Rosario arrived in Missouri bursting with a sense of adventure and a sparkle in her eye. As she grew to know Dolan, she came to appreciate his calm confidence and profound love of the church, and she took him under her wing. A friendship that would span a lifetime soon developed. "He was always at home with himself," Rosario later said. "He's always been at peace with himself, always smiling."

The nuns and priests paid particular attention to the young boys in the community who were on the path to the priesthood and, wherever possible, helped train them in specific church rituals. On Saint Patrick's Day every year, St. Louis's auxiliary bishop, Glennon Flavin, visited the nuns at their convent to say Mass, and Dolan and another few neighborhood boys were invited to assist, a considerable honor. The sisters taught the servers the extra Latin phrases they needed to know for the service, and Flavin usually slipped them a few dollars by way of thanks. Father Callahan moved to St. Matthias Parish in St. Louis in March 1967, midway through Dolan's high school years, and was replaced by Father Adolph Schilly. He was a precise, reserved man of German heritage and starkly different in character from his gregarious predecessor. He exhibited great care and concern for people but in a far more controlled manner. Where Callahan knocked back drinks and wined and dined with his community, Schilly was more likely to be seen socializing at a football game or at a local parishioner's home for a quiet Sunday dinner. Dolan very much respected him as a pastor but found him somewhat distant by comparison and initially struggled to feel the same rapport he had had with Callahan, who never lost touch with his old community and kept a keen eye on Dolan's progress. Instead, Dolan gravitated toward the young, new associate pastor who arrived at Holy Infant two months later: Father Robert Foley.

Foley was assigned to Holy Infant in May 1967, having been ordained a priest a little more than a year before. He had followed the same path that Dolan was currently on track to complete: Prep South followed by Cardinal Glennon College and Kenrick Seminary. When Foley arrived in Ballwin, Dolan was a senior in high school, and the teenager found this new priest young, vibrant, and illuminating. Foley was about to open up Dolan's eyes to a whole world his parish and high school had not exposed him to. Foley was passionate about the ideas of social justice and civil rights, which were exploding onto the scene at the time. He introduced Dolan to inner-city ministries and took the seminarians to poor black parishes or to visit migrant workers in Chesterfield, Missouri. Due to Foley's influence, Dolan started reading about Martin Luther King Jr. and the associate pastor also daringly took a group to the movies to see *The Graduate,* widely considered risqué. He treated the seminarians like equals. He let them borrow his car, and he took them out for pizza or accompanied them on canoe trips where they floated about twenty miles a day past stunning cliffs and bluffs, and camped out at night and sang songs. Barely a decade older than Dolan, Foley instantly recognized the boy's intelligence and natural leadership qualities. He appeared far more mature than many of his peers and Foley felt able to communicate with him as an adult. The pair also found an affinity in their shared Irish heritage and love of jokes. They quickly formed a close bond and trusted friendship, which came to have a profound impact on Dolan as he matured.

The wider Ballwin community was developing quickly, and while it continued to struggle financially, life was thriving in other ways. Ballwin's Catholic Youth Council (CYC) had become especially active and Foley was appointed chaplain. Monthly dances were organized, and on one occasion, Foley invited a busload of black teenagers from urban St. Louis to enjoy the live music. Their presence felt cutting-edge to the youngsters, even though it incurred scowls of disapproval from some adults in the community. The CYC also organized group swimming outings, trips to the skating rink, or excursions to see a show. Dolan embraced these activities and became president of the CYC in his senior year.

In the summer when school was out, the teenagers were free to spend the time as they chose, but getting a job was a priority for Dolan. He often worked at Holy Infant doing maintenance or cutting the grass. One year he worked in the warehouse of GrandPa Pidgeon's department store unloading delivery trucks; another year he worked on the assembly line in a Sunnen Products factory where his grandmother was also employed. "That was hard work, but I was proud of that," Dolan would later recall. Sometimes the seminarians got together with their families for weekend gatherings. Bob and Shirley gradually became friendly with the parents of Dolan's closest classmates and they arranged to meet for dinners or New Year's Eve celebrations.

Dolan was thriving at Prep South and his parents were very proud of their oldest son, but his father was conscious of never overdoing his encouragement. Every summer without fail, usually around July, Bob Dolan would pull his child aside for a quick chat. "Tim, you think you're going to go back?" he would inquire. "I think so," the teenager would reply. "We're very proud of you," Bob Dolan would tell his boy. "But we'd be equally proud of you if you didn't go back." For twelve summers in a row, from when Dolan enrolled in high school seminary until his ordination as a priest, father and son would go through the same ritual. "I think he wanted me to be free," Dolan would later say fondly. "And he didn't want me to ever get the idea that I was doing this to please my parents, or that they would be disappointed."

After four happy years at Prep South, Dolan graduated high school

and moved on to Cardinal Glennon College. It was the fall of 1968, and
the young men were now weekly boarders. Their new home was mod-
eled after the state capitol building of Nebraska with a single tower in
the center of the building, a domed roof, and a cross looming large on
the roof. Wings of residential rooms, libraries, and classrooms led off to
either side. The college students were in dorms during their freshman
year, then were assigned individual rooms, which occupied four floors.
There were about fifty students on each floor and one phone for an entire corridor, supposedly only for emergencies. They spent a lot of time
together, developed firm friendships, and quickly came to know one another's strengths, weaknesses, and annoying habits.

The 1960s and early 1970s—the exact time Dolan was moving through
high school and on to college—were years of radical change within the
Catholic Church. Pope John XXIII's decision to convene the Second
Vatican Council in 1962 set in motion a wave of reforms that made spiritual life virtually unrecognizable for clergy and laity alike. He was a
progressive pontiff who believed the church was better served by being
in touch with worshippers instead of unapproachable, and he called the
bishops together to discuss how Catholicism should adapt to meet the
changing demands of the era. Prior to this moment, the church had a
fortresslike mentality that pervaded every aspect of Catholic life from
the Vatican itself to the seminaries and parishes. Men studying for the
priesthood led a cloistered existence. They had to wear formal cassocks,
their newspapers were censored, TV was limited to an hour a night, and
they were expected not to talk from evening prayers until breakfast, a
period known as the "great silence." There was an "index of forbidden
books" that seminarians were banned from reading that included titles
by authors like Jonathan Swift and Jean-Paul Sartre. The church was a
top-down authority with tight centralized control over every decision,
and Pope John XXIII felt that change was imperative.

After seeking advice from bishops and leading theologians during three years of intense debate in Vatican City, a series of sweeping reforms were hashed out, and the Second Vatican Council concluded in 1965. The church's next challenge was the implementation. In some instances it was a complete 180-degree shift from what had been considered the norm. Gone was the emphasis on Latin, for one. Prior to Vatican II, parishioners learned Latin phrases, the so-called language of the church, to repeat at Mass by rote. Now the service was in English. In the classroom, Latin lessons suddenly carried less weight than subjects such as philosophy or theology. Priests were also urged to turn to face the congregation, instead of showing only their backs. When clergy were outside church, they could wear informal black trousers in place of cassocks, and nuns could abandon their full-length habits for more informal headscarves and below-the-knee skirts. These changes were embraced by some and rejected by others, causing new ideological rifts within Catholicism with clergy increasingly defining themselves along a liberal-to-conservative spectrum.

The reforms also caused a dramatic shift for students considering a vocation in the priesthood. Foley had been the first person to introduce Dolan to the theology of Vatican II and made him feel comfortable with this new way of thinking. On a practical level, Dolan and his classmates found the rules governing their daily school regime constantly being relaxed. When Dolan first enrolled in Cardinal Glennon College in 1968, students could leave campus a maximum of three times per semester to attend a doctor's appointment, days known as "town days." Weeks into their freshman year, these rules were suddenly abandoned and they were allowed to come and go as they pleased as long as faculty knew where they were, in case of emergency. In previous years, students had to wear cassocks throughout college, but by the time Dolan was a freshman they wore more informal clerical shirts instead, with cassocks reserved for liturgical purposes only. They were also encouraged to go out into the communities as a form of social outreach. The students donned black jackets, white shirts, and black ties and hopped on buses all together to teach at a YMCA, a poor parish, or a camp for disabled children. For the students it felt like a stimulating and dynamic time to be in the priesthood, while for the faculty it was conflicting. Many of the older members of staff didn't know how to relate to, or deal with, these young men with so much newfound freedom, something they had certainly never had themselves. They struggled to know where the boundaries should be set in this new unstructured style of formation, the term used to describe the spiritual education the men receive as they are introduced to sacramental life.

Although life within Cardinal Glennon College relaxed, there did, however, remain an abundance of rules that were enforced, and the students invariably tried to see how far they could push them before being caught or reprimanded. Some rules were easy targets. Rooms were strictly no smoking, so students mischievously stuck their heads out the window or used the fire escape when smoking. And the "lights out at eleven P.M." rule was destined for failure. The night before an exam there was no way the students could go to bed at that hour when there was so much last-minute cramming to be done. So they became adept at utilizing every nook and cranny of the sprawling building where they could turn on a reading light without getting noticed. Some boys raced to the confessionals, knowing it was the last place that a priest would look to find a studying student, and they could remain there until two or three o'clock in the morning. Others rushed into the sub-basement of the library. They knew the faculty often checked the stairwell for the glow of a light, but they never went into the basement, let alone one level below.

Having greater autonomy over their lives gave the students the confidence to challenge the rules if they thought they were unwarranted. St. Louis University held a Mass for college students in the basement church every Saturday night. It was often attended by more than one thousand young people but ended after midnight, past curfew for the Cardinal Glennon College men. They approached their dean of students, Father Thomas Croak, to plead their case that this was unfair. "You only want to go there to meet girls," Croak told them. They didn't deny that was a motivation, as a large number of girls did attend, but Croak cut them a deal all the same. "Okay, if you go down there and I see you there, you're just another member of the congregation, I'm not the dean anymore," he told them. "But the rule is, you have to beat me home. If you come back after me, you're gonna get in trouble." Croak deliberately took his time returning home from the Mass and took great amusement in seeing a carload of his students whiz past him, trying to beat the lights, as they rushed back to their dorms ahead of him.

There were occasions when the young men pushed it too far. One evening, Dolan was among a group of college friends who returned to the dorm drunk at about one A.M., long past curfew. They had been out to celebrate the end of their midterm exams at a classmate's home and their noisy, animated banter failed to subside as they brushed their teeth in the communal bathrooms. Some of them were flushing the toilets while shouting, "Blast off!" and it woke up one of the resident priests, who was furious. Croak said he would deal with it. The group was swiftly informed they were "campused," meaning they could not leave the college grounds for a month. Dolan knocked on Croak's door a short while later. His youngest sister, Lisa, was about to have her First Communion, which he was supposed to attend. Could an exception be made so he didn't miss out? he asked. The answer was definitively no. "You made your bed, you lie in it," Croak told him. Dolan understood but had to relay the news to his family, who were disappointed he was missing this important rite of passage in his sister's life. The First Communion went ahead as scheduled, but the Dolan family brought the party to the college's small parlor afterward so he wouldn't miss out on the entire day.

•   •   •

As at Prep South, the curriculum remained intensive. The men were all majoring in philosophy and had at least twenty hours of classes a week, which included lessons in history, English, Latin, Greek, French, political science, science, and math. They also took courses in scripture, canon law, church history, and sociology. It was rigorous. In English class for example, one teacher made the freshman students submit a six-page research paper on a particular topic each week. Sister Bosco's captivating Bible stories in Holy Infant had first piqued Dolan's interest in history, and this was a passion that had continued to grow through his time at Prep South and now at Glennon College. It quickly became one of his favorite subjects. The students turned to one another for help when they became stuck on a subject and arranged study nights where students who excelled in one topic mentored a classmate who found it tough.

In the evenings to relax, the young men perfected their card skills, and pinochle was a perennial favorite as well as poker. On Friday nights Bunco parties became a big deal. Sometimes large groups of students gathered together and split into teams to play the dice game. The emphasis on sport continued, and although Dolan still chose to sit out most sporting activities, his adoration of watching baseball continued to know no bounds. The year split roughly into those who were good at sports and those who threw themselves more into academia, but around Thanksgiving one year all the nonathletes, Dolan included, decided they'd show off their skills. It became the stuff of legend. It was one of the coldest days of the year and they wore jeans, didn't have appropriate footwear, and were out of shape. But the team huffed and puffed their way around the field while the jocks of the college stood and watched in amusement, quietly impressed by the show of resilience. At its conclusion, Dolan and his pals posed heroically for a photograph, arms around one another, wrapped in blankets and hats.

As the rules about leaving campus relaxed, Dolan and his core crew of friends started to plan excursions. His Victor Court home soon earned a reputation as the best place to gather for an impromptu party. Even though Ballwin was still considered a backwater, a group of anywhere from six to ten students followed Dolan back to the bungalow to hang out nearly every weekend. It was always a more-the-merrier affair. The doors were flung open, everyone was made to feel at home, and there was an abundance of food and drink. Dolan's father fired up the barbecue with hamburgers and hot dogs and provided plenty of beer, and several of the gatherings invariably descended into a spontaneous party with lively chat and music. Bob Dolan was a slender man with Irish red hair and overwhelming generosity. He and Shirley loved entertaining the teenagers and never let on if the cost of feeding and watering so many mouths was a strain on their working-class income. It was never too huge a crowd, and Dolan's younger siblings looked forward to the invasion by the older boys. Other parents sometimes swung past, eager to catch up on what their sons were up to, and Mom and Dad Dolan became second parents to many of the seminarians, who spent more time with them than with their own families.

When they didn't go to Ballwin, the college students headed out for pizza and a movie, or made a beeline for the popular frozen custard hangout Ted Drewes. Two or three times a year, Dolan arranged tickets to see the St. Louis Cardinals at Busch Memorial Stadium in downtown St. Louis. He was a ringleader for organizing activities, and as he and his friends matured, local girls from parishes, nearby schools, and camps where they volunteered to help the mentally ill became an increasingly prevalent part of their social group. From the girls' point of view they were fun, smart guys to hang out with, not to mention safe. Given the emphasis on celibacy in the priesthood, the young women knew that hanging out with the Cardinal Glennon College guys was unlikely to put any pressure on them sexually. Some girls also seemed to find added appeal in knowing they were unobtainable, playfully doling out nicknames like "Father What a Waste." As the hormones continued to kick in, girls became an increasingly dominant part of their lives, as well as a growing temptation and distraction.

Every fall the seminarians put on a musical, and although Dolan was not the most gifted of performers, he helped out as an usher and playfully heckled his friends from the audience. Students were encouraged to sell tickets to their family and friends, and the teachers often noticed the presence of a significant number of girls. The boys knew better than to admit the females were personal friends and took to describing them as cousins. Faculty marveled at just how many cousins these young men seemed to have and sometimes pushed them to clarify exactly how they were related, causing some students to quickly scramble to conjure up a plausible family tree. Typically, the teachers let it slide. The adults were not oblivious to what was going on but realized they were dealing with young men who needed to find out about themselves and explore their ability to have platonic female friendships. They kept a close eye on how these relationships developed. If a frank conversation needed to be had, it was, or if a girl was lingering around the college too much, she was sent on her way. It was not unheard of for a student to be told he had to leave the college if his behavior was deemed inappropriate.

Inevitably, with the passage of time, some of these casual friendships did develop into flirtations and full-on romances, and the attrition rate was one aspect of life at Cardinal Glennon College that differentiated it from a typical college experience. Of the 167 teenage boys who entered St. Louis Preparatory South with Dolan in 1964, ninety-two made it through to senior year. Of those, seventy-five enrolled in Cardinal Glennon College, and forty-two graduated four years later. Over the summer recess, more men rethought their vocation and just thirty-two enrolled in Kenrick Seminary in 1972. Ultimately, just sixteen—Dolan included—were ordained priests in 1976.

Sometimes it happened subtly. A student would quietly transfer schools and disappear during the year. Others would wait until the end of the semester to confide to their closest friends that they wouldn't be returning after the break. This often wasn't a huge surprise to faculty or other classmates. In fact, the seminary was a twelve-year track from high school to ordination precisely so that the men could discern if becoming a priest was a vocation they could sustain for life. Still, a student's departure could be devastating. Suddenly a best friend who shared the same values was choosing a different path in life, and it could make the classmate left behind question his own future. Some defections did put a shock wave through the class. Thomas Walther dropped out weeks into Kenrick Seminary. He had made it through four years at Prep South and a further four at Cardinal Glennon College, but when he arrived at Kenrick Seminary it felt different. It wasn't the life of celibacy he questioned but rather being surrounded by men who were months away from becoming priests who seemed so much more prayerful than he could ever envisage being. Another student, Tim Caimi, dropped out as soon as puberty kicked in, and he felt there were too many "distractions," mostly of the female variety. One of the students who caused the greatest upset was Richard E. Henneke, who left one week before the men were ordained deacons, the last milestone one year before becoming a priest. Carl Pieber deferred his place at Kenrick Seminary by three years because at the end of Cardinal Glennon College he wasn't ready to take the next step. Then there were those who abandoned their hopes of joining the priesthood because they had fallen in love and wanted to get married.

Although there was an array of reasons why someone decided not to go the distance, celibacy was a major factor and caused the biggest crisis. It wasn't a vow to be entered into lightly, but at the same time it was hard for these young men to know what that kind of lifelong commitment really entailed. Within the rooms and corridors of Cardinal Glennon College it was a topic of conversation that dominated more than others as the friends shared their feelings, hopes, and concerns with one another. They were encouraged to pick someone they felt an affinity toward as their spiritual director, be it a local parish priest or a faculty member. This mentor talked them through the concept of a life without physical intimacy, even if the conversation sometimes served only to help the student come to the bittersweet conclusion the priesthood was not for him. Faculty tended to describe it as a gift, but it would take years for many of the men to really see it that way. "For ten or fifteen years it's a discipline. It grows into a gift," one of Dolan's classmates explained. "It didn't happen overnight, it was something that we had to grow into. We are not trying to kid ourselves. We're not saying we're happy because we're not married, it was a challenge."

Blossoming romances tended to start as intimate friendships rather than as full-blown affairs. The young women involved were Catholic, too, and intuitively understood the issues the men were grappling with. So in their infancy, these relationships involved two people spending a lot of time together and trusting each other with their innermost thoughts. However, the dilemma of whether to act on a sexual impulse was very real. When one of Dolan's peers felt his relationship with his best childhood female friend had the chance to become something more, they discussed it. The friend was in his early twenties and realized they could probably have a happy life together as man and wife. "We loved each other that much," he explained. The young woman wrote him a letter one day containing important pearls of wisdom and undeniable maturity. "If you're going to leave the seminary, do not leave the seminary for me," she said. "Leave because you don't want to be a priest any longer. And, whatever happens, I will always be here for you." He decided to stay in the seminary to work through his conflict and ultimately became a priest.

The power of the calling was hard to articulate and yet not something to be overlooked or underestimated. Some felt the urge to run from the vocation in the face of these conflicts and even did for a few years, but it often tugged them back. "I don't feel like I chose, I was chosen," one of Dolan's classmates explained. "And I responded to the choice." The young men also had an idealistic vision of what being a priest meant in that era, which played heavily into their desire to pursue a priestly life. It was the 1960s and in the post–World War II boom, society was changing rapidly. Many members of clergy were at the forefront of the Civil Rights movement—some were in politics—and the first Catholic U.S. president, John F. Kennedy, had been elected. (He was assassinated only one year before Dolan had started at Prep South.) Kennedy's inaugural address included a powerful call to a life of public service: "Ask not what your country can do for you—ask what you can do for your country." These role models became heroes to the young men. They were examples of bold, forward-thinking people of faith, and being a Catholic felt cutting-edge. "You don't know what you're getting into completely," one classmate said. "You're caught up in the moment, caught up in the adventure, the process of growing."

There were typically two approaches to dealing with celibacy among students in Dolan's year. There were those guys who went off and secretly got girlfriends or developed close platonic friendships with the opposite sex to explore the idea. And there were those who tried to shut out all female contact as if it didn't exist. The latter group tended to be the ones who caved in their early twenties at the first glimpse of a fluttering eyelid from a pretty girl. They acted like young teenagers with a delayed crush, while the others had perhaps worked out what it meant to turn these relationships into lifelong friendships. "The whole tension of falling in love with someone and having someone to be very intimate with is attractive and desirable," Dolan's classmate said. "But to commit to anything, you're going to have to give something up. To get married you have to give up being single." And to become a priest, you had to give up sex.

Dolan always gave the impression he found these dilemmas a little more straightforward than others did. He seemed to be a natural priest with an unwavering conviction and fierce calling, and as he embarked on his freshman year in college, life felt good. His confidence was growing, he had a good solid group of friends, his studies were going well, and he had strong spiritual guidance from his faculty and the nuns and priests at Holy Infant. Then he received a letter from Father Foley, who broke some unexpected news: He was leaving the priesthood. Foley loved the church and was happy at Holy Infant, but unbeknownst to the community, he had been grappling with his vocation internally. His seminary life had been precisely the kind of sheltered and restrictive experience the Second Vatican Council was trying to reform, and as he had moved toward ordination, Foley felt caught ideologically between the old, regimented way of teaching and these new, exciting, and passionate ideas that were being spawned. At night in his room in the seminary he had huddled under the covers to read the works of theologians like Hans King, Edward Schillebeeckx, and Karl Rahner by flashlight, knowing the older priests on the faculty did not want their young charges exposed to these ideas. However, Foley couldn't resist; they captivated him. Now a fully ordained priest, he often felt an urge to say what he really thought during Mass at Holy Infant—that priests should be able to marry, that he didn't consider birth control and divorce to be sins, that he did not see a difference between mortal sin and venial sin. He kept quiet, knowing these were not ideas that the community he was serving embraced, but the doubts kept swirling in his head.

Foley eventually came to the inevitable conclusion that he had to leave the priesthood. He went into Father Schilly's room to break the news to him, and left feeling heartbroken. Schilly was reduced to tears, and Foley was scarred with the memory of his kind pastor sitting in his chair sobbing as he exited and closed the door behind him. Soon after, Foley also sat down and wrote Dolan a beautiful letter. "It's a very difficult decision," he explained to the teenager, who received the note while away on retreat. "I've sure enjoyed knowing you and your family, something tells me this is going to hurt you but I don't mean to. Please know that I respect your vocation, I'm praying for your vocation as a priest, you need to know I still love the faith, I love the priesthood."

He offered to meet Dolan face-to-face, and they met at Pizza Hut in the St. Louis area for dinner, where Foley talked through what had been going on in his mind. If Dolan was upset at the time, he did not convey it openly. Although their evening was not filled with as much laughter as usual, Foley felt the young man had taken the news remarkably well. Foley never explained to Dolan why he was leaving the priesthood, but rumors soon emerged it was over a woman. That was not entirely correct. Foley did know he wanted to get married—and he would soon tie the knot with a woman he met during his previous assignment as associate pastor at St. Ferdinand Parish—but his misgivings had been a long time coming. Even walking down the aisle to his ordination, he thought he might be making a mistake but had pushed those fears to the back of his mind and kept walking.

Despite his calm external demeanor, Dolan was crushed. He felt like everything was suddenly uncertain and the ideals and values he had been brought up around were slowly altering. All the reforms seeping into parish life post Vatican II meant Catholic life was changing, and the idea of a sustaining, coherent Catholic culture that was not just a part of life, but a way of life, was slipping. Some of his seminary friends had left already, and now the parish priest he most admired was also leaving the priesthood. It was sobering, and to make matters even more complicated, Dolan had been quietly grappling with his own internal conflict. He had gradually started to develop strong feelings for a girl he had been spending more and more time with recently.

Dolan had never liked a girl this much before, and it brought the first creeping doubts about his own vocation. They had met in his parish and at first friendship was all it was. Ever so slowly, it began to feel like more. Dolan was nineteen, and they spent a lot of time together over Christmas break. He adored being in her company and he grappled with the urge to take the relationship further. "I was just very attracted to her, very comfortable with her," Dolan would say. "It was kind of what it meant to [have] good chemistry there, I guess it sticks in my mind because it was a tough time." Dolan would ordinarily have sought out Father Foley's advice, but he had recently left the priesthood and the speculation that it was to get married compounded things. Dolan went to Father Schilly with his dilemma instead. Schilly again broke down as he frankly shared his own devastation at Foley's departure. He spoke about his profound respect for Foley, and how much he had enjoyed his company and how beautifully honest Foley had been with him about his reasons for leaving. He went on to talk Dolan through his own heartache and concerns, and a tight bond between the two men began to form from that day forward.

Dolan headed on retreat shortly after New Year's Day 1969 and also sought advice from the priest leading the trip. He confided in friends and the girl herself. "She knew me pretty well and she was a woman of faith so she would have very much understood," Dolan explained. "She was very attentive and very supportive of my vocation." It took some soul-searching, but ultimately he decided that if he was serious about the priesthood, he needed to give the vocation his full attention and step away from this budding romance. He came to see it as part of God's plan even though it was far from easy. "The seminary just sort of worked its magic and I re-chose the priesthood," he would say many years later.

In the years before his ordination there would be three women Dolan felt a strong attraction toward, but he came to appreciate that a priest can be celibate only if he truly does desire to have the alternative. "Never was it a crisis, but boy, they made me think I sort of enjoyed this," he said. "You can't be celibate unless you want to get married and do want to have kids. We're not called to be bachelors; we're called to be spiritual fathers. So they kind of taught me that because I kind of would enjoy this. But will it be possible for me to be happy without the beautiful intimacy of a woman and children? Or can I be happy with a greater love? And they helped me decide that I probably can, even though I had to say: 'I'll miss that, I would enjoy that.'"

Dolan threw himself back into his friendships, studies, and prayer. As he and his classmates turned twenty-one and could have their first legal beer, they had birthday gatherings at local hangouts like Shakey's Pizza, Cousin Hugo's, or Jacks R Better. The schoolwork also never let up. Dolan was among the top 10 percent of students in his class, but in a school of high achievers he hardly stood out. As far as his peers were concerned, he was just another fun, outgoing guy to hang around with. He slotted neatly into the existing fabric of talent. It was only with the slow passage of time that other students became aware that Dolan was perhaps a more natural leader than others, and his charisma became increasingly evident. He was elected president of the student body during his senior year in college, with classmate Michael Turek as his deputy, and therefore became responsible for liaising between the students and the faculty. If his peers had gripes about the food, the schedule, the discipline, or an array of other issues, they expected Dolan to champion their cause. Dolan had a flair for negotiation and was easy to talk to. At the same time, he wasn't a jock—a prevailing characteristic among the college kids who gravitated to leadership roles. Even though he could talk effortlessly and expertly about baseball, he could hold his own with the nonsporty students and was well liked by all. The faculty started to take notice.

The Archdiocese of St. Louis had a history of sending two of the best students from the graduating class to Rome each year to complete their seminary studies at the prestigious North American College, often described as the West Point of the Catholic World. It was a huge honor that many of the top students strove for. The men sent each year were not simply the best academically, but they were also the ones who seemed to have the most potential, stamina, and the personality to handle the environment and associated pressures. Faculty looked at students' activities beyond the classroom, their service to the community, their involvement in extracurricular activities, and their respect among peers. When the faculty gathered for a meeting to weigh in on the choices, Dolan made the short list. His academic abilities were indisputable and his leadership skills had become increasingly self-evident as president of the student body. After much discussion, two names were decided upon: Dolan and his locker mate, Dennis Delaney, who was also one of his closest friends. The young men were honored to be selected, but Dolan immediately thought of the others who didn't make it, especially his friend Mike Joyce, who, he had discovered, was number three on the list. He decided to call Joyce and ask him to meet for a drink. "Mike, I've just had a meeting with our rector," Dolan said, explaining he was being asked to go to Rome. His friend was thrilled for him, but Dolan wasn't there to boast. "Mike," Dolan added, "you're next on the list, and if you want to go I'll say no." Joyce was overwhelmed by his friend's generosity but declined, saying Dolan had been the first choice, so it was only fair that he should be the one to go. "To this day, that really still moves me," Joyce would say decades later.

Soon after Dolan and Delaney received word about Rome, the news came down from the cardinal of St. Louis, John Carberry, that the college could actually send only one student from the archdiocese that year. It was left up to the faculty to decide which. The dean of students, Father Tom Croak, met with the rector, Father Jack Melito, to weigh the merits of the two candidates. It was tough, but finally Croak had to break the bad news to Delaney. The young man was devastated. A short while later, Dolan knocked on his close friend's door. "If you want to go to Rome, I will stay," he said. Delaney knew the offer was genuine but turned him down. "No, they want you," he replied. "You go."

Dolan was naturally flattered to be chosen but felt he needed time to deliberate the offer. It was a big trip, and a big decision. He had been out of Missouri and on a plane once during a senior trip to Washington, D.C., and New York, but moving overseas for four years was a whole different deal. The North American College rules dictated he would not be able to return home for the first two years, and he was also incredibly contented in St. Louis and had been looking forward to continuing his studies at Kenrick Seminary with the rest of his friends. Father Croak offered to have a word with his parents, and they told him their son had their blessing. Still, Dolan expressed concerns about what happened afterward. "Can I still be a priest?" he asked. Yes, Croak replied but explained that the guys who went to Rome usually ended up getting fast-tracked and working in administrative roles within the Vatican. Dolan said he needed to think about it.

Dolan arranged to meet with Carberry before giving his final decision. The cardinal was fanatical about the Vatican and the Holy Father, possessing a "love of Rome on steroids," as Dolan would later describe it. He desperately wanted Dolan to accept the placement. Dolan approached him shyly but voiced his concerns. "Your Eminence," he said. "I'm worried, what if I get there and don't like it? Can I still be a priest?" Carberry stared directly back. "I guess," he replied. "But not in this archdiocese, it would be tough for me to ordain a man who didn't like Rome." It was an obedience test of sorts, as Carberry wanted to be sure that Dolan, with all his talents, would be willing to serve the church, but the words were worrisome. As he finally made the decision to accept the placement, Dolan knew there was significant pressure on him to make it work or risk losing his lifelong dream of being a parish priest. When Croak heard the news he was happy for his student. "You're going to go far," he told him. "Don't forget about us." His family was proud and honored to know their eldest son had been selected to go to Rome but devastated at the thought of losing him. Their pastor tried to offer some reassuring words that this would be only a temporary separation. "It's okay, Shirley, if he goes to Rome," he said. "Just think, your other kids are going to get married and you'll always have Tim around." The reality would be anything but, as once Vatican officials got to know Timothy Dolan, they knew he was destined for greater things than Missouri could provide.

Dolan was never going to be able to leave quietly. His classmates organized a surprise party for him at classmate Richard Hanneke's house, which students of Cardinal Glennon College and Kenrick Seminary were invited to. It was a bring-your-own-booze-and-food affair, and a hat was passed around to help cover any costs the family would incur covering Dolan's Rome living expenses.

When the morning of his big depature finally arrived, it was emotional. Father Schilly said a final private Mass inside the small family home before joining them on the ride to the airport. Dolan's mother, two sisters, and grandmother Nonnie Lu wore dresses for the occasion, and Bob Dolan and his two youngest sons, Bob and Patrick, put on crisp shirts and pants. It was a warm and sunny day right at the end of the summer and Dolan, looking the most formal of them all in a shirt, tie, and blazer, shielded his eyes behind a pair of sunglasses. As the family posed for a picture, their strained smiles left little doubt about how heavy their hearts were on the inside.

A gaggle of close friends came for the send-off, too. They hugged each other one last time and it was impossible for many to hold back the tears. They all knew it would be a long time before they would see their buddy again, and their carefree days of bending the rules in the college dorm and hanging out in the Dolan family backyard were over, at least for the time being. When the Rome-bound young man eventually disappeared out of sight, the crowd was simply left waving farewell.

4

THE NORTH AMERICAN COLLEGE, ROME

As the plane's wheels lifted off the St. Louis tarmac, Timothy Dolan was alone with his thoughts. His mind drifted to all the changes that lay ahead of him, as well as everything he was leaving behind. It felt both exciting and incredibly daunting. Soon he would be taking his first steps in Italy, where he didn't understand the language, had minimal grasp of the culture, and would have to make a whole new circle of friends. His best pals were all continuing their studies at Kenrick Seminary, a short distance from the familiar world of Cardinal Glennon College and Prep South. They would still go to Ted Drewes for frozen custard desserts, catch Cardinals baseball games in Busch Memorial Stadium, or head home for dinner with their families on Sundays. Meanwhile, Dolan was entering a world where he knew barely a soul.

A couple of hours later Dolan's plane landed at JFK Airport and he made his way to a preassigned location to meet the rest of the seminarians. The men, who had all been instructed to wear jackets and ties, were complete strangers for the most part and drifted toward one another tentatively to board an Alitalia flight direct to Rome. Those who lived near

New York still had family members with them, and in those days of relaxed security, these relatives were able to walk virtually to the plane's doors. Dolan, however, was on his own for the first time in his life.

It was 1972, and this was the first year that seminarians were making the journey to the North American College by plane. Since 1859, when the seminary accepted its first students, each year's fresh intake—known as New Men—had made the journey from the United States to Italy by boat. The crossing took nearly a week, during which time they ate meals together, prayed together, and strolled the decks of the ship, getting to know one another. It provided an opportunity to bond so that by the time the students arrived in Rome they already had a wealth of shared experiences to reminisce about. Dolan's year had an eight-hour ride instead, and there was limited opportunity to socialize and connect with each other while strapped in an airplane seat. The best story they took away from the experience was that the plane ran out of ice midflight, and although they knew no better at the time, they would come to lament missing out on this boat experience and wonder if it might have made their year a more unified group. The plane journey also made the culture shock of leaving home and arriving in a new environment with new people, new food, and a new language feel that much more immediate, jarring, and stark.

When they touched down at Fiumicino–Leonardo da Vinci International Airport, they were met by a small welcoming committee comprising the rector, Bishop James Hickey, and a handful of students who directed them to a waiting bus. As it weaved its way through Rome's streets, passing the ruins of the Roman Empire and churches, piazzas, and cobblestoned streets, they were informed there would be a quick pit stop on the way to their new digs: Saint Peter's Basilica, one of the holiest sites in Catholicism. Despite the jet lag, their excitement was palpable. The driver pulled the bus right up to the steps of the basilica and the men were led straight through the doors of the world-renowned basilica to the tomb of Saint Peter. "We're not touring now," the rector told them. "We can do that later. We've just come here to pray." Some members of the group were transfixed; others could barely keep their eyes open with fatigue, and it took considerable concentration to focus on putting one foot in front of the other. Without fail, it was an overwhelming and treasured moment for all. They were led up the aisle toward the high altar with its imposing bronze canopy from the Baroque era. From there, Hickey directed the group down a small interior side staircase and into the crypt level, where they were taken directly up to the Confession of Saint Peter and gathered around the rail to pray. They said the Apostles' Creed and asked for God's blessings on their stay and studies in Rome before climbing back into the bus to make their next and final stop: the Pontifical North American College.

The college was established in 1859 after Pope Pius IX decided he wanted a seminary in Rome for students from the United States. Pius believed the men would reap unique benefits by studying in the Italian capital and gain an appreciation for the universality of the Catholic Church. The college was initially housed in a former Dominican and Visitation convent in the center of Rome, but in 1953 construction was completed on a new building set on a ten-acre plot of land on the Gianicolo hill, overlooking Vatican City. It is an imposing sight, and as the bleary-eyed crew pulled into the sweeping driveway they were struck by the magnitude of the place. A large cluster of students stood on the front steps to greet them and broke into applause as the new arrivals stepped off the bus. That very first evening there was a big welcoming dinner and the men were then able to settle into their fourth-floor digs and explore their new surroundings a little. When Dolan had tried to imagine life in Rome, he had no idea how rustic he should expect Italian living to be and was immediately reassured to discover the college was a little slice of modern America. Each seminarian had his own room, assigned alphabetically and fitted out with a closet, desk, bed, and sink. It was simple but perfectly adequate. The communal bathrooms had showers with plenty of hot water and the college had a wealth of other amenities on-site. There was a large chapel and library, a small number of classrooms, as well as handball courts, tennis courts, and big open fields for sports. The college was set around a central courtyard with a water fountain and forty-eight orange trees to symbolize every state in the union at the time the new campus was dedicated. Their personal belongings had been sent by ship and did not arrive for two more weeks, but when Dolan's two trunks did finally turn up, opening them felt like Christmas and brought more welcome reminders of home. They also served as useful makeshift tables.

As the New Men adjusted their body clocks to Rome, they were thrown into an intensive Italian course ahead of the formal start of the semester. To the surprise of most, one of the first things they were taught by their language instructors was curse words. This wasn't in the hope the men would use them but so they could avoid being caught off guard, smiling politely and nodding if someone started abusing them in a language they didn't yet fully understand. It was a skill that became particularly useful when dealing with kids who often tried to catch the foreigners out by playfully asking them questions using crude terms and then ran away, laughing hysterically, when they got the men to affirmatively answer, "Sì, sì, sì" in response. After more than a month of total-immersion Italian, the real academic work began. The students were initially studying for three-year bachelor degrees in theology, and while they slept at the North American College, classes were held off-site at two of the Roman universities about a half-hour walk away. There were chartered buses on hand to take the students in their first year until they became a casualty of budget cuts. From the second year onward, the men walked or caught a city bus. The majority of students were to study at the Pontifical Gregorian University in Rome, a Jesuit institution where lectures were exclusively in Italian and Latin. A handful of students were sent instead to the Pontifical University of Saint Thomas Aquinas, known as the Angelicum, which offered parallel classes in English. At the instruction of Cardinal Carberry in St. Louis, who considered the teaching style at the Gregorian heretical, Dolan enrolled in the latter.

The Angelicum had only recently started accepting students from the North American College, and among the entire class of New Men there was some degree of snobbery about who studied where. Although the curriculum was universal across all American seminaries—both in the United States and overseas—there was an unspoken implication that those who attended the Angelicum were less academically gifted because they didn't have to grapple with lessons in a foreign language. There were also only about thirty students per class at the Angelicum, which made for a much more hands-on, intensive experience compared with the Gregorian, where lecture halls could be packed with hundreds of men. Only seven out of the forty-eight New Men that year went to the Angelicum, and they soon became a close-knit group. Dolan knew that his superiors back home had high expectations of him and he didn't want to disappoint, but he was excruciatingly homesick. Cardinal Carberry's warning that he didn't think Dolan could be ordained a priest in the St. Louis archdiocese if he couldn't learn to appreciate Rome often whirred in his head. It may have prevented him from impulsively jumping in a cab straight to the airport to catch the next flight home, but the added pressure to make it work did not make the transition any easier. He spoke about his sadness with his spiritual adviser, who urged him just to try to make it to Thanksgiving. Dolan vowed to give it his best shot.

Communication with the United States was difficult. There was no Internet, cell phones, video chats, or instant messaging, and obtaining news from the United States took perseverance. Some New Men had simple transistor radios, and there was a small black-and-white television set in a rarely used room off one of the long corridors, but for the most part, regular mail became the most reliable way of keeping in touch. Phoning home was a luxury, not to mention expensive and logistically complicated. There was no direct dialing, so calls had to be reserved ahead of time and connected via an operator working at the central switchboard for the city of Rome. Dolan made a point of calling his family on two specific occasions each year: after returning from Midnight Mass in the early hours of Christmas Day when, with the seven-hour time difference, it was still Christmas Eve back in St. Louis, and on the Fourth of July. Bob, Shirley, Deborah, Bob, Lisa, and Patrick gathered around the phone hooked to the kitchen wall and patiently waited for it to ring at a prearranged time. The calls never lasted long, as every few seconds there was an audible click down the line as more money ticked away, but Dolan eagerly anticipated hearing the sounds of their voices, and the receiver was passed around so everyone got a chance to say a few words. There was one member of the Dolan family who never got to speak, however: his youngest brother Patrick. He was only eight years old when Dolan first headed off to Europe, and every time it was his turn to speak, he would burst into tears. "Let's talk to Tim," Shirley gently coaxed, but Patrick was so overcome with emotion he couldn't utter a word. Occasionally Lisa, just two years older than Patrick, also broke down at the sound of her big brother's voice. In between the biannual phone calls, and to ensure his son was up-to-date on the goings-on back home, Dolan's father recorded messages into cassette tapes that he slipped into an envelope about once a week and sent across the Atlantic. Sometimes Bob left the recorder on the table during dinner so Dolan could listen to his family's chatter about friends, neighbors, school, and Ballwin. Other times when his dad ran out of his own news he remarked, "Well, I don't know what else to say. Let me set it here near the radio," and music played until the tape ran out. Dolan lived for these audio recordings and listened to them for hours while reminiscing about home. Eventually, he taped over them with his own updates and sent them back.

By Thanksgiving, as Dolan's spiritual adviser had predicted, he had turned a corner. The homesickness was subsiding and he loved being in Rome. Walking through the piazzas and along the dimly lit, winding, cobblestoned streets, Dolan felt the history and beauty of the city seep into every pore. For the less adventurous seminarians, there was a temptation not to leave the confines of the North American College if it wasn't necessary. Studies were demanding enough, and they had everything that was needed within the walls of their expansive American enclave, including a general store with imported treats from the United States. That was not the way Dolan wanted to spend this time in Rome, and he sought out a classmate in his corridor who was equally enthusiastic about taking full advantage of everything the historic city had to offer. At about nine A.M. every Thursday, one of the students' days off, Dolan and classmate Christopher Peck would head out the gates to explore a museum or a new neighborhood with a copy of Augustus J. C. Hare's *Walks in Rome* as their guidebook. In their four years in Rome the pair was nearly as faithful to this weekly ritual as they were to their studies and prayers, and it became a running joke that they could never go out in Rome "without Hare under their arm." They also developed a passion for visiting the station churches during Lent. Each of the forty days has its own dedicated historical church, and the two men took care to visit the appropriate church on the corresponding day. Sometimes other seminarians joined them, but without fail Dolan and Peck worked out the location of every church they needed to visit and diligently ticked them off their list. It felt as though every street corner, church, and region had a story to tell and, for a budding history enthusiast like Dolan, there was little better.

·   ·   ·

Life settled into a predictable routine as the days turned into weeks and months. They rose early for breakfast before heading out to attend morning classes, which began around 8:30 A.M. They returned to the college for 12:30 P.M. Mass, followed by lunch. Their afternoons were typically free. If the weather was good and their studies permitted, the seminarians threw themselves into sport. In the evening there was a community Mass around seven P.M., followed by dinner at eight, and then more recreation or study time. Sundays were a day when the students were more flexible and relatively free of obligations, or could devote themselves to parish work. Some mornings Dolan visited Saint Peter's Basilica when the doors opened, before the tourist rush. He used the time to wander through the basilica slowly and really get to know it from the inside because there was so much to absorb. Sundays were also good days to hang out at the college, and after morning Mass and before lunch Dolan and his six other Angelicum University classmates typically gravitated toward one another. They usually spent their afternoons studying and some Sunday evenings headed into the city center for dinner. The exchange rate worked in their favor at that time. A bowl of pasta could be as little as fifty cents, which was a blessing on a seminarian's minuscule budget.

The sweeping liberalization introduced in the seven years since the conclusion of the Second Vatican Council continued to shape Dolan's experience of priestly formation as well as the Catholic Church globally. Rules had loosened up significantly at the North American College, and by the time Dolan and his classmates arrived, their formation was anything but regimented. In practical terms, this meant the New Men were treated with a much more laissez-faire attitude than their predecessors had been. They were expected to pray daily, for example, but were allowed to do that in small groups or on their own, and no one kept tabs. They were supposed to attend Mass once a day, but no one prescribed when. They were allowed off campus whenever they wanted and could go for meals in the city center without a bishop in attendance, all things forbidden to previous generations of seminarians. The emphasis throughout Dolan's formation was on "responsible freedom," which forced the men to be self-disciplined if they wanted to succeed and to seek out their own mentors. There were some faculty who argued the rules had been relaxed too much, as letting a group of twenty-something-year-old men loose in a European city to do as they pleased did not always elicit the most exemplary behavior. But this was the school of thought at the moment and the pushback did not come for more than a decade.

Although the curriculum across all American seminaries followed the same pattern, in Rome the exams were often oral, which added an extra element of dread. Instead of having several hours to compose their thoughts coherently on paper, seminarians were given just ten minutes to review the questions before they had to come face-to-face with their professor and start talking. In the weeks before exam period, the college went into lockdown and felt like a monastery. Anyone who suggested they might visit during that period was turned down and informed "the push" was on. The proximity and intensity of the living quarters caused friendships to form quickly at the North American College. Men who were strangers before arriving in Rome suddenly became the only people around to rely on for company, banter, and advice. It was an intense, self-sustaining community, and Dolan's jovial personality, infectious laugh, and natural leadership tendencies quickly endeared him to others. He had a habit of giving people nicknames that stuck for life. His New York classmate Charles Balvo became Moose, after the New York Yankees' first baseman Bill "Moose" Skowron. It was the same position Balvo played when he and Dolan picked up softball games together. Dolan had always made friends with ease, but across the corridor from his room he discovered a true kindred spirit in fellow Midwesterner Robert Busher, who was also studying at the Angelicum. He soon

simply became known as "Bush." They often walked from the Angelicum, in downtown Rome, to the North American College up on the
Gianicolo hill, talking constantly, trading stories, and really getting to
know each other. They both loved to tease and crack jokes and placed
great value on hospitality. Occasionally seminarians from the North
American College were invited to serve Mass for Pope Paul VI, and on
Christmas Eve 1973, Dolan and Busher were bestowed the honor. At
the end of the midnight service the students lined up as the pope walked
past. Sometimes the Holy Father paused to greet them; on other occasions
he just waved. Busher and Dolan were standing side by side and it appeared that Pope Paul VI was going to continue without stopping this
time, so Dolan took matters into his own hands. *"Buon Natale, Santo
Padre,"* he yelled out, meaning "Merry Christmas, Holy Father." Hearing
the words, the pope came over to meet the young men. Even on seemingly serious occasions, however, Dolan couldn't resist the urge to play a
subtle practical joke. As the Holy Father moved toward them, Dolan
took a slight step forward to block Busher's view. Later he feigned ignorance and claimed Busher must have tried to push him forward, but he
knew it was only a matter of time before his friend worked out a way to
get even.

Busher, from Davenport, Iowa, immediately related to Dolan's Midwestern roots. He knew how Dolan's upbringing had shaped his character, quirks, and humor, but it took some of the other seminarians longer
to appreciate what made Dolan tick. Shortly after their arrival, Busher
overheard a couple of classmates airing some concerns one day. They
beckoned him over as he passed by and said they thought the guy in the
room opposite him might have a drinking problem, motioning toward
Dolan's door. "He has a yellow washtub," they said. "He takes that every
afternoon down to the ice machine and uses it to float his Budweiser
on." Busher soon put them at ease. Dolan had bought the tub at one
of Italy's big department store chains, Standa, shortly after arriving,

and filled it with beer, to re-create a little bit of his father's legendary Ballwin hospitality at the North American College. The way he saw it, he wanted to make sure he could offer anyone a cold beer if they came past because no visit was complete without offering a guest a refreshment. He had also discovered where Busher kept his stash of Planters cashew nuts from the general store and would sneak into his room and take them out of his closet to make his warm welcome complete.

The men had three main vacations each year: A couple of weeks at Easter, ten days at Christmas, and a long summer break that stretched from late June through mid-October. At the conclusion of their first year of studies, the students were not allowed home and their only requirement was that they spend a month either studying or doing apostolic work. The college pretty much shut down during that period. There were no regular meals and the hot water was turned off, so the impetus was on the students to travel. Dolan made a beeline for Ireland for two weeks with another seminarian, where he visited Sister Bosco. She was back home from Ballwin for vacation and when he arrived at the airport in Dublin he was overjoyed to see a face that he knew. One of his cousins and her husband also came over to join him and they rented a car and explored the country. Dolan also visited England, Vienna, and Venice before spending the final month studying Italian on Lago di Garda.

When he returned for his second year, Dolan's leadership skills and ability to put others at ease had already been recognized by faculty, and he was put in charge of orientation for the new intake. The college had reverted back to making the New Men travel by boat instead of plane and he was selected to meet them as they arrived at the port of Genoa and accompany them by train to Rome. The whole academic year was about to begin again. This time, however, Dolan didn't arrive at the North American College homesick; he was at home. He also had one more thing to look forward to before resuming his rigorous study

regimen—a visit from his family. Dolan's parents and siblings continued to miss him deeply and it was decided that since he could not travel
back to Missouri yet, his mother would make the trip to Rome. Shirley
flew in September to see her son for a few weeks with his grandmother
Nonnie Lu. Dolan's father wasn't a big traveler and they couldn't both
afford to go, so he opted to stay behind and look after the other four
kids. They spent a couple of weeks touring Rome and making day trips
to nearby cities like Assisi and Florence before more tearful good-byes
and a promise to write soon.

The North American College was full of gifted students. The men had
been specifically selected for their academic and social ability, yet there
was a quality about Dolan that made him stand out more than the
others. He would sit attentively in the front row in many lectures taking
copious notes, and he always appeared eager to learn. He had perceptive
questions about the theology behind the Second Vatican Council, he
absorbed all the theory, and he never missed a class. Father Joseph Henchey
taught Dolan in a second-year theology of hope class and felt all the
students were passionate about becoming priests, but Dolan was equally
passionate about learning. He would visit his professor after class to ask
more questions or for clarifications about assignments, and he was already developing a booming voice. "Timothy, we can hear you before we
can see you," Henchey would sometimes tell him jokingly.

Throughout Dolan's time at the North American College one
teacher made a life-changing impact on Dolan's life—Monsignor John
Tracy Ellis. He was a scholar in residence in Dolan's fourth year and a
master church historian. His semester-long class in church history was
optional, but Dolan didn't hesitate to sign up. He would listen to the
stories about Catholic leaders of the past, absorbing every word during
the forty-five-minute lecture, and ask pertinent questions. In his mind,
these narratives came alive. These weren't just stories or anecdotes. These

were real scenes, they were real people, and he developed a gift for listening to Ellis's lecture and deciphering the personalities behind the people he was describing. Dolan's love of history had begun in Holy Infant listening to Sister Bosco's Bible stories, and it was only intensifying with age.

By the end of Dolan's third year, his middle brother, Bob, was a senior at John F. Kennedy High School in Manchester, Missouri, and desperate to experience Europe. He loaded up his courses so he could graduate a semester early and worked full-time at a grocery store for nearly two months to save enough money for the trip. In the spring of 1975 he had enough in the bank to get on his first plane and spend six weeks with his big brother in Rome. Dolan was twenty-five years old and well acquainted with the Italian capital by this stage, so a perfect host. The first part of the visit was busy, with Dolan going off to class every day and wrapping up the academic year, but Bob was instantly made to feel like part of the gang. He would eat dinner and go to Mass with Dolan and his classmates. They treated him as a friend and he explored every nook and cranny of Rome. Then Dolan had a couple of weeks off and the brothers decided to explore. They headed to Innsbruck, Austria; Munich, Germany; and Zurich, Switzerland, and ate and drank their way around every city.

Seven years younger than his brother, Bob found the trip illuminating. The last time he had spent real time with his brother was when he was a Cardinal Glennon College student who returned home for the weekends with friends in tow to eat their dad's barbecue food and drink beer in the yard. Here, for the first time, he saw his brother in his new life and realized he was in his element. "That's when it really hit me that the priesthood was indeed his calling," Bob recalled. "He was so content, so joyful." It was bittersweet, however, as it also dawned on Bob that he would forevermore have to share his brother with the church.

Bob remained in Rome as his brother was ordained a deacon on April 10, 1975, the final milestone before becoming a fully ordained priest one year later. Father Schilly from Holy Infant also made the trip over for the occasion. As Bob headed back to St. Louis bursting with stories about his adventure, Dolan geared up for an eight-week pastoral assignment in Liverpool, England. He traveled with three classmates who were also working in the city and headed back to the North American College in September to spend his final year studying toward a license in sacred theology.

By the time Dolan was in the homestretch, his relationship with Busher had grown into a tight friendship and they had become the go-to team when it came to event planning. Busher was excellent at organizing, and found Dolan was the perfect person to rely on when he needed to delegate. "I'll take care of it," Dolan would tell him, and sure enough it would get done. Together they were called upon to coordinate an array of dinners and celebrations. When Bishop James Hickey was stepping down as rector, the college faculty entrusted the Midwestern pair to organize his leaving party, and they coordinated with the college staff to hold a reception for him and bought a gift from the student body. Then, a month before their own ordination, they were asked if they could perform their biggest event yet: a reception for Archbishop of Washington William Baum after his consistory elevating him to the College of Cardinals by Pope Paul VI. Several hundred guests were invited to the dinner, and Dolan and Busher were in charge. It took a huge amount of planning and they enlisted the help of about fifty seminarians. At the end of the night, they collapsed exhausted near the fountain in the courtyard in the center of the college building to take stock of their achievements, which were hailed a resounding success. Little did they know, the real thrill was still to come.

The next morning, Busher received a phone call from the porter informing him that Cardinal Baum would like to see him downstairs, and could he please bring Dolan with him. As they made their way down in the elevator, the two of them had chills. They had met American cardinals before since the cardinals typically stayed at the North American College when they passed through Rome, but to have one of the princes of the church personally request their presence was remarkable. Baum said he wanted to thank them for all they had done for his consistory dinner. He asked where they were from and said if they ever ended up in Washington, D.C., where he was assigned, they should look him up and they could have lunch. It was an unforgettable moment. They considered Baum a remarkable and humble man who, just the day before, had received his red biretta from the pope. Now here he was taking time out to thank two lowly seminarians. In that moment, Dolan and Busher could never have envisaged that thirty-six years later that encounter would come full circle and Dolan would be a cardinal receiving his own red hat. They were simply left in awe.

Out of the forty-eight classmates who stepped off the plane from JFK Airport nearly four years earlier, twenty-nine made it through to ordination. They were weeks away from finally becoming priests and everything they had been working toward was about to culminate in one moment.

5

RISING UP THE LADDER

Dolan landed back in Missouri after four years in Rome to a far more jubilant scene than the one he had left. His family greeted him at the airport with WELCOME HOME banners and they threw a party in Victor Court. The majority of Dolan's childhood friends who had graduated from Kenrick Seminary had already been ordained the month prior at the Cathedral Basilica of St. Louis, a New Byzantine–era building with more than eighty-three thousand square feet of stunning mosaics depicting Bible scenes and prominent St. Louis church leaders. Dolan lamented the fact he had missed out on sharing the occasion with them but was able to choose where he would like his ordination to take place as a result. Many of his classmates from the North American College had opted to have their ceremony in Rome, but Dolan knew his entire family could never afford to fly there, so he chose the most meaningful place in his life: the church at Holy Infant parish. "It was far better than being ordained a bishop or made a cardinal, it was a fulfillment of all the dreams," Dolan would later recall. "When I stood there to go in, it was the happiest time 'cause all my memories were of that church: my First Communion, coming to Mass there when I was a kid in school, serving there, cleaning it, painting it, confirmation, all of that was there. It just symbolized everything."

The auxiliary bishop of St. Louis, Edward T. O'Meara, ordained Dolan on June 19, 1976, inside the small church, which was full to bursting. Sister Bosco was in the pews, alongside Sister Rosario. Fathers Schwegel and Callahan concelebrated at the Mass alongside some of his St. Louis classmates, and Father Schilly was the homilist. Dolan's parents insisted on buying his chalice for the occasion, which they had handmade at a famous chalice maker in Rome at a cost of about $300, no small sum in those days, especially given the family's meager income. Small diamonds and sapphires from Shirley's engagement ring were embedded in a Celtic cross design at the base and it had depictions of Saint Peter, Saint Paul, the Blessed Mother, and Jesus. The base was inscribed with the words FATHER KEEP US IN YOUR LOVE, followed by the names of all his immediate family and including Father Schilly. It was a beautiful and treasured gift that would remain with Dolan throughout his life and when the check his parents wrote to pay for it bounced, it also served as a reminder of all they had given up to help him along the way. Dolan's childhood pastor, Father Callahan, had also written to Dolan a few months before to say he wanted to give him his personal chalice as a gift, an object Dolan had admired since childhood. Callahan used one that had belonged to his deceased brother so his own sat unused. He wanted it to go to a good home. "You could use two chalices," Callahan told him, and Dolan was honored to accept it.

Immediately after becoming a priest in 1976, Dolan reported to his first assignment as associate pastor at the Church of the Immacolata in Richmond Heights, west of downtown St. Louis. It was a busy, thriving parish and his pastor was Rev. Cornelius Flavin, the brother of Bishop Glennon Flavin, who had been involved in the mission to recruit Holy Infant's Sisters of Mercy from Ireland. Dolan was working alongside another associate pastor, LeRoy Valentine, and found Flavin a wise man to learn under and an excellent role model. He noticed how trusted he was by his fellow priests, who regularly visited him for confession. Children from the parish school attended Mass at Immacolata every day and the pastors took charge of the service on a weekly rotation. When it was Dolan's turn, Flavin had some advice for him. He explained that Dolan might have obtained an impressive theology degree from the prestigious seminary in Rome, but it was meaningless if he couldn't make religion understandable to children. Dolan thought hard about how to speak to the youngsters, and Flavin watched from the sidelines as he delivered Mass. "You did pretty good. You spoke and the children understood you," Flavin told him afterward. "Now if you're wise, that's the way you'll preach to adults." Dolan took the advice to heart. He recalled how Sister Bosco had been a masterful storyteller of church history, and he had absorbed all her tales from a young age, so he started to use them in his own homilies. His studies had also reminded him that Jesus was a simple man who spoke in a way that everybody could understand, without talking down to his audience. Although Dolan had studied under some of the most accomplished and highbrow religious teachers of the time, he started to develop a skill for making the Catholic message relevant to everyday life, and accessible to many.

Dolan was contented being back in Missouri. He was near his family again, his older sister was newly married and had just had her first child, and his longing to be a priest had finally been satisfied. He spent his days serving Mass and getting to know the parishioners, and on occasion found himself giving Holy Communion to his childhood hero, Stan Musial. The St. Louis baseball great often stopped in at the church to attend the Sunday five P.M. Mass. Dolan did his best to feign ignorance that one of the greatest ballplayers in the world was making a beeline for him but was always struck by, and in awe of, the reverence this lauded and talented man gave to his faith. His grandmother Nonnie Martie also lived about ten minutes from the parish, and he brought her

Holy Communion every Friday. She had been an earthy woman in her heyday, smoking Pall Mall cigarettes and drinking bottles of Falstaff beer, but she now suffered from dementia and was cared for by her daughter, Frances Noonan, Dolan's aunt on his father's side. Nonnie Martie's husband, William, had died when Dolan was just eight years old and he only had hazy memories of being taught how to fish by him at their home on the Meramec River. But Nonnie Martie had continued to be a great inspiration to him throughout his childhood and young adult life, so the weekly ritual was important to him. Christmas Eve—Dolan's first as a priest—fell on a Friday that year, and he arrived at his grandmother's house as per his routine to receive some saddening news. Nonnie Martie had passed away in her sleep. He solemnly entered his grandmother's home and found himself saying the prayer of Commendation for the Dying over her frail body instead of Holy Communion. Although she had been ailing for several years and her death was not a surprise, it was a loss to all the family.

Despite his rigorous schedule as an associate pastor, Dolan made frequent trips back to Holy Infant to spend time visiting family, Father Schilly, and the Sisters of Mercy. A few months after Nonnie Martie's death, and as Dolan's first Easter as a priest approached, Schilly asked Dolan if he would serve Mass and give a sermon every Thursday evening as part of the Lenten series at Holy Infant. He gladly accepted. On April 1, exactly one week before Good Friday, Dolan was also invited to speak at an eight A.M. Mass to commemorate Father Schilly's tenth anniversary at Holy Infant Parish. It had been Sister Rosario's idea, and he was more than happy to participate in the celebration. In order to be ready in time for the morning service, Dolan decided to spend the night at the Holy Infant rectory after his regular Thursday night Mass that week. He headed over to Victor Court for dinner with his family and rose early to help prepare. He and Schilly were still in the rectory when the phone rang. It was one of the parishioners from Immacolata, looking for Dolan. The caller worked with his father at McDonnell Douglas Corporation and had been phoning around, trying to find the young pastor. His voice was grim. He explained that Bob Dolan had been taken sick and they needed to go to the hospital immediately.

Dolan rushed over to Victor Court to pick up his mother and they drove out to St. Joseph's Hospital. His brother Bob, twenty, stayed home with Lisa, who was fourteen, and Patrick, who was twelve. They phoned their older sister Deb, who was twenty-five years old and married with a one-year-old, and she rushed over to the family home. Dolan and Shirley made their way to the hospital and were concerned but unable to fathom that it could be anything too serious. Perhaps he had slipped and fallen over at work or had food poisoning or had fainted, they thought. As they walked into the emergency room and announced who they were, a nurse broke the news that Bob Dolan was dead. He had arrived at work as usual at about six o'clock that morning and about thirty minutes into his shift told a colleague he was feeling unwell and might head back home. Bob was a hard worker, and the announcement struck his workmate as strange. He had high blood pressure and smoked a pack of cigarettes a day, but that was nothing out of the ordinary for that generation of men, and he always appeared strong and healthy. As Bob got up from his chair, he took a couple of staggering steps and collapsed. He had suffered a massive heart attack.

Shirley and her eldest son were allowed to view the body, which was laid out on a table and still warm. Dolan removed the cross around his father's neck and they were handed a bag with his meager personal belongings before heading home. When they pulled up outside Victor Court, the four other siblings already knew. A nurse had phoned the house earlier, looking for Dolan, unaware he was already en route to the hospital, and Bob had pleaded with her to tell him what happened. As the family met in the driveway, the only thing left to do was to embrace.

The days that followed were largely a blur. That first evening, Dolan took his youngest brother, Patrick, home with him to the rectory at Immacolata to give his mother space to grieve in private, and to make sure the youngest in the family was all right. Dolan had been ordained little more than nine months and suddenly found himself presiding over his own father's wake for two consecutive evenings, as well as the funeral. He phoned his good friend Busher from the North American College, who was working at a parish in Iowa City, and told him the news. They were all heading into Holy Week, an incredibly busy time in the Catholic calendar, so Dolan said he need not come. "Tim, be quiet," Busher replied. "I'll be there." The Ballwin community was devastated. Father Schilly delivered a heartfelt and tearful eulogy inside Holy Infant Church, which was standing room only, and the funeral procession of cars driving to the cemetery stretched far into the distance. Bob Dolan had been just fifty-one years old.

The death left a huge gap in all their lives. As the tributes poured in from well-wishers, the family came to appreciate how much respect both the adults and children in the neighborhood had for Bob. He was a man of great hospitality who loved to make people feel welcome. To the grown-ups, he felt like everyone's friend and a man who went out of his way to be a good neighbor. People didn't gravitate toward him when he entered a room the way they did with his eldest child, but he treated every guest that entered his home like royalty and loved to tell stories, joke, and laugh. For the youngsters in the neighborhood, Bob Senior had created a home where they always felt welcome. He was a man they were never afraid to approach to ask a question or a favor. Dolan also kept thinking about his father's perseverance, day in, day out, to keep food on the table. He never missed a day of work yet worked to live, rather than vice versa. His priority was to provide for his wife and kids, and he was always at his happiest when he was simply surrounded by them in his home. Dolan remembered vacations to the lake and playing

ball games in the backyard. When the family sat around the dinner table each evening, their father never took food from a bowl until everyone else had served themselves, no matter how hungry he was after a day
at work. He adored ketchup and smothered it on everything he could,
but when it came to the end of the week and the bottle was nearly empty,
he never touched it to ensure his children could enjoy the last remnants
instead. He was a good man and a good father, and the void in their
lives was large.

The siblings also came to understand exactly how much their father
had struggled and sacrificed for them, especially financially. The day
after the burial, Dolan and his brother Bob were asked to pick up their
father's belongings from work. All they found were a few coins and
some family photos. The hospital had also given the family a plastic bag
to take home with his possessions. Inside was his wristwatch, car keys,
wedding ring, and wallet. When Dolan looked inside the wallet he
found his father's driver's license, health insurance card, more photos,
and only one dollar bill. "It was terribly sad," Dolan said. "Probably the
greatest shock in my life."

The community helped out Shirley where possible. An insurance
policy was used to pay off the house and she was also eligible to collect
various benefits as the widow of a disabled war veteran, since Bob had
been left deaf in one ear from his military service. Shirley was working
in the cafeteria at Holy Infant at the time and soon after got a job
housekeeping for a wealthy woman in Chesterfield, Missouri. She later
worked for the pastor of St. Joseph Parish, which neighbored Holy Infant, and remained with him for about fifteen years, following him from
assignment to assignment, including ultimately to Immacolata, long after
Dolan had moved on. Bob Dolan was supposed to take a job out of state
and instead stayed home for a year to be close to his mother. The whole
family pulled together.

Dolan had to return to parish work, where he set about immersing himself in his new duties, but just three months after his father's funeral, grief struck the family once again. Sitting at the dinner table in late August, Dolan received a phone call from a neighbor informing him that no one had seen his maternal grandmother, Nonnie Lu, for a few days, and she wasn't answering her door. She lived only about a mile from Immacolata, so he immediately headed over to her house and found her dead. With his pastor, Monsignor Flavin, at his side, Dolan went to find his mother to break the sad news. It had been a trying time, and the Dolan family now faced yet another funeral and yet another loss. She was only sixty-five years old. "That was tough for my mom especially," Dolan later recalled.

Throwing himself back into parish duties at Immacolata once again, Dolan was given responsibility for coordinating the Catholic Youth Council (CYC), which became very active in the community. He organized meetings and pizza nights where the children found this young associate pastor engaging and vibrant. There was also great buzz about the election of a new pope: John Paul II. The former Polish cardinal Karol Wojtyla was a young, confident, and vigorous choice for pontiff who arrived at a time the church needed a boost of vitality. Dolan was swept up in the fervor as much as the rest of the Catholic world and started to follow everything the new Holy Father said and wrote.

In late April 1979, as the end of his third year at Immacolata approached, Cardinal Carberry pulled Dolan aside one day after confirmations to say he was considering sending him away for graduate studies. Carberry wanted to gauge Dolan's interest and asked the young priest what he would like to study. Although Dolan was happy where he was, it was a flattering and exciting offer. He dutifully told the cardinal he would study whatever was chosen for him but given a choice, he would opt for church history. A few days later Dolan received a phone call from the priests' secretary informing him the cardinal had just received a letter from Catholic University in Washington, D.C., which was offering a scholarship for a diocesan priest to study church history under none other than Monsignor John Tracy Ellis, whom Dolan had studied under in Rome. Carberry urged Dolan to apply. When he was accepted into the program, Dolan was over the moon. In June he packed his bags and moved to Washington, D.C., and could not wait to say a personal thank-you to Ellis for choosing him. "I'm so thrilled," he told the monsignor. "I won this scholarship out of all the priests in the country." Ellis looked at him. "Tim, you're the only one that applied." Dolan later found out Ellis had personally handed out the scholarship and was more than happy to have the former North American College student under his charge again.

Dolan once more thrived under the instruction of Ellis and the other professors who recognized his natural aptitude for studying and passion for history. The course covered the evolution of Catholicism in the United States but also required him to learn about church history more generally, including its development in modern Europe. He always appeared to grasp the topics with ease and never seemed to be overly burdened by the workload. His questions were insightful and his teachers were hopeful the world of academia might be in Dolan's future. Indeed, that was what Carberry had suggested Dolan would do. Before sending him to Washington, D.C., the cardinal had told him to get his master's degree and plan on returning to teach in one of St. Louis's Catholic high schools or colleges. Dolan figured he might well spend the rest of his life teaching history, and that path did not seem unappealing so he immersed himself in his new studies. However, as much as Dolan enjoyed studying and learning under Ellis, there remained a part of him that still longed to be working in a small community and getting to know his parishioners. When his Midwestern buddy from the North American College, Bob Busher, was allocated his own parish in 1979, Dolan told him frankly, "You are what I want to be: a pastor." To compensate, in his spare time he assisted at the National Shrine of the Immaculate Conception, the largest Roman Catholic church in the country, adjacent to Catholic University of America. He heard confessions, said Mass occasionally, and on Saturday gave tours of faith to visitors.

In October 1979, three months after Dolan had arrived in the nation's capital, an exciting visit popped up on the calendar. Pope John Paul II was on a tour of the United States and made a visit to the basilica to address students and faculty at the university. Dolan made sure he was present for it all, including the pope's Mass on the National Mall. It was the first time he had seen the pontiff up close, but not the last. That first Christmas as a graduate student, Dolan didn't have a parish to attend to and knew this would be one of the only times in his priestly life he would be free of obligations at this typically busy time of year. So when he spotted an advertisement in the Catholic paper offering a nine-day tour of the Holy Land followed by a visit to Rome, he signed up. The tour group was in the Italian capital for New Year's Eve and Dolan knew that tradition dictated the pope headed to the Church of the Gesù to close the year out with Mass. "Why don't we go there?" Dolan suggested to the rest of the group. "I bet we can stand on the steps and see the Holy Father arrive." Sure enough, John Paul II arrived outside the church and walked over to greet a number of the well-wishers, including Dolan. "It was a quick handshake but I can very much remember being very much inspired by him," he later recalled. The encounters served to further intensify Dolan's desire to learn more about the Catholic leader. "I made it my business to read everything about him and follow him very intensely," Dolan explained.

By the time Dolan's two years in Washington, D.C., were drawing to a close and his master's degree was almost complete, Carberry had retired and his successor, Archbishop John May, was at the helm. Dolan informed

May that he assumed he would soon return to St. Louis to follow through on Carberry's plans for him, but May had other ideas. He asked Dolan if he had any interest in staying on in the nation's capital for two more years to get his doctorate. Dolan told his archbishop he would love to. "We're blessed with a good number of priests in St. Louis. Stay," May told him. Dolan was delighted and was sure his professor and mentor, Ellis, had had a hand in the decision behind the scenes.

Studying for his Ph.D. in American church history involved writing a doctoral dissertation, and Dolan selected as his topic the life and ministry of the late Archbishop Edwin O'Hara, who had headed the Diocese of Great Falls, Montana, and later Kansas City, Missouri. O'Hara was a powerful and innovative Catholic leader who founded the Catholic Biblical Association. He was theologically liberal and pushed for the greater involvement of the laity in church life. Dolan was one of twenty-five doctoral students under the direction of Monsignor Robert Trisco, and to research his doctoral thesis, Dolan had to move to Kansas City for a year. There, he trawled through the diocese archives and interviewed people in the community who were old enough to remember O'Hara, who had died in 1956, twenty-three years earlier. He went to live at St. Elizabeth Parish, south of the city center, where Father Richard Carney was the pastor. One of the priests he found himself living alongside in the rectory was Father Michael Caruso, who had been ordained only a few months earlier and assigned to St. Elizabeth as associate pastor. Dolan spent his days researching and writing diligently, but in the evenings he and Caruso sat down for meals, went for walks, or smoked cigars together.

Although he was living in the rectory, there was no obligation for Dolan to get involved in parish life to the extent that he chose to. He became engaged with all aspects of the local community, helping with the sacramental work of the church and getting to know the families by name. He occasionally joined a group of elderly parishioners at their

Sunday morning "breakfast club" meal of pancakes, bacon, and eggs at restaurant chain Waid's following the seven A.M. Mass. He acted more like an associate pastor and, as Caruso saw it, he had the makings of "an exemplary priest." Dolan's passion for exploring a city by foot, the way he had in Rome, continued. He took himself off on marathon walks. It was a densely populated Catholic parish and near impossible to walk around the neighborhood without bumping into a familiar face. One beautiful spring evening, the first at the end of a long and hard winter, Caruso and Dolan decided to take a walk after dinner. Caruso didn't have any appointments and Dolan had decided to put his books down for the night, so they headed to Jacob L. Loose Park. They bought some cigars on the way and were strolling around the lake when they came upon a retired Irish priest who lived at a nearby parish. Dolan immediately offered Father Clary a cigar, but he declined, saying he didn't smoke. Dolan suggested he could take one back to Monsignor Tighe, a well-loved pastor who was also retired and lived in the same location as Clary. "I don't believe so," Clary replied. "The monsignor only smokes the expensive brands." Dolan and Caruso chuckled at having been put firmly in their place by the old priest and soon continued on their way.

Caruso frequently invited Dolan over to his own family's home on Sunday afternoons, when his mother whipped up delicious Italian meals. He met Caruso's pastor friends, and the pair occasionally headed to one of their parishes for the night to hang out. Some days they grabbed their bathing suits and towels and visited the home of a local family who had a swimming pool and an open-door policy, jokingly telling the parish receptionist that they were "going out on a sick call" and not to expect to hear from them for a while. There remained no stemming his adoration of baseball, either. Some afternoons Dolan and Caruso accompanied a group of youngsters who helped to serve Mass to a Kansas City Royals game. They often had nosebleed tickets and on at least one occasion found themselves seated alongside a rabble of very drunk fans, but catching a ball game was one of life's necessities for Dolan and a fun excursion for the kids.

Dolan's joyful view of the world was infectious, and Caruso enjoyed spending time with him and learning by example. They talked about sports and matters of the church and cracked jokes endlessly. In his spare time, Dolan read avidly and always had a title on the go. Without fail, he woke up early for prayers and tried to incorporate some form of exercise into his day. The death of his father still weighed heavily on his mind, and when the eighth anniversary rolled around, the schedule said Caruso was to offer the Mass that morning. Dolan asked if he might take it instead. Dolan always spoke fondly of his father and told heartwarming stories about him.

As his research drew to a close, Dolan went back home to await his next orders. Archbishop May had suggested Dolan might be put to use teaching back at Kenrick Seminary but instead assigned him to be an associate pastor at Curé of Ars Parish in Shrewsbury, outside St. Louis, in 1984. The pastor was Father Lambert Hrdlicka. It was a relatively small parish but near the seminary library, and May felt it was a good place for Dolan to be stationed while he put some finishing touches on his dissertation and defended it, which he did successfully. His final thesis was lauded a success and the Catholic University of America press deemed it worthy of being published in a revised form under the title *Some Seed Fell on Good Ground: The Life of Edwin V. O'Hara.* Dolan then approached May and told him he was ready. His doctorate was done, he could go teach at Kenrick Seminary full-time. He even had it in his head that he might remain at Curé of Ars on the side. But it wasn't to be. A brisk call came through from someone on the personnel board, telling Dolan he wasn't needed at Kenrick Seminary and he was going to be moved from Curé of Ars to become an associate pastor at Little Flower in Richmond Heights instead. Dolan was disappointed. He felt he had been gearing up for becoming a history professor and now he was suddenly being diverted elsewhere again, but a young priest knew better than to question the authority of his church superiors, so he diligently said he would go wherever he was needed.

Bishop George Gottwald was the pastor when Dolan arrived at Little Flower, a picturesque church in a leafy middle-class neighborhood on the borders of St. Louis, in 1985. As soon as he arrived, parishioners realized they had someone different on their hands. His homilies were engaging and thought provoking but blissfully never too long. He turned Bible stories into narratives that were relevant to the congregation's everyday lives. He had a way of simplifying the church's message without detracting from its meaning. Nearly thirty years later, some of his parishioners still remember the lessons he taught them. "You know a doctor can't help you if you don't allow him, and the Lord is the same way," Mark Mueller recalls Dolan saying. Mueller was only in his early teens at the time but still marvels at Dolan's ability to make his sermons stick in the mind. "You can be at a parish sermon that lasts for fifteen minutes and not remember it an hour later," he said. Although Dolan only stayed at Little Flower for two years, he made a lasting impression. When he wasn't in the church, he marched around the neighborhood with a shillelagh stick in one hand and a flat cap on his head, an old soul in a young man's body. "How you doing? I'm Father Dolan," he bellowed at anyone he passed by before stopping to knock on doors for a quick visit. "Oh, I'll come in for a beer," he said if one was offered, and residents were flattered to think this young priest could make time for them. He quickly got to know nearly everyone living in the neighborhood and they could not help noticing him. How they managed to get assigned this intriguing young assistant pastor was something they discussed among themselves: "He is too good," they would remark.

It was through these walks that Dolan came to know the Kelly family. Bill and Jeannie were regular churchgoers with vibrant personalities and five rambunctious children. Their oldest was sixteen and their youngest only a toddler. Bill loved to impersonate people and wrote *Saturday Night Live*–style skits about parishioners at Little Flower. The Kellys became a regular fixture in Dolan's life and he nicknamed them Fred and Ethel after the couple in the *I Love Lucy* television series. He frequently stopped by to see how they were and, on occasion, entered their home to find Jeannie juggling what looked like a thousand tasks at once. Her baby boy was in the high chair eating, she was cooking dinner, and their one-hundred-pound dog—a mixture of German shepherd, husky, and collie—was trying to grab food from the baby, who was feeding himself one moment and the dog the next. In swept Dolan and, without asking what he could do to assist, he grabbed the baby and started to feed him. Jeannie was eternally grateful. "What manner of man is this that even notices my problems?" she wondered.

The job as associate pastor involved the usual duties: presiding over Mass and performing baptisms, weddings, confirmations, and also funerals. Since he was new to the community, there were often occasions when Dolan was charged with saying a few words of remembrance for someone who had died but whom he did not know personally. He always approached Bill beforehand to ask his advice. Bill, a quick-witted man with astute observation, gave Dolan the lowdown, explaining what the person did for a living, what hobbies they had, and what their character was like. As he and Jeannie sat in the pews during the homily, Dolan skillfully used all the little nuggets of information he had obtained to paint an accurate and fitting portrait of the person they were gathering to pay tribute to. Bill nicknamed Dolan Fireball for the quick-fire way he grasped a topic and ran with it, and the nickname stuck.

On Halloween, Dolan bought candy and gave it out to the kids who came to trick-or-treat. He borrowed the Kelly family's 1984 Chevy Caprice station wagon occasionally to take local youngsters on excursions. If he saw the boys playing roller hockey in the schoolyard he'd shout and see if they wanted to come into the church for soda. He offered teenagers in the community eight dollars an hour to take calls in the rectory. One day Dolan approached Jeannie and Bill's oldest daughter, Mary Theresa: "Hey, I need someone to answer phone calls at the rectory, can you do it?" It was hard to say no to Father Dolan. Once or twice a week, Mary Theresa spent the day in the rectory getting a feel for the day-to-day life of the church. She and the other youngsters fielded calls from parishioners requesting a visit for a dying relative, or answered the door to couples who were asking for some marriage guidance. The youngsters, who were inevitably at an age where their blossoming social lives seemed more appealing than church, were suddenly made to feel like they were in on a secret. Seeing how things worked from the inside of the church was fascinating, and the pocket money came in use, too.

Dolan was quick to reach out a helping hand when he spotted someone in need. When a young homeless boy in the community was dropping out of school, he sought help from Jack Lally, a former teacher of his from Cardinal Glennon College who was a member of Little Flower Parish and now involved in Catholic Charities. He asked if Lally might know any agency that might be able to assist. Dolan also taught part-time in the grade school and at St. Louis University and offered a class in scripture study on the Acts of the Apostles to a group of women after morning Mass. He also met with members of Project Rachel, the Catholic Church's program for women who have had abortions, offering an opportunity for prayer. Dolan liked things to be orderly, and if there was an area that needed attention, he tackled it. One day he set his mind on the church basement, which was loaded up with years' worth of broken records, props, and discarded costumes from plays. He enlisted the help of a parishioner and his son, and they spent the day hauling unwanted objects out onto the curb for trash pickup.

When Dolan was two months shy of two happy years at Little Flower, he was reluctantly informed he was on the move again. He adored his life in the parish but received word a hugely prestigious new assignment awaited. He was being sent to work as a secretary at the apostolic nunciature in Washington, D.C., essentially the Vatican's embassy in the United States. It was 1987, just three years after the United States and the Vatican formally established diplomatic relations, and he was to report to the apostolic nuncio, Pio Laghi, who had the equivalent rank of an ambassador. Laghi was an archbishop at the time, though he would later be elevated to cardinal, and he became an invaluable person under whom to learn. He was Dolan's boss for three years, until Archbishop Agostino Cacciavillan became the papal nuncio for the remainder of his time there.

The Massachusetts Avenue building housing the apostolic nunciature is located across the street from the U.S. vice president's official residence and has two primary functions. The apostolic nunciature maintains diplomatic relations between the Holy See and the U.S. president, and also acts as a liaison between the pope and the American Catholic hierarchy. The office is, effectively, the pope's eyes and ears in the United States. Anything that needs to be said, done, understood, or investigated takes place there, and the appointment gave Dolan his first real insight into the inner workings and politics of the Catholic Church. He also had access to an abundance of archives, including research documents and reports from all dioceses, which provided a big-picture view of Catholic faith in United States.

On Memorial Day weekend 1987, shortly after Dolan had arrived in the nation's capital, Laghi invited Dolan to dinner at a country club with Monsignor Joseph Coyne, the pastor at Little Flower in Bethesda, Maryland, and Father Peter Vaghi, a priest from nearby St. Ann's Parish who was two years ordained. The four priests sat at a corner table and traded stories all evening and it was an opportunity for Dolan to start making friends in his new community. Vaghi had grown up in D.C. and had also graduated from the North American College. The two men, a couple of years apart in age, instantly hit it off. Coyne invited the St. Louis native to help out at his own parish if he had any spare time between his duties at the nunciature. Eager to continue developing his skills as a pastor despite his highly administrative role, Dolan accepted and began presiding over one of the Sunday services and volunteered to take an evening Mass during Lent. Here, too, the parishioners were drawn to his pastoral style, especially those short, punchy homilies.

At the nunciature, Dolan was assigned to be a secretary to Laghi. His responsibilities ranged from more mundane duties like keeping the archbishop's calendar in order or taking notes as he sifted through his letters and dictated a response, to meeting influential heads of state and the U.S. president. He also discovered he was working alongside one of his classmates from the North American College, Bernard Yarrish, who had also recently been appointed secretary to Laghi. They both had rooms on the fourth floor of the embassy and bonded over their mutual love of good food. Dolan loved nothing more than a hearty meal—meat and potatoes, if available—and they ventured out for dinner together several evenings and swiftly became close friends and a great source of companionship.

Dolan used to sit with friends and casually banter about which priest they thought would be made a bishop, or which bishop they felt was best suited to a post that had opened up. Now he was involved in the core of that exact decision-making process. One of the duties that consumed a large amount of his time was compiling reports on priests who were up for promotion. This would involve hours of meticulous research into the individual's background, his health, his affability, and even his language skills. The nuncio's office needed to determine why a particular person would be a suitable candidate, and where they might fall short. They sent letters to priests and laypeople in the diocese asking questions about how the candidate handled themselves on a day-to-day basis, if they had good relationships with the congregation, and how they got on with other priests. If a recommendation letter was returned with unfavorable remarks, calls had to be made to the priest in question so the issue could be addressed directly. It involved walking a tightrope between potentially offending someone and unearthing the truth, and Dolan quickly acquired some essential tools of diplomacy. "It gave you the flavor of the universal church," Yarrish recalled. He also developed an understanding for how the Catholic Church operated, top to bottom.

As much as Dolan got to understand the inner workings of the church and the names of priests and bishops around the United States, so, too, did they come to know him. Clergy paid close attention to who was working in the nuncio's office, given that this was where appointments were made, and some attempted to strike up friendships via their regular correspondences to find out if they were being considered for any post or promotion. When bishops were called in to meet with Laghi face-to-face, Dolan became the warm-up act of choice. "He just seemed to be so different from most of the other people who worked there," Yarrish explained. "Pretty much his goal was to make the people comfortable." Dolan's gregarious personality marked him out, and as the visitors waited to enter the nuncio's office, he made it his responsibility to laugh and chat jovially to ensure they were comfortable and at ease. By the time they stepped into Laghi's office, the guests were relaxed and happy from having been in his presence.

Once the reports on priests up for promotion were compiled, they had to be sent to Rome to get the pope's seal of approval. Dolan's Italian counterparts, also based in D.C., were responsible for first translating these reports from English into Italian to send to the Holy See. Slang phrases like "happy-go-lucky" often baffled the foreigners and they worked closely together to ensure that the recommendation wasn't misconstrued or diluted before being sent. Then, when the appointment of a new bishop was finally approved, the apostolic nunciature made the news public and Dolan worked with diocesan staff to find a date Laghi was available to attend the ceremony. Laghi did not have to install every bishop personally, but he chose to. He loved to travel, so the plane trips were no inconvenience; plus, they gave him an opportunity to meet these bishops face-to-face and get a feel for the way their dioceses were run. Sometimes, if the budget allowed, Dolan, Yarrish, or another member of the staff was invited along for the installation.

It was an around-the-clock job, and both physically and mentally tiring, but it came with some obvious perks. Some evenings Laghi would be entertaining an important government official and extend the invite to Yarrish and Dolan. They met President George H. W. Bush and First Lady Barbara Bush and soon got used to being introduced to high-powered politicians and diplomats. In September 1987, Laghi also invited staff from the nunciature to fly down to Miami to greet the pope as he arrived on U.S. soil for a whirlwind ten-day tour. Working for the papal ambassador, Dolan was becoming even more familiar with Pope John Paul II's talks and teachings. In preparing letters for parishes, issuing greetings, and giving press calls, the nunciature staff had to be up to speed on every statement the pope made and how they should be interpreted on a local level to ensure dioceses fell in line with the pontiff's vision. He also came to know all the American cardinals and these skills and contacts garnered in Washington, D.C., proved invaluable later in his life. Equally important, bishops around the country came to know Dolan's name.

Always an avid reader, Dolan joined a book club with Vaghi, the priest he had met at dinner at the country club shortly after arriving, and bestowed upon him the nickname Don Pedro, since his first name was Peter. Every four to six weeks the pair met with a few other priests to discuss a text someone had recommended. It was an opportunity to read an array of fiction and nonfiction and since he was still soaking up John Paul II's writings, Dolan's contribution one month was the pope's *Crossing the Threshold of Hope.* Vaghi had left his first parish and was now settled at St. Patrick's, a few blocks from the White House, and asked Dolan to come and help out in his spare time. Never one to pass up the opportunity to be a priest, Dolan happily agreed and heard confessions on weekends and some evenings.

As he adjusted to living in a large urban area, Dolan often popped in to visit an old pal from his Ballwin days who was living nearby in Baltimore and then in Wilmington, Delaware. Tim Caimi's childhood home had been right by the Dolan household and he and his siblings had constantly played ball together in the Victor Court cul-de-sac. When Caimi's father passed away, Bob and Shirley had opened their doors to him and he had never forgotten it. Now that Dolan was working in the vicinity, the two childhood friends were able to spend time together once again. Dolan frequently pulled up into the drive, cigar in mouth, decked out in a Cardinals baseball cap and jacket and immediately threw himself into a game of Candy Land or Mouse Trap with Caimi's kids. If he had his priest's collar on when he arrived, he changed into regular attire. The friends reminisced about Ballwin as they played music, drank beer, smoked cigars, and barbecued. Dolan might have had an audience with President George H. W. Bush the day before, or have spoken to an influential cardinal rising up the Vatican ranks, but he preferred to ask how Caimi's week had been and he rarely talked about himself. On one visit Dolan brought a picture of himself throwing a ball to the president and first lady's dog. Caimi was impressed but not by the photograph as much as by his friend's demeanor. "He's [at the Bush house] throwing a tennis ball to Bush's dog and the next day he's at my house playing games with my kids for hours," he said. "That's about as real as you can get."

Old friends often found themselves in D.C. and made a point of spending time with Dolan. One classmate from Cardinal Glennon College, Father Michael Joyce, was completing his doctorate at Catholic University, and during Holy Week they concelebrated Holy Thursday Mass with Laghi at the National Basilica. It was quickly obvious to Joyce that his old friend was going places. "It was evident to me that Cardinal Laghi had a certain affection and affinity for Father Tim that surpassed that of his other staff," Joyce recalled. "I could just see Laghi would put his eyes more on Tim, would joke with him more than the rest of his staff." It was Joyce whom Dolan had offered to sacrifice his place for at the North American College many years prior and, during a car ride back from visiting a mutual friend one day, Joyce said playfully he wasn't sure Dolan would be able to keep his head on his shoulders if he became bishop one day, something Dolan was now clearly destined to become. Without hesitation Dolan replied, "All I want to be is a parish priest."

It was around this time that Dolan also had to deal with some difficult news concerning one of his best friends from his days in Rome. Christopher Peck, whom Dolan had explored every inch of the city with, called the nunciature one day in the late 1980s. "Tim," he said. "I've been diagnosed with HIV/AIDS." Peck had taken a leave of absence a few years after their ordination in 1976 and soon after fell off the radar completely. Last Dolan knew, Peck had been working in the San Francisco area. However, despite Dolan's best attempts to find him, Peck had vanished. It took at least five years before Peck resurfaced. He rejoined the priesthood and became a chaplain at a Catholic hospital but always stayed quiet about where he had been and what he had done. Dolan did not push the subject. Now it seemed clear that his friend had been grappling with homosexuality and had engaged in behavior the church would not condone. Still, Dolan did not pry or judge, and the news did not hamper their friendship. Dolan continued to visit Peck and, the week before he died, they concelebrated Mass on his deathbed.

"Tim, you know I'm dying," he said. "When I do, would you bring my remains over to Rome?" Peck asked to be laid to rest at Rome's famous Campo Verano cemetery. Dolan promised he would but admitted he wasn't sure of the logistics. "You could bring me over in your carry-on bag, for all I care," he said. "As long as there's a bottle of Sambuca by my remains." After his friend's passing, Dolan kept his word.

Agostino Cacciavillan replaced Laghi for Dolan's penultimate two years at the papal nunciature in Washington, D.C., from 1990 to 1992. He was an intelligent, Italian-born man who had had a long career in the papal diplomatic world before arriving in Washington, D.C., having most recently served in Kenya. Dolan diligently continued his duties as secretary alongside Yarrish, who was having his own health issues. He had begun to experience a tingling sensation in his limbs and eventually discovered he was suffering from multiple sclerosis. Dolan provided support as Yarrish dealt with the news and sought out treatment.

After five years in Washington, D.C., Dolan's time was drawing to an end, and his fate once again rested with Archbishop May back in the Archdiocese of St. Louis. Again, dutifully, Dolan told his archbishop he would do whatever he was asked. It was the standard reply all priests say, but May was a shrewd man and wanted to know what was really on Dolan's mind. "I'd love to be a pastor," Dolan said. He explained his first choice would be Little Flower, as he had such fond memories of working and living in that parish; his number two choice would be to work in campus ministry at the Newman Center at Washington University in St. Louis. May took it on board, but by now there were others vying for Dolan's talents. The rector of Kenrick Seminary, Ronald Ramson, had approached May, requesting Dolan as his deputy. "What? You're crazy. I want him," the archbishop replied, and then offered Ramson a deal. "You go to Washington, D.C., and you talk to him," he said. "If he says yes, you can have him. But, I hope he doesn't." Ramson traveled to D.C. and made his pitch to Dolan, who explained truthfully that his real dream was to be a pastor, but if Archbishop May wanted him to be vice rector, Ramson had made a good case. Ramson was delighted, and declared victory.

Dolan had never worked at a seminary before, but his reputation as an excellent student and expert in church history preceded him. His primary role was to serve as Ramson's right-hand man in the administration and operational aspects of the seminary. Seminary life was divided into four pillars: human, spiritual, academic, and pastoral, and together Dolan and Ramson ensured they were all adequately addressed. During the two years that Dolan was vice rector at Kenrick Seminary, from 1992 to 1994, the building went through a major overhaul. The property that had formerly housed Cardinal Glennon College became the seminary school, and Dolan acted as liaison between the archdiocese and the seminary during the renovation. Ramson had made the pitch for Dolan because he knew he had the organizational skills and the smarts, and that he was good with people. "I knew he would be a good vice rector and he and I could work closely together because he was a team player," Ramson said. During his time as vice rector, Dolan also served as the director of spiritual formation, gave lectures as a professor of church history, and found time to be an adjunct professor of theology at St. Louis University. In between all this, some of the children from the three local parishes he had served at in St. Louis were now growing up and getting engaged. Several retained very fond memories of his ability to distill Catholicism down into basic principles and asked if he could guide them through premarital exercises. "It all begins with prayer," Dolan told Mark Guyol and his bride-to-be. Then he got into the practicalities. "You need to talk about money. Are you on the same page? Are you in agreement about children?" Guyol was forever grateful for his pragmatic yet spiritual approach. "It solidified our relationship and friendship," he said about his marriage.

Dolan's work in Washington, D.C., and now as vice rector in St. Louis ensured he had caught the attention of many United States bishops. Bishop Edward Egan of Bridgeport, Connecticut, who was chairman of the board of the North American College in Rome, was among them. He knew the college's current rector, Monsignor Edwin O'Brien, was scheduled to leave, and finding the right person to replace him was vital. The college had been through a turbulent few decades and O'Brien had been a great steadying influence, but all that progress could go to waste if the next rector was not up to the job. Ultimately, the decision would be made by the head of the Congregation for Catholic Education, who names the rectors for all the national Catholic colleges. By chance, that position was now being filled by Archbishop Pio Laghi—Dolan's former boss from his days at the papal nunciature in Washington, D.C. Egan heard whispers about some of the candidates being floated around and wasn't happy with the choices, so he jumped on a plane to Rome. He phoned Laghi, an old friend he had known for years, and cheekily invited himself to lunch the following week. Before they had even walked into the restaurant, Egan had presented Laghi with thirteen signed letters, one from every member of the North American College board, all throwing their weight behind the candidate Egan believed was the only man for the job: Timothy Dolan. "Now I'm going to play my ace," he told Laghi, and placed a letter in his hands from one more cardinal who was not on the board but who held great sway. "You don't do things this way," Laghi told him. "Your Eminence, in Rome this is exactly what you do." Egan pressed on: "I really do want Dolan. I know what I want."

Egan, also a graduate of Rome's North American College, had come to know and admire Dolan. He found him prayerful, happy, and supremely intelligent. He knew he was an excellent church historian and had acquired first-rate administrative skills working under Laghi at the papal nunciature. Dolan's recent assignment at Kenrick-Glennon Seminary had also given him a feel for the duties of a rector, and Egan had every confidence he had exactly the qualities the North American College needed at that moment in time. "I wanted him because I felt he would be a wonderful influence on the young men," Egan later said. "I thought the college needed a burst of enthusiasm, a man who could handle men very well." "I wanted a guy who will hit the baseball farther than anybody else," Egan would later recall. Laghi and Egan sat down for lunch, but since Egan had effectively invited himself along, the two were not alone and he wasn't able to further bolster his arguments in Dolan's favor. As the coffee came around at the end of a long Italian meal, Laghi turned to Egan and told him the words he had been hoping for: "Egan, you can have your Dolan."

Dolan received word of his new assignment and had to break the news to Ramson, who knew something was up as soon as he laid eyes on his vice rector. Ramson was unquestionably disappointed to lose him but understood it was a prestigious offer and impossible to turn down. Dolan then had to break the news to his family and start packing his bags for Rome once again. He decided against having his family wave him off at the airport this time because it was too emotional. Instead he said good-bye to them at Little Flower Church and asked his high school and college friend, Father Rich Hanneke, to drive him. As they said their tearful good-byes, Shirley looked at Hanneke. "We'll never get him back, will we?" she asked. He looked at her and replied truthfully, "I don't think so."

6

RECTOR DOLAN

Roger Landry was barely two weeks into his first semester at the North American College when his class received an invitation to a meet-and-greet with the rector. The twenty-five-year-old was a smart, driven Harvard graduate from Lowell, Massachusetts, who was keen to make a good first impression. He had been sent to the prestigious American seminary with his twin brother, Scot, and as he climbed the stairs with the other students and knocked on the door of the rector's suite he was eager to put his best foot forward. The scene that greeted Landry caused him to stop in his tracks. There to welcome them to their new lives was an oversized man exuding boundless energy, delivering one-liners, passing out cigars, and using his desk as a bar to serve soda or cocktails. Landry was dumbstruck. He thought the rector might be stiff, perhaps a little nervous, certainly someone encouraging them not to have too much fun. Instead, here was a man full of joy, thriving on being the life and soul of the party and not hesitating to poke fun at the guy choking on cigar smoke. "It blew the concepts that I had anticipated the rector of the North American College to be," Landry later said. "It decimated them."

Dolan had been rector of the North American College for a year by the time Landry and his classmates landed in the Italian capital. It was

1995 and he was well settled into the role. Dolan made it a priority to ensure everyone felt warmly welcomed under his roof when they arrived as New Men and placed great importance on being accessible and approachable to students throughout their formation. He would come to expect much of them, but he never wanted them to stop being satisfied in their vocation. He himself had always felt a deep inner joy and fulfillment with the path he had chosen, and he wanted these men to be good priests. Above all else, however, he wanted them to be happy priests. Dolan could easily recall how despairingly homesick he was leaving Missouri for the first time to head to the North American College and hoped to make these New Men feel at ease instead. As each year's new class pulled up by bus at the front entrance, the bells of the college rang and a group of older students waited to escort the men inside to the main chapel. Tired, disorientated, and often feeling trepidation about what lay ahead, the men accepted Dolan's invitation first to pray together. He then read them a passage from Saint Paul's letter to the Corinthians, asking them to ponder these words: "'I consider everything as a loss when compared to the supreme good of knowing Christ Jesus my Lord.' You've all lost a lot," Dolan told them, explaining frankly that he understood they had left behind families, homes, friends, and, in some cases, girlfriends, by making a decision to prepare for the priesthood. He knew they'd also lost all the familiarity of their old lives, including even the language, and the path ahead was unknown. "Let those words of Saint Paul resonate with you," he told them. "You may have lost a lot but you've still got the greatest gift of all . . . your faith in your knowledge of your love for Jesus Christ." Dolan was confident these young men could relate to exactly what Saint Paul was talking about.

Dolan had replaced Monsignor Edwin O'Brien at the North American College, a Bronx native who had previously served as rector of the Saint Joseph's Seminary in the Archdiocese of New York, just north of the city. O'Brien had arrived in Rome on January 1, 1990, with instructions to steady a seminary that had lost its way in recent decades. Enrollment was down, funds were dwindling, and cynicism was high. Bishops back in America had lost confidence in the thoroughness of the formation students were receiving in Rome and some decided they no longer wanted to spend archdiocese funds sending their best and brightest overseas. O'Brien himself had spearheaded a move not to send any more New Yorkers to the North American College while he was in charge at Saint Joseph's Seminary after one alum returned from Rome and left the priesthood just six months after ordination. It was seriously worrisome to O'Brien that the doubts in this young man's mind had not been adequately noticed or addressed by faculty before he took his vows. "A young man will give himself to a mystery, but not to a question mark," he later said.

The difficulties the North American College faced were consequences of the wider changes the Catholic Church was grappling with in the wake of the Second Vatican Council. The council had convened to revitalize the church, bring it into the modern era, and promote greater interaction with the larger world. However, it had also sparked a revolution that redefined religious life. Students passing through the North American College and seminaries back in the United States in the late 1960s through the 1980s experienced huge freedom and autonomy compared to their predecessors. The spirit of the age encouraged the relaxation of rules and formalities. There was no curfew, liturgies became increasingly informal, openness was encouraged, and as a result, private devotion was frowned upon as too insular. Prior to O'Brien's arrival, if a student was seen to be overly pious it was a red flag. Faculty might even pull the man aside for questioning or give a harsh year-end evaluation. While this cultural shift was motivated by a desire to create a more inclusive church community rather than one where worship took place in isolation, the decline of a regimented style of formation was failing to sufficiently challenge students about their vocation and left many unprepared for the realities of a life in the priesthood. The right balance between focus and openness had to be established, and it was not until O'Brien's arrival that this issue was addressed.

O'Brien had a military background, having served as an army chaplain at the military academy West Point, at Fort Bragg, and in Vietnam. He immediately introduced more structure into the daily routine. A meeting of the synod of bishops in 1990 produced a document that outlined how formation for U.S. seminarians needed to improve, and it had fallen on O'Brien to implement it. He instructed staff to concelebrate Mass instead of sitting in the front rows of the chapel observing, and he demanded the entire college celebrate Mass together at the start of every day. O'Brien said students should wear clerical attire—black shirts, pants, and white collars—to school instead of civilian clothes, and he addressed simmering rumors about homosexuality among students. O'Brien informed them that anyone with specific knowledge of same-sex encounters had an obligation to speak up, in confidence, to their spiritual director or to himself. He said it wasn't a witch hunt and there would be "no blood on the walls," but it was an issue that needed to be dealt with. Many years later, O'Brien went on the record saying seminaries were no place for men with strong homosexual tendencies, even if they had been celibate for more than a decade.

During his five-year stint as rector, O'Brien encouraged visits from American bishops so they could see the changes taking effect and the value of making an investment in the college once again. They slowly resumed sending their seminarians to study in Rome, providing a vital source of income, as the men's archdiocese covered the cost of tuition. By the time Dolan arrived in Rome, he was thankful to find a well-organized system in place that had already dealt with most of the push-back the new system had evoked. However, he also knew the hard work was far from over. There was a lot riding on his ability to build on the changes his predecessor had introduced, and take the college to the next level.

Since Egan had wagered a lot of his reputation on championing Dolan for the rector's job above other contenders, he sought to reassure other bishops about his choice. In the summer months before the North American College semester started, Egan invited Dolan to one of the biannual bishops' conferences in San Diego, California. Egan was chairman and wanted to give the bishops a chance to meet the new rector face-to-face and appreciate firsthand not only his charisma but also his scholarly ability. Dolan was asked to speak to the men about church history, an unusual event for the bishops, who did not typically receive a talk from someone outside their ranks. It did the trick, however. They were suitably impressed and reassured about the caliber of man who was taking charge of the spiritual development of their most promising seminarians in Rome.

As Dolan settled in and went about putting his own stamp on the North American College, he never hesitated to share the fun side of his personality with the seminarians. Several times a week Dolan bounded into the student lounge where the men hung out and relaxed to greet them and share a joke. On occasion he declared, "Everything's on my tab!" and invited the seminarians to have an ice cream, soda, or candy on him. Seminarians didn't have a lot of money, so his generosity was always well received. He frequently stopped by as they tuned in to watch a recording of the news anchored by ABC's Peter Jennings at two P.M. after lunch. Dolan passed a few comments before encouraging them to get back to work. Or he wandered the corridors of their dorm rooms to check everyone was all right but was careful never to overstay his welcome, knowing that the rector was there to be a mentor, not a friend.

Although Dolan encouraged the young men to let loose where appropriate, it quickly became abundantly clear that behind his hearty laugh, the back slaps, and the cigar smoke, he expected much in return. He rarely talked to the men about rules; he preferred to talk about expectations. He typically refrained from reprimanding students who were oversleeping or missing class, hoping instead to instill a sense of internal accountability. He wanted them to take ownership of their spiritual development and be able to exist on their own when they were out in the world, in a parish, without a faculty member breathing down their neck. For many of the men this was initially unnerving, but for Dolan it was about making the priesthood a way of life, not a series of rules that must be followed and would, inevitably, be broken. Dolan's gentle yet direct way of enforcing authority let students know he noticed if they were not pulling their weight. And it mattered. Walking from the chapel to the dining room one day, he interrupted his conversation with a faculty member midflow to address a student. "Oh, Joe, you weren't at Mass today, where were you?" Such a pointed question from Dolan was enough to make you realize you needed to up your game.

The students also soon discovered the rector's joie de vivre was matched only by his piety, and it was something Dolan deliberately put on full display. Where other priests hid their private devotions or had eliminated them from their life of prayer because they were not in keeping with the times, Dolan challenged the notion that piety and openness were mutually exclusive by making a point of letting others see him pray. Every day before evening prayer, he paced back and forth at the entrance to the main chapel, reciting the rosary for about fifteen minutes. He had his hands behind his back, rosary beads between his fingers, and was sweating profusely, as he did even in winter. Dolan also moved statues to more prominent positions around the grounds, a symbolic gesture that subtly acknowledged the importance of religious symbols to Catholics. One day, the Sacred Heart of Jesus statue appeared on the front lawn unexpectedly; a while later a new plaque went up in a corridor. The faculty joked it felt like every month something was relocated. Dolan started a habit of gathering the whole college community together each Saturday outside in front of the statue of Our Lady of Lourdes, by the college's rear exit. There, he genuflected on a granite kneeler to lead the recitation of the rosary, never rising, while most seminarians lacked the stamina to kneel for its entirety. His love for the Blessed Virgin Mary and his piety were on full display. For the seminarians, these small gestures had an important and lasting impact. They taught them to be proud of their faith and to embrace it, and increased their respect for Dolan's spiritual guidance. "It gave me greater confidence," Landry said. "When he needed to give me fraternal corrections, I knew it was coming from a priest who prayed. . . . I knew that he was listening to the Lord, and it increased his authority on a personal level."

Dolan conducted an entry interview with the seminarians when they arrived, and made a point of visiting each of the New Men in their room. It served two purposes for him. He felt he could tell plenty about a person by seeing the way he chose to live, and he felt it taught them the value of priestly visits. At the end of each year, the students had to attend an evaluation on their performance. They were invited to take a seat at a round boardroom table in front of the rector and a couple of faculty members, including the student's spiritual director and formation adviser. Each faculty member prepared a report on the individual, which they read aloud. Dolan took his turn last. He spoke without notes yet insightfully summed up exactly who the seminarian was and where they were excelling or struggling. His observations were acute, leaving some men baffled and somewhat embarrassed that the rector appeared to know them so well. He tried to make the evaluations fundamentally positive and encouraging for those who were working hard. He knew it wasn't an easy path and he wanted to nurture them to keep pushing on. "We trusted Monsignor Dolan to be able to look at the big picture," one seminarian said.

• • •

Dolan's responsibilities at the North American College made for a demanding schedule, and Dolan relied heavily on the staff around him for support. He therefore made sure to surround himself with people he respected and trusted whom he either knew personally or who came highly recommended. O'Brien had brought in a whole new faculty shortly after his tenure started, and Dolan was adept at spotting someone's talents and dividing up responsibilities to play to their strengths. He noticed how beloved one of the spiritual directors, Monsignor William Ogrodowski, was by the students, so he appointed him vice rector for student life. He asked his former professor from the Angelicum, Father Joseph Henchey, to come back to Rome as a spiritual director. He recruited Monsignor Cornelius McRae to be a spiritual director also. Plus, there was another welcome familiar face. Monsignor Bernard Yarrish, whom Dolan had worked alongside for years as secretary to the papal nuncio in Washington, D.C., was already in Rome working as vice rector for administration at the North American College. Their firm friendship and solid working relationship was long established and Yarrish became another trusted confidante.

Dolan preferred to involve faculty in the decision-making process rather than take a top-down authoritarian approach and with that in mind, he held a meeting every Friday morning to get everyone up to speed on new developments. While he was walking the corridors it was not uncommon for him to poke his head into someone's room unexpectedly and ask, "Hey, what do you think of this?" as a way of canvassing opinion about a new initiative. Even though he went by the book, he created a fair and open administration. Dolan had a whole administrative staff to get to know also. His personal assistant, Lory Mondaini, had heard much about her new boss long before she met him. "You're going to love him," people had told her. "You're going to hear a lot of laughter in these hallways," others said. Dolan lived up to the hype. He was exciting to work for and a straight talker who looked you in the eye when he spoke. It was rare to see him without a smile, either. When Mondaini brought her eleven-year-old son and eight-year-old daughter to the office on one of her first few days working with Dolan, he took them around the building, showing them the sports field and plying them with yogurt and Coca-Cola.

Dolan made coming into the office a joy. The administrative staff working around him often couldn't wait to hear his contagious laugh again on a Monday morning. "Lory," he bellowed down the corridor before she came into view. "I'm coming down, put the nail polish away." He wrote all his correspondence in longhand and Mondaini typed it up on a computer. If she got stuck in the office late because of an important letter that needed writing, he headed into the kitchen to get her something to eat. Dolan had an easy way with people, and it didn't take long before his staff all had nicknames. Mondaini became Della Street, after Perry Mason's fictional secretary. Mondaini was originally from New Jersey and that also provided fodder for teasing. "I'm going to be sending you back to school to learn English," he joked, to which Mondaini fired back: "*You're* going to send *me* back to school?" mimicking his Midwestern tones. He tried to be in the office as much as possible, but there was often one interruption after another, so when he had to concentrate, he took his work to his quiet private suite. This was where he always crafted his monthly rector's conferences and apologized to Mondaini before giving them to her to type up. "I have to give you one of those boring conferences to write again," he would say. However, they were far from boring and she couldn't wait to get a sneak preview of a hotly anticipated speech that never failed to captivate the college.

The rector's conferences took place roughly once a month throughout the academic year, which spanned from October to late June. They typically lasted about twenty minutes and each focused on a different virtue essential to the priesthood. O'Brien had started the tradition of delivering a monthly rector's conference followed by a question-and-answer session. Prior to his arrival they had been sporadic and primarily about housekeeping, but O'Brien made them a regular occurrence and an opportunity to help the men understand what changes were being implemented around the college and why. O'Brien was an excellent homilist, but the two men's approaches were starkly different. Where O'Brien took a more cerebral approach, using quotes from popes, Catholic experts, and saints to get his message across, Dolan told a tale about how he lost his temper once while hearing confession to make a point about anger, or described his father sharing quiet time with his mother after a long day at work to teach about love. Dolan peppered his talks with personal anecdotes as he stood in front of a room filled with smart young men eager to learn, and he held their attention. The seminarians had demanding schedules, but this was one of the fixtures they looked forward to most. Even fifth-year priests who didn't have to attend the talks wouldn't miss them, and the conferences were later published as a book entitled *Priests for the Third Millennium,* which became a must-read handbook for future generations of priests.

If classmates from Dolan's days as a student at the North American College passed through Rome for work they stopped by to check in. They were on their own career path up the church ranks and were pleasantly surprised at how well he was taking charge of their alma mater. Back in the United States, another former classmate was also keeping an eye on his old friend from his days as a student in Rome. Father Timothy Doherty had happened to be in St. Louis for an ethics meeting right as Dolan received word he was Europe bound. Over a brief early morning breakfast, Dolan had told him about the appointment. "I've just been named rector of the North American College," he said. "I can't imagine why they'd ask me to do that." Doherty stared straight back at his old corridor-mate. "It's very apparent to me," Doherty said. "You have a wonderful talent for getting all different kinds of people around a table for a meal and a conversation. That's a tremendous gift. And that will be of tremendous value to the college." In that moment, Doherty had no idea just how accurate that statement would be, but a few months later he received an e-mail from a priest friend who had gone to work in Rome. Attached was Dolan's first rector's speech. Doherty felt heartened. When Dolan and Doherty were at the North American College their formation was more unstructured and they had to seek out mentoring, but here was Dolan using his personal experiences to explain frankly the struggles the seminarians would face, detailing what was expected of them and reminding them the work they were undertaking was serious. Doherty wished he had had such guidance as a twenty-two-year-old and instantly knew the students were in good hands. "It had a vision," he said. "It spoke to these men as adults with responsibility and in such a way that the failure to live up to certain elements of this program would not be tolerated."

Just as a twenty-something-year-old Dolan had used his Thursdays without classes to explore, he implored the students to get to know Rome and the Italian people. He encouraged them to take people on free tours around Saint Peter's Basilica, or just approach tourists in Saint Peter's Square and help answer any questions they might have. He also developed the idea of seminarians giving Scavi tours, guided walks of the underground excavations of Saint Peter's Basilica, as an apostolate (a form of pastoral ministry seminarians do before they are able to perform all the functions of an ordained priest). "He had an eye for those who want to learn about the church," one student said.

The job of rector made Dolan responsible for far more than the well-being of students, faculty, and administrative staff. It was a highly administrative role and he also had to deal with maintenance issues, the budget, and fund-raising. To get a grip on these new duties concerning financial management, Dolan was always ready to listen to advice. He did not slavishly follow what he was told, but he was a quick study when it came to grasping new concepts, and he was easy to work alongside. When a suggestion was made to start a capital campaign as a way of raising large sums to invest in the college, Dolan sought the counsel of the seminary's lawyer, Jim Crowley. Crowley warned Dolan against such a move, explaining it could be disastrous to implement if the college's financial records and accounting systems were not yet able to handle such a large flow of funds. Money would be collected, but there was a risk no one would know where it had come from or where it ended up, the attorney explained. Dolan agreed. Accountability was paramount, and a capital campaign was put on hold. Still, repairs around the building needed to be addressed, and Dolan looked at ways to pay for them and plan for future expected expenses. To make the plumbing last longer, he approved the installation of a centralized water-softening system to counteract the effects of Rome's hard water. Small changes were also introduced around the college to improve fire safety, including clearly marked exits and signs.

Dolan occasionally had somewhat grandiose ideas about a program he wanted to implement, or someone he wanted to bring over from the United States to be on faculty. As vice rector for administration, Yarrish was there to translate these ambitions into dollars and cents and occasionally had to stop his old friend in his tracks: "Listen, we've got a budget we've got to keep," Yarrish explained. They made a good team. Having worked together in Washington, D.C., for so many years, Dolan knew he could depend on Yarrish and leave him to deal with many of the financial, business-management issues around the college, which freed up his own time for some of the larger challenges. Dolan and Yarrish also sought to build on O'Brien's policy of encouraging American bishops to see the North American College with their own eyes. Every five years bishops from every diocese in the world are required to make an *ad limina* visit to the Vatican to meet with the pope. While Dolan was rector, it became policy that when a group of American bishops came over for their designated trip they had a place to stay at the college, something that was not the norm previously. Dolan and Yarrish worked together effectively to ensure the bishops' stay was as easy as possible. Yarrish took care of all the logistics, including planning visits to various basilicas and churches and organizing transportation. Dolan made sure the bishops got to see firsthand how students were being trained. The visitors left Rome confident that the formation program was falling in line with the synod document they had all decided upon in 1990, and it made them more favorably disposed to sending students there, safe in the knowledge that it was money well spent. This became a vital source of income. Yarrish and Dolan also devised another money-generating plan by deciding to refurbish a group of rooms on the fifth floor and turn them into luxury suites. Bishops were invited to sponsor one of these rooms financially and have it named in their honor, or for a person of their choosing. The room would always be free for them to stay in when they visited Rome. It was a successful fund-raiser and created beautiful rooms dedicated to the late Cardinal Bernardin of Chicago and Hickey of Washington, D.C., among others. A Florida businessman, Greg Jewell, also paid for the refurbishment of a four-room suite with windows overlooking the dome of Saint Peter's, which was named after Bishops Thomas Larkin and Joseph Patrick Lynch.

Jewell became a huge investor in the North American College during Dolan's tenure. They first met through Dolan's former boss, Ron Ramson, the rector at Kenrick Seminary, who invited Jewell to join him on a visit to Rome. Dolan welcomed the pair with open arms. He invited them to the faculty dining room for breakfast every morning, where they could hear his deep, resonating laugh well before he walked through the door. Dolan also grabbed the first available student or member of staff to be their tour guide each day. Although Jewell was a stranger to the college, Dolan made him feel at home instantly. Jewell had made his fortune in the funeral home business, and simply seeing Dolan's passion for the students and the college was inspiring. Dolan didn't ask for money directly, but soon after the trip, Jewell pledged to help the development of the college and he became a significant donor from that visit forward. It became his second love, after his family. "He so involved you in the college and what it means to him that you wanted to do something," Jewell recalled.

Being in Rome full-time gave Dolan, as he liked to call it, a "fifty-yard-line seat" view of Pope John Paul II's papacy. He saw the pontiff in action during his weekly general audience in Saint Peter's Square, and on special occasions he was invited to the pope's private chapel for Mass. Dolan often entered to find the pontiff kneeling in deep prayer, as though in a mystical trance, and only afterward did he stand and welcome those present. Dolan led small groups inside the Vatican's palatial reception rooms for a private audience and quick photo op with John Paul. He was in good health when Dolan first became rector, but as he grew increasingly frail in later years, the number of requests he granted diminished. Yet there was always one group of Americans he made time for: the sabbatical priests. They could number up to forty and spent a couple of months each year in the Italian capital. As one group's visit came to an end one year, it transpired they had not yet had their face-to-face meeting with the pope because Dolan had completely forgotten to put in the request. After making a few phone calls to John Paul's personal secretary, the rector was informed he could bring the group in on Tuesday, the day before their departure, and the pope's one day off each week. Dolan led the group over to the pope's residence at eleven A.M., where they were ushered through a bronze door and at least three ornate rooms filled with people also waiting for their moment in front of the holy man. "This man just never stops," Dolan thought. "He's indefatigable." The experience intensified Dolan's great respect for the pope and affirmed some of the virtues he already held dear and would come to value increasingly as his own career developed. "A fearlessness, a confidence, a sense of joy and peace, and just a sense of telling the truth with love," Dolan said were the qualities that most impressed him about John Paul. "He would never fudge on the truth, but for some reason he could get away with saying tough things because he said it with such genuineness and indefatigability. You know that he never gave up, he never gave you the impression that he never had time for you." Dolan was more than just a passing priest to John Paul, too. When an American bishop had a meeting with the pontiff during a trip to Rome, he told the Holy Father he was staying up the hill at the North American College. "You know the rector, Monsignor Dolan?" the bishop asked. John Paul was a man of few words but nodded and replied, "Dolan. Good rector. Good rector."

Aside from the rigorous schedule within the college gates, there was time for relaxation. Dolan sometimes invited Yarrish to his room so the two old friends could enjoy a cigar and a glass of Scotch. At other times they took a stroll down the hill from the college for some pizza or pasta at the simple family-run trattoria Sor'eva, where staff knew them by name. On Wednesday evenings the faculty changed out of their clerics into casual sports shirts to have a relaxed evening and maybe an impromptu cookout. If mini getaways were possible, a small group occasionally drove north to Greccio or Montepulciano or to visit the Basilica of St. Francis in Assisi. Sometimes they went south to Sorrento. Dolan loved Tuscany, and frequented a beautiful town called San Gimignano on weekends away, or made a trip into the hills for a bite to eat at Castel Gandolfo, a beautiful cobblestoned village set around a lake where the papal summer residence is located. Once a year, before exams, Dolan invited the whole seminary out to the beach, where they picnicked, played a volleyball tournament, and sunbathed. Dolan relaxed in the sand and kicked back with a book. "What are you reading?" one of the seminarians inquired, because the dust jacket of the book had been removed. Dolan revealed a copy of *White Smoke* by Andrew Greeley, a novel about a fictitious papal election and the behind-the-scenes struggle to elect a liberal Holy Father. Part of the narrative was set in the North American College, and it was considered a somewhat racy and scandalous read for a priest at the time. "I can't believe it," Dolan told the student before returning to his page-turner. "They're describing the rector as fat, obnoxious, and a cigar smoker." He paused. "I'm not fat!"

To let off steam, the men frequently played sports, from tennis and football to basketball, soccer, and softball. One of the pinnacles of the year was an annual sporting fest known as the Spaghetti Bowl around Thanksgiving. It took the form of a hotly contested football game between the New Men and the Old Men, and united the seminarians like little else. Dolan was quick to deflect any concerns other faculty members had about the injuries the men could incur or the propriety of such a contest. He knew it was a critical bonding experience. The remainder of the year, during more casual games, Dolan occasionally took a turn pitching at softball. He was competent, but his real skill was playing chief ragger. "You have no chance to be able to hit this curve ball I'm about to throw you," he taunted. The North American College students also competed against outside seminaries, and long-standing rivals the Legionaries of Christ were always the one to beat. They were a big religious order comprised of seminarians from around the world and the two colleges battled it out with softball and basketball games. One year, as the head-to-head approached, Dolan made it well known he really wanted to win. The Legionaries of Christ were the perennial favorites but one of the seminarians, Christopher Nalty, decided to give his side a psychological advantage. He dragged two chaise longues out onto centerfield, wore a pair of shorts and no T-shirt, donned a beer-can helmet, which he drank from using the attached hose, smoked cigars, and did the wave. Their opponents, ultra-strict seminarians, were scandalized that this was able to take place, and under the nose of their rector, no less. The Americans heckled and cheered their way to victory, and Dolan simply looked on and laughed. He even gave the unconventional cheerleading squad a shout-out in his subsequent rector's conference. Not all faculty members were so enamored by Nalty's antics, but Dolan stood up for him. "I was at chapel every morning at 5:30 A.M.," Nalty later remarked. "That's what Dolan knew."

The night before the Spaghetti Bowl was another opportunity for the men to let off steam. But this time their energies were diverted toward the faculty. The evening was known as the coffeehouse and involved a show by the Old Men and the New Men. They wrote and performed skits and at least half were Dolan-themed. The impersonators took jabs at his waistline, questioned some of his decisions, or mocked his rhetorical style. When Dolan speaks, he never settles for one word if three are possible. He doesn't just want "happy priests" but priests who are "happy, holy, healthy Catholic priests," so the men took that character quirk and ran with it, stringing twenty-six words in a row that all began with the same letter. As the indeterminately long sentence rolled on, Dolan's deep, loud guffaw filled the auditorium. He knew he needed to let the guys have their moment and it was good for their morale. He understood the psychology behind humor and criticism and, more important, could take a joke. There were other skits, too. One year a seminarian dragged an exercise bike onto the stage, put on sweats and glasses, and mimicked Dolan's distinctive Midwestern twang while swigging a Budweiser and pedaling. After one coffeehouse, when there was a particularly large number of Dolan-themed skits, a student approached the rector warily to let him know they were moving on to a new target now. "Monsignor, I wanted to let you know that you are done," the student said, fearful they'd crossed the line this time. Dolan turned red and stared back. "No, *you're* done," he said fiercely. Then erupted into laughter.

•   •   •

Dolan was in Rome when he received word every family member dreads. His nine-year-old niece, Shannon, had cancer. His sister Lisa phoned on a Wednesday in September to break the news that her daughter was having a biopsy Saturday, but the doctors were already 99 percent sure it was cancer. He was back home in Missouri by Sunday and did not leave his sister's side for a week. He arrived at Lisa's home by at least ten A.M. each day and ferried the family back and forth to doctors' appointments as needed. Lisa and her husband had not yet told Shannon the full extent of her diagnosis, so Dolan made sure he was present as they broke the news. He attended their first meeting with an oncologist, and his niece's first chemotherapy session. The next morning, Dolan said Sunday Mass in the hospital room with family before boarding a plane back to Rome. He knew he had to get back to his duties at the North American College, but Shannon's illness weighed heavily on his mind. He felt as close to her as he would a daughter of his own, and the occasions when he was pondering her illness were some of the few times that staff saw him without his trademark beaming smile.

Dolan's mind never drifted far from his family in other ways, too, and he felt it was about time his youngest brother, Patrick, who was now thirty-four, found a wife. One day in Rome in the fall of 1998 he received a call from Mary Theresa, the daughter of Bill and Jeannie Kelly, whom he had become so fond of at Little Flower parish. She was twenty-eight years old and working as marketing director at KYKY 98.1 FM and KEZK 102.5 FM radio stations in St. Louis. There was great buzz about Pope John Paul II coming to town in January. Her bosses were not Catholic, and she was in charge of finding a way to capitalize on this event for the station. She came up with the idea of passing out heavily scented potpourri along the parade route from the radio station and a friend at a local florist was able to help. Her mother had told her to call Fireball for advice, using the nickname they had given Dolan so many years prior. After all, he was the closest person she knew to the pope, and she didn't want to get excommunicated for the sake of a publicity stunt. She dialed Rome and he picked up. "Mary Theresa, how's it going?" Dolan boomed.

"I'm fine, I wish you were back here, I know you're a bigwig in Rome, but I need to know if I can pass out heavily scented potpourri?" Dolan had little interest in the appropriateness of her potpourri caper, dismissing the idea with "It's fine, it's fine," and became far more intrigued with her love life. "Who are you dating?" Dolan quizzed. She said she wasn't dating anyone, and Dolan quickly shot back: "Well, you need to go out with my brother. He works on computers and he's got nothing but money and nobody to spend it on." Patrick didn't work in computers—he simply used computers for work—but it was all the same to Dolan, who rarely had a need for one personally. Mary Theresa was taken aback at the turn the conversation had taken. "You need to call him," Dolan continued, at which point she stopped him. "I know you've been a priest for a long time, but girls don't call boys," she explained. "*He* needs to call *me*."

Soon after getting the green light, Dolan sent a fax off to Missouri with Mary Theresa's number and an instruction for his brother to call her. About three weeks passed before Patrick decided he would, for his brother's sake if nothing else. When Mary Theresa's phone rang, the voice at the end of the line had the same tone and intonation as Dolan's and for a moment she was convinced it was Fireball trying to wind her up. Then the man she was speaking to asked her on a date. Patrick and Mary Theresa met for the first time at a local sports bar, O'B Clark's, and were engaged a year later. They immediately phoned Dolan in Rome and asked when he could make it over to marry them because they could not make any plans without him. The couple tied the knot at Little Flower Parish in November 2000, and in his homily, Dolan recounted how all he wanted to do before he was assigned to Little Flower was teach but it had turned into two of the best years of his life. And, he added, if it weren't for that parish and his introduction to the Kelly family, they would not be standing where they were today. Still, he spent no time gloating on his superior matchmaking skills. "I didn't set them up, God set them up," he told the wedding guests. The newlyweds planned to head to Europe for their honeymoon, and Dolan insisted they come to Rome and stay with him at the North American College, where they got to see the city through his eyes. He was the best tour guide in town and knew all the good restaurants, and the restaurant owners clearly knew him, too. He also had the inside scoop. One day strolling through the cobblestoned streets, Patrick and Mary Theresa saw an incensed man wearing civilian clothes having a furious screaming fit with a parking attendant who had given him a ticket. "That's Cardinal Ratzinger," Dolan told the newlyweds. "He will be the next pope. Just mark my words," he added. Sure enough, it was Cardinal Ratzinger who would one day become Pope Benedict XVI.

Dolan's niece Shannon would have eighteen months of chemo in total, and Dolan checked in on her progress frequently. He became close to the doctor at her hospital and when he entered the children's ward, he walked around meeting all the sick children before paying extra-special attention to his niece. Back in Italy, Dolan also concerned himself with his buddy Yarrish's failing health. His multiple sclerosis continued to advance, and one day Dolan approached him with a suggestion: He wanted to take him to Lourdes, a place of Roman Catholic pilgrimage where miraculous healings are believed to have happened. The town is situated in southwest France, and the springwater that flows there is said to have healing properties. It was there that a fourteen-year-old peasant girl, Bernadette Soubirous, claimed the Virgin Mary spoke to her in a cave in 1858. Dolan had been to Lourdes before and hoped that when they immersed Yarrish in the baths he might find new strength. Yarrish was skeptical. He had spoken to numerous doctors and grappled with the degenerative nature of the disease for a long time, but Dolan pressed on. "He pretty much said, 'Listen, there's nothing to lose, you might as well try it,' " Yarrish said. So, off they went. They flew to France and made their way to the sacred site, asking the cabdriver for advice on where to stay. They checked into a hotel within walking distance of the entrance so Yarrish, who was now using a walker for support, could make it without the need for any additional assistance. As they headed up to the baths the pair passed people in wheelchairs and on gurneys, all on their way to be immersed in the water. When their moment arrived, Yarrish went first. A prayer was said over him as he collapsed into the hands of staff members who carried him to the baths and slowly lowered him into the water in a sling. Dolan went in after.

Although it resulted in no lasting improvements, Yarrish was moved by the experience. It was poignant to witness Lourdes firsthand, and he was also deeply touched that his friend cared enough to take him there. It gave him a renewed resolve to deal with the disease. Soon after, Yarrish was scheduled to head back to the United States and before he left, Dolan asked if he was sure about his decision because there remained a place for Yarrish at the North American College if he changed his mind. Yarrish confessed he loved being in Rome and adored working under Dolan, but for the sake of his health he needed to head home and seek out new treatments. Without hesitation, Dolan understood.

Rectors at the North American College typically stayed five years, but Dolan was asked to stay two more. Then in 2001, he was summoned back to St. Louis to become auxiliary bishop. Greg Jewell was in Rome at the time and spent a day and a half helping Dolan pack his room and library to put it into steamer trunks to send back to the United States. He gave a farewell address to faculty and students in the refectory, quoting an excerpt from Cardinal John Murphy Farley's diary from his time also studying in Rome. "Farewell lady Rome, I hope not forever, I hope we meet again."

7

ST. LOUIS

A joyous Timothy Dolan turned to the congregation at the end of the three-hour Mass inside the Cathedral Basilica of Saint Louis and lifted his crosier in the air like a trophy. He waved it so high above his head, even the short people in the back could see. Muted laughter rippled through the two-thousand-strong audience at this unconventional ending to an otherwise formal ceremony attended by seven cardinals, fifty-seven bishops, fifty American seminarians, and countless friends and family. Rapturous applause then broke out in the pews and the overflow crowd in the three balconies in honor of St. Louis's newly ordained bishop.

Dolan had arrived back in St. Louis a few months earlier after seven years as rector of the North American College in Rome. As he settled back into life in his hometown, the archbishop, now Justin Rigali, immediately appointed him vicar general, which made him responsible for helping with pastoral administrative duties around the archdiocese. Less than two weeks later, on the twenty-fifth anniversary of Dolan's ordination to the priesthood, Pope John Paul II also elevated the St. Louis native from a monsignor to auxiliary bishop. "Twenty-five years ago this very day, just having returned home from four years of preparation at the North American College in Rome, I was ordained a priest," Dolan said as the appointment was made public by the papal nuncio in

Washington, D.C. "Humbled and overwhelmed, I stood before my family, friends, brother priests, and the people of my home parish of Holy Infant, hardly able to say four words: Thanks be to God! Now on the day of my silver jubilee, here I am again, just back from Rome, in awe of the 'gift and mystery' of the priesthood."

The music-filled installation ceremony took place on August 15, 2001, inside the packed downtown St. Louis basilica. It was a moment no one who had come to know Dolan over his years in St. Louis, Washington, D.C., and Rome wanted to miss. There was standing room only and an unprecedented eleven rounds of applause. His mother, Shirley, sat in the front pew with a large family entourage. The only thing she wished was that her husband were beside her to witness the occasion, the way he had been at Dolan's ordination twenty-five years before. His grade-school teacher Sister Mary Bosco delivered a reading from the Old Testament. One of his nieces read from Saint Paul, and nine more nieces from his ever-expanding family carried offertory gifts of bread and wine to the altar. Rigali, an influential player in Vatican circles who had spent a long time working within the Roman Curia, was the principal celebrant, and Dolan's locker mate from St. Louis Preparatory South and Cardinal Glennon College, Dennis Delaney, also played a leading role. Wherever possible, the people who had supported Dolan throughout his life and helped him get to this moment were invited to share in his happiness. As he walked down the aisle at the end of the service, hundreds of flashbulbs went off from every corner of the cathedral and he tried to acknowledge everyone. When his gaze fell momentarily on the mothers of two childhood friends he paused to chat. "Not bad for a kid from Holy Infant?" he remarked with a smile before moving on to share the moment with the rest of his well-wishers. Dolan adopted as his Episcopal motto the profession of faith of Saint Peter: *"Ad quem ibimus,"* meaning "To whom shall we go."

•   •   •

Dolan no longer had a parish of his own to look after, but as vicar general he was assigned a number of deaneries, or geographical districts, to supervise. He was also put in charge of overseeing Catholic schools and fund-raising, and was assigned to be vicar for clergy. This last role made him responsible for dealing with an array of priest personnel issues, essentially acting as Rigali's representative to the priests around the archdiocese. He quickly got to work. Dolan visited parishes on the archbishop's behalf to celebrate sacraments and stood in for Rigali at functions he was unable to attend. Dolan made use of his preaching skills by leading special Masses and participated in days of spiritual renewal. He also sought to reestablish ties with the communities he had served in his early years as an associate pastor at Immacolata, Curé of Ars, and Little Flower. He threw a small party at his rectory after Mass one day where everything was a St. Louis delicacy, from the toasted ravioli to the Ted Drewes frozen custard, gooey butter cake, and Farotto's pizza. The place was jammed and full of laughter as locals soaked up having Dolan back in town. However, a scandal of unprecedented proportions was brewing. In January 2002, five months after his elevation to auxiliary bishop, the front page of *The Boston Globe* exposed the first of a series of investigations detailing widespread sexual abuse by local clergy and attempts at a cover-up by the Catholic Church hierarchy. The report initially centered on one Boston priest who had been moved from parish to parish for more than three decades and was accused of abusing more than 130 young people. The floodgates were opened and more damning stories started to emerge from all across the country. Many of the allegations against priests were not new to the church and related to incidents that had occurred decades prior, but the endemic nature of the problem came as a shock, not to mention the widespread media attention the issue was attracting. The outrage was intense, and victims who had never spoken up before suddenly started to feel there was safety in numbers and added their disturbing tales to the growing tally. The Catholic world was sent into a spin.

In various dioceses, St. Louis included, committees already existed to deal with complaints against clergy, but it was clear the church now needed to present a united front and come up with a coherent single policy for tackling the issue. The United States Conference of Catholic Bishops immediately started laying out new guidelines for the 195 dioceses across the country, detailing exactly how they would deal with priests who abused minors going forward. Their recommendations were hashed out in a series of meetings and formally established in the Charter for the Protection of Children and Young People, colloquially known as the Dallas Charter. The document introduced a "one-strike" rule, which meant any priest who had a substantiated allegation on their record, no matter how long ago, was now barred from ministerial duties. If a priest was sick or very old, an exception was sometimes made and they were not moved for laicization, commonly known as defrocking, but asked to devote their life to prayer and penance. They also could no longer wear clerics or say Mass anywhere other than in private. Bishops also had to alert civil authorities about any abuse cases involving their priests. This was a dramatic change compared with how cases had been handled previously. Prior to 2002, priests with proven allegations against their name were typically sent to a treatment program where they were put through weeks- or months-long assessments by a team of psychologists, psychiatrists, spiritual advisers, and social workers. At the conclusion of their therapy they were evaluated and, in the majority of cases, deemed safe to return to ministry. Experts often advised moving them to a new parish for the chance of a "fresh start," and they continued to be monitored closely for years, but for all intents and purposes remained free. Victims, meanwhile, typically settled out of court for a lump sum and signed nondisclosure agreements, which meant the majority of cases had been resolved well out of the public eye. Parishioners were rarely informed about the troubled past of a new priest arriving in their parish and, in some cases, their abusive tendencies were far from resolved and they reoffended. The Dallas Charter introduced a new, unified zero-tolerance policy, but it was not formally approved by vote until June 14, so in those first few months of 2002, as story after story was plastered across the front pages and television screens, dioceses were largely left to devise their own strategies for grappling with the fast-evolving situation.

In Dolan's capacity as vicar for clergy he was already the archbishop's main liaison with the priests across the archdiocese, but in February, as the crisis unfolded, Rigali appointed him to be the point person for the sex abuse crisis. He was now dealing not just with clergy issues but also with victims. A committee set up by the St. Louis archdiocese had been addressing allegations of this nature since the 1980s. It became known as the Gennesaret Committee in 1996 and Dolan immediately called the board together to strategize. They quickly established rules for dealing with priests with sex abuse claims against their names, coming to the same conclusion the United States Conference of Catholic Bishops would soon endorse: No matter how long ago the crime occurred, if the accusations could be backed up, the priest must be removed from a parish. "Do we have anybody out there who has substantiated allegations?" Dolan asked the committee. "I don't think so" was the response, but the team resolved to go back over the priests' files and double-check.

A study of priest personnel files revealed that two priests who had substantiated sex abuse allegations against their names from many years earlier were still serving in parishes. Dolan was firm. They needed to be removed, and he would be the one to tell Archbishop Rigali. "You're going to have to back me on this, guys," he told his committee. Father Joseph Ross and Father Michael Campbell were the men in question. Ross was a priest at St. Cronan Church and had been accused of abusing a minor fifteen years prior when he worked in a different parish. Campbell, a pastor at Our Lady of Sorrows, had also admitted that thirteen years earlier he had "inappropriately touched" a young man who was nearly eighteen years old. Both had received treatment and been evaluated and given the green light to return to ministry by psychologists. Now it was left to Dolan to tell them that despite whatever reassurances they had received in the past, their ministry was actually over. It was a tough conversation and, in the case of Campbell, a move that hit close to home, as when Dolan arrived back in St. Louis he had moved into the Our Lady of Sorrows rectory, where Campbell also lived. The news about the removal of Fathers Ross and Campbell was made public, and Dolan declared it a sign that the archdiocese's new, stricter rules dealing with offenders was working. "There is nobody we are worried about in the ministry," Dolan said publicly, though the *St. Louis Post-Dispatch* soon reported the names of three more priests who remained in active ministry despite being having been accused in civil court of sexual abuse in the past. The archdiocese responded by saying those cases could not be substantiated and it had no plans to remove a priest without a credible claim against their name, but trust in the church was at an all-time low and it was hard for this not to raise suspicions.

Dolan pushed on with his work. He encouraged any victims of sexual abuse to come forward, and the phones started to ring off the hook. In the first few weeks of February, the archdiocese's main office was flooded with more than two hundred calls. Some of the voices at the end of the line were concerned and disillusioned Catholics wanting to know how their church had allowed this to happen, but there was also a deluge of calls from victims, or their relatives, who had finally summoned up enough courage to speak after hearing others tell their stories. There was no precedent for dealing with a tragedy of this scale and it was a steep learning curve. The Gennesaret Committee had been meeting quarterly, but the current situation demanded the team get to-

Timothy Dolan on a swing with his younger brother, Bob, in his lap.
(The Dolan Family)

The Dolan kids (left to right: Timothy Dolan, Deborah Dolan, Bob Dolan) sit on the sofa with their father, Bob Dolan.
(The Dolan Family)

Timothy Dolan's childhood home in Ballwin, Missouri.
(New York Daily News/*Debbie Egan-Chin)*

The four Sisters of Mercy who arrived in Ballwin, Missouri, from Ireland to teach at Holy Infant Parish in 1957. Left to right: Sister Berchmans, Sister Bosco, Mother Xavier, and Sister Gertrude. *(Sister Rosario)*

Timothy Dolan assisting at Mass during his days as a student at St. Louis Preparatory South in 1968. *(St. Louis Preparatory Seminary South yearbook—Blackhawk 1968)*

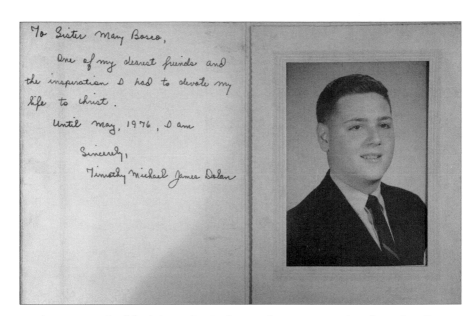

A photo inscribed by Timothy Dolan to Sister Bosco thanking her for
inspiring him to dedicate his life to Christ. *(Sister Mary Bosco)*

A young Timothy Dolan enjoys a beer during a
gathering at a friend's house in Missouri.

(The Guempel Family)

A young Timothy Dolan (bottom, far left) poses with his Cardinal Glennon College classmates after a game of sports.

(Cardinal Glennon College yearbook 1970)

Dolan (third from right) and his classmates from St. Louis Preparatory Seminary South. *(St. Louis Preparatory Seminary South yearbook—Blackhawk 1967)*

A portrait of the Dolan family. Top row, left to right: Deborah Dolan, Timothy Dolan, Bob Dolan (father), Bob Dolan (middle son). Bottom row, left to right: Lisa Dolan, Shirley Dolan, Patrick Dolan.

(The Dolan Family)

Timothy Dolan during his first Mass as a priest in 1976.

(Sister Rosario)

Timothy Dolan introduces his mother, Shirley Dolan, and sister, Deborah, to Pope John Paul II during his time as rector of the North American College in Rome. *(The Dolan Family)*

Timothy Dolan's spiritual mother, Sister Bosco, and sister-in-law Mary Theresa Dolan admire the gold ring Dolan was given by Pope Benedict a few days earlier during the consistory that elevated him to cardinal.

(New York Daily News */Debbie Egan-Chin)*

A jovial Archbishop Timothy Dolan on the roof of the North American College in Rome a few days before his elevation to cardinal. He is wearing a Super Bowl baseball cap since the game was won earlier that month by the New York Giants, and a windbreaker from the NYPD's Emerald Society, which celebrates Irish-American roots.

(*New York* Daily News/*Debbie Egan-Chin*)

Cardinal Timothy Dolan (center) stretches out while listening to Pope Benedict say Sunday Mass inside St. Peter's Basilica alongside the twenty-one other newly named cardinals.

(*New York* Daily News/*Debbie Egan-Chin*)

Cardinal Timothy Dolan chats to throngs of reporters in Rome on February 18, 2012, the day he received his three-pointed red biretta and was elevated to cardinal by Pope Benedict.

(*New York* Daily News/*Debbie Egan-Chin*)

gether every two weeks and be on call for an unscheduled meeting at any moment in between. Calls and letters were being received from an array of people, and they initially came into Dolan's office, where his secretary, Genevieve Curtis, organized them and passed them on. The volume was too much for one man to handle, however, and Dolan did not have the requisite training as a psychologist to handle some of the complaints, so he frequently passed them on to one of the committee members best equipped to handle the issue at hand. "The whole response to this terrible tragedy was an evolutionary thing," recalled Deacon Phil Hengen, a licensed clinical social worker on the committee who often received messages from Dolan asking him to take on a case that had come across his desk. "We didn't have a playbook at the beginning, we had to write the playbook as we went along."

When Campbell was removed from Our Lady of Sorrows many of the parishioners were angry and upset. He was a well-liked priest and some felt he had been cut loose to serve as an example to others. Dolan stood before five hundred parishioners at the end of a Saturday evening Mass and read a letter Campbell had written to his flock explaining he had been haunted by what happened many years before and had cooperated fully with officials the entire time. "It is the toughest letter he ever had to write," Dolan told them. "He has been living for the past thirteen years with an incident that had never happened before and never happened after." Dolan told the audience he had spoken to Campbell numerous times in the past week and continued to trust his brother priest so much he would still go to him for confession. "I'm sorry this ever had to happen," he told the people, explaining that he couldn't promise to give them answers, but he could promise to listen. As much as Dolan had been working to try to satisfy the needs of victims, now he was also bearing the brunt of the vitriol from parish residents who took objection to Campbell's removal. They did not hold back, expressing their distaste at the developments. "Wow, I felt like it was Our Lady of Snarls, not Sorrows," he remarked after leaving. While Dolan was speaking to the congregation, nearby was the associate pastor at Our Lady of Sorrows, Gary Wolken, who also lived in the rectory with Dolan. He didn't speak much that evening, but Dolan said parishioners should feel they could talk to any one of the clergy present about their concerns. Unbeknownst to anyone at the time, by the end of the month Wolken would also be removed and suspended. Wolken later admitted to touching and having oral sex with a young boy over a three-year period, beginning when the child was five. Wolken knew the child and his family well and had shared dinners and vacations with them. He pleaded guilty to two counts of statutory sodomy and six counts of child molestation and was eventually sentenced to fifteen years in prison. It was reported that Dolan wrote a letter to the judge in the case, asking for leniency.

The accusations were coming thick and fast. Two days after reading Campbell's letter to the congregation, Dolan received a frantic phone call from a man who said he needed to speak to Bishop Dolan. His name was Arthur Andreas, and he was very agitated. "I can't speak, I'm not free to speak," he said repeatedly. "I'm going to have to call you back." Over the space of a couple of hours, Andreas and Dolan spoke several times as the man kept hanging up mid-conversation and then dialing back. As Dolan later recalled in a deposition, he was able to ascertain that Andreas was claiming he had been abused by Father Alex Anderson while living at St. Joseph's Home for Boys in the 1980s, an orphanage that had since been closed. Anderson was now a pastor at Most Sacred Heart Church in Eureka, Missouri. The caller said Anderson used to invite him and other boys to his private quarters in the summer and while there he had been sexually molested.

"Mr. Andreas," Dolan said. "This is very serious, we need to take this very seriously. I would encourage you—we need to follow proper procedures. I would encourage you to report this to the police, and I would encourage that—to come in and be more specific. I want to interview you. I want to know—I want to get some data here that we can pursue." Andreas was reticent. He sounded nervous and emotional and didn't want to meet at the Catholic Center, so Dolan offered to meet him anywhere he felt at ease. "Would you like to meet [in an office], would you like to come to the parish?" Andreas said it had to be a public place. "Would you like to meet at the Chase Park Plaza, can I take you for lunch, anywhere?"

As their conversations went back and forth that morning, Dolan asked Dr. Sue Harvath for help. She was a child psychologist on the Gennesaret Committee and Dolan had already been fielding several of the inquiries he'd received to her. She happened to be in her office that day as these calls were coming in. "Sue, can you help me?" he asked. "I'm not getting anywhere on this. This man is very confused. I don't know if I'm reading him right. I don't know what questions to ask. Would you mind talking to him?" Harvath spoke to Andreas by phone but also struggled to get a good handle on his allegations. She, too, wanted to meet. Together they worked out a plan that Andreas would meet them three days later at a psychological counseling center outside the archdiocese, where Harvath had an office and worked part-time.

The consensus from Harvath and others at the Gennesaret Committee was that this claim had to be taken seriously. Andreas's explanation about the alleged abuse was hard to grasp fully, but they needed to meet him to ascertain more. In the meantime, Dolan went to check Anderson's files. There was neither a record that this incident had ever been reported, nor did Anderson have any other allegations of impropriety against his name. Dolan also checked Andreas's files and found he had lived at St. Joseph's while Anderson was chaplain there. The next day, Andreas called again and left a message for Harvath. The call came through to Dolan's secretary. "He wanted me to tell Dr. Harvath he appreciated her warmth and concern," Curtis wrote in a note for her boss.

"He said he is going against what people are telling him in talking to us—he says most people are encouraging him to not consult with us but to make this a legal issue."

The next day Dolan received a letter. "My office is representing Arthur P. Andreas," attorney Jack Fishman wrote. "He is meeting with me to discuss his responsibilities and rights concerning allegations of sexual misconduct of a parish priest in the St. Louis area. It appears there may be civil and/or criminal issues involved. Therefore, Arthur has asked me to let you know he would prefer to cancel his appointment for lunch with you tomorrow."

"I was eager to meet him," Dolan would later recall in a deposition hearing about the details of this case. "You try your best to listen, you try your best to respond, but none of it seemed to work." Dolan called Anderson in for a meeting at the Catholic Center. They were not close friends but had known each other since high school, since Anderson was one year ahead of Dolan at St. Louis Preparatory South and Cardinal Glennon College. "Alex, sit down, I have something difficult and painful to talk to you about," Dolan said. "There's been an accusation against you of sexual misconduct against a minor." The mood was tense. Dolan had been obligated to have this conversation a few times already, and it was always a painful task. But Anderson was remarkably serene as he took in the words. "Tim," he replied. "I have long feared that something like this would happen. Some of the happiest years in my life were spent as chaplain of St. Joseph's Boys' Home. I love my work, I love those boys," he explained. "The nature of the boys is that they were all very troubled, they were all very hurt. Thank God, because of good care, many of them became healed and whole and are living very healthy lives today. Some of them, that didn't happen to." He continued: "In the current climate, I have been afraid that sooner or later somebody was going to make an accusation against me. . . . I can say to you with utter candor that never did I physically, emotionally, or sexually abuse anybody during my years as chaplain at St. Joseph's Boys' Home."

Anderson said he did not specifically recall Andreas but admitted he did invite groups of five to six boys to sleep on the floor of his study during the height of the summer, since his rooms were the only ones with air-conditioning. They ate popcorn and watched movies, but Anderson said he always slept in his own room, and always alone. "He said it with a lot of peace," Dolan recalled. "He said it with a lot of conviction." Dolan took it all in and explained he had to report the allegations to police. Anderson gave his full support. "Not only do you have to, I want you to," Anderson said. "You can count on my full cooperation." Dolan continued to pursue whatever leads he could to shed more light on the situation and also spoke to two women who had been nuns at St. Joseph's two decades earlier, when the abuse was alleged to have occurred. They described Anderson as an impeccable priest and had no recollections of any slurs against his name. They said they remembered Andreas had been a troubled boy, like many of the youngsters at the house. Dolan became convinced of Anderson's innocence and wrote a memo to the Gennesaret Committee outlining the details of their meeting. "Father Anderson remained serene and consistent in his expression of innocence, but deflated at the charges," Dolan wrote. Yet his involvement in the case would be scrutinized for years to come, as Anderson later took the unprecedented step of bringing a defamation lawsuit against his accuser in an attempt to clear his name. The victim advocacy group Survivors Network of those Abused by Priests (SNAP) remains outraged that this course of action was able to take place while Dolan was overseeing the handling of these sex abuse cases. "You can't say, 'We want victims to come forward,' and when they do, in a private setting like Art [Andreas], then let a priest sue an accuser," said David Clohessy, director of SNAP. "We think it's inherently wrong." Andreas countersued, and the parties later settled, with both lawsuits dropped and the archdiocese paying $22,500 for Andreas's counseling.

By the end of March, Ross, Campbell, and Wolken had been removed from ministry and a fourth priest had resigned. Leroy Valentine, one of the three priests the *St. Louis Post-Dispatch* reported had previously had civil suits filed against them, was called before archdiocese officials after an accusation he had molested an altar boy in 1978 while working as an associate pastor at Church of the Immacolata, in Richmond Heights. It was the same parish Dolan had been assigned to immediately after ordination and their paths had crossed at that time. The man, now thirty-two, said he had been molested by Valentine while taking confession. It also transpired that Valentine had made a secret settlement with three brothers four years prior after being accused of sexually molesting them at a different parish two decades earlier. Valentine resigned during a meeting with archdiocese officials and wrote a letter to parishioners saying he was innocent but felt in light of the current climate it was in the best interest of the parish to "take some time away for rest and for prayer." He never returned to active ministry.

There were cases that received media attention but also countless cases that did not. One day a man called the Gennesaret Committee to say he had been abused as a child. He had never spoken publicly about what had happened before but felt that in order for him to heal and move on, he needed to finally confront the priest who was now an old man in a nursing home. Dolan and Hengen said they would be there. They made the forty-five-minute drive to the facility, where they met the victim and his wife. Sitting there with the elderly priest, the man talked through what he remembered happening to him as a child, hoping this encounter would finally enable him to put this dark chapter in his life behind him. The priest listened, but old age made his mind wander and he frequently started to veer off topic and reminisce about the good times they had shared and the trips he used to take the children on.

Dolan brought him back to the task at hand. "You abused this man, you hurt this man," he said until the message finally got through. "I'm sorry every day," the old priest finally replied. "And I pray every day for people that I hurt."

As case after case emerged, it was a trying time, and sometimes an allegation emerged that didn't even involve a priest from the St. Louis archdiocese but still had to be explained. One month after Dolan dealt with the fallout at Our Lady of Sorrows, it surfaced that two priests from the Joliet diocese, about forty-five miles southwest of Chicago, were living and working in St. Louis despite sexual abuse allegations from their past. In the 1980s, Reverend Fred Lenczycki had been accused of molesting boys at a Hinsdale parish by luring them into his apartment within the church rectory. He was removed and placed in counseling. The diocese had quietly settled a lawsuit leveled against him by one of the victims, but he was never criminally charged. Instead, he was transferred to St. Louis to act as a hospital chaplain at DePaul Health Center in Bridgeton in 1992. Dolan came out publicly saying the St. Louis archdiocese had been kept in the dark about Lenczycki's past and there was nothing in the records to indicate the now fifty-seven-year-old had anything but a stellar record. The Joliet diocese chancery shot back that they had spoken to the archbishop at the time, John May, and he had been fully aware of the situation. May had died in 1994, so there was no way to confirm or deny the reports. Lenczycki was recalled to Joliet, Illinois, and one day later Reverend Jay Meis, also from the Joliet diocese, resigned. The sixty-five-year-old had been hired by St. Anthony's Medical Center in St. Louis in 1994 despite being accused of having sexually abused a minor in the late 1980s while serving as pastor of a parish. The Diocese of Joliet had reached an out-of-court settlement with the minor, and Meis had received treatment. Then, like Lenczycki, he was moved out of state. Administrators at St. Anthony's Medical Center said they were aware of Meis's troubled past when they hired him but had been assured that he posed no risk working in a hospital ministry. "Now the church is changing their position on priests who suffer from this problem," David P. Seifert, president and chief executive officer of the medical center, said in response. Again, the St. Louis archdiocese denied knowing anything about Meis's past. They said letters in his file from the Joliet bishop described him as a priest in "good standing" with nothing that would ring alarm bells about his reputation. But again, the wider reputation of the church was in such tatters it was hard to take this at face value.

Dolan was working twelve- to sixteen-hour days. He said he often made himself hoarse asking for victims to phone him and was becoming increasingly exhausted and losing weight from the stress. In addition to keeping on top of his responsibilities as vicar general and heading up the Gennesaret Committee, he had also agreed to teach a course on the history of Catholic leaders in the Catholic Church at Kenrick-Glennon Seminary. As he left the building one day, he bumped into another priest from the archdiocese, Father Michael Witt, who was on his way in to teach his own class. Witt instantly got the impression the auxiliary bishop was drained. "You know, Mike," Dolan said to him. "This is the worst thing that has happened to the Catholic Church in American history." "It can't be as bad as that," Witt replied, though years later those words resonated with him as he came to appreciate how accurate Dolan's assessment had been. Still, Dolan's faith in the church did not waver. Members of the Gennesaret Committee, which was renamed the Review Board in June 2002, found him bright, compassionate, and open to entertaining any idea or listening to any suggestions. "Sometimes people don't want to hear bad news," Deacon Hengen recalled, but not Dolan. "I remember him saying, 'All we want to know is the truth.' That was kind of his mantra." To get through difficult and long Review

Board discussions, Dolan ensured there were always bowls of M&Ms on hand, a custom that prevailed long after his departure, and, occasionally, he was also able to lighten the mood momentarily when compassion fatigue set in from handling terrible story after terrible story. Sitting in one of the committee's meetings in the Catholic Center one day, Dolan stared out the window to see a flamboyant local St. Louis character, affectionately nicknamed Baton Bob, striding through the streets wearing a pink tutu and whirling a stick in his hands like a drumming major in a marching band. Dolan absorbed the scene during a lull in an otherwise heavy and serious agenda. "Please tell me that's not one of ours," he said. Everyone erupted into laughter and the atmosphere lifted. Then they got back to work.

For young men embarking on a life in the priesthood at this time, there were significant feelings of confusion, disillusionment, and betrayal that could not be overlooked or understated. The newly ordained priests were a concern to Dolan because as much as the victims were hurting, he knew he had to focus on the future of the church, too. Witt, in his capacity as the director for the continuing formation of priests, organized a series of overnight conferences at a Holiday Inn in Collinsville, Illinois. The city was about a half-hour drive northeast of St. Louis, just over the state border, and the conference provided an opportunity for the men to meet with more senior church leaders in their diocese and ask questions. A study had recently been published by Georgetown University that said it was important for a priest who had been ordained less than five years to have contact with a bishop, be it an ordinary or auxiliary, and Witt was doing his best to ensure this was enforced. Other bishops had spoken to the men at these conferences beforehand, but in September 2002, it was Dolan's turn to address the group and his tone was frank and honest as they debated the sex abuse crisis. He was peppered with questions from the troubled group, which numbered about thirty, ranging from simply "How could this happen?" and "What led him to act out in this way?" to the more philosophical: "What's wrong with these guys?" and "Didn't they know?" These newly ordained priests were from a different generation and had taken courses at seminary about establishing boundaries and how to be aware when a friendship with someone is at risk of overstepping a line. These young men were also taught the importance of caring for their own psychological well-being. All of these were concepts that had not been around when many of the priests now being outed as abusers were going through their formation. Dolan sat and listened. He made eye contact with the men and made sure he understood their questions fully before answering. "Is this what you mean?" he asked, or, "Did I hear this right?" he probed before launching into the best explanation he could give for the tumult happening all around them. The new priests embraced the conference and they felt like their concerns were really being answered. Everyone was excited to meet with Dolan again, especially the more than a dozen priests who had been invited to the weekend away but had missed the encounter due to prior commitments.

However, the second question-and-answer session was never to be. One year after being named auxiliary bishop, and with not yet six months' experience dealing directly with the sex abuse fall-out, Dolan got a phone call beckoning him to meet with the papal nuncio in Washington, D.C., Archbishop Gabriel Montalvo. Dolan assumed it was a friendly, informal invite to catch up and declined the cigarette and drink offered to him when he first arrived. Montalvo then explained Dolan had been tapped to head Milwaukee, one of the most troubled archdioceses in the country. And he was about to become an archbishop. "I think I'll have that drink and cigarette now!" came his immediate reply.

8

MILWAUKEE

The communications director for the Milwaukee archdiocese stared at the piece of paper placed in front of him with ten scribbled digits. "You need to call this number," Bishop Richard Sklba told him. "There's going to be an announcement tomorrow, you need to get the background and be ready." Jerry Topczewski took note of the familiar 314 area code but could not place the city and was still none the wiser. "I can't tell you who it is," the bishop continued. "We'll be very happy." After Sklba left the room, he picked up the receiver and dialed. A voice on the end of the line informed him he was through to the Archdiocese of St. Louis's communications department. As soon as Topczewski explained who he was, he got patched through to his counterpart, Steve Mamanella, who explained Auxiliary Bishop Timothy Dolan would soon be Milwaukee's new archbishop. After giving Topczewski the relevant information and promising to e-mail more documents, Mamanella paused. "Do you know Bishop Dolan?" he asked. Topczewski confessed he did not. In fact, his only real knowledge of the man was through Dolan's younger brother Bob, who was cohost of the morning drive show "Weber and Dolan" on News/Talk 1130 WISN in Milwaukee. "Hold on to your hat," Mamanella told him. "It's going to be quite a ride."

The preceding months had been draining for Topczewski. First, in

January, *The Boston Globe* had lifted the lid on a massive sex abuse scandal within the American Catholic Church. Milwaukee had been actively dealing with the issue for more than a decade, but every diocese was suddenly put under intense renewed scrutiny as new victims came forward and old cases were revisited. Then the situation grew exponentially worse. On May 23, a fifty-three-year-old man appeared on *Good Morning America,* detailing how he had been the victim of date rape two decades prior by the outgoing archbishop, Rembert G. Weakland, O.S.B. Former Marquette University theology student Paul Marcoux claimed he visited Weakland in his apartment after a dinner, looking for advice about the priesthood, and was assaulted. To make matters worse, Marcoux said he was given $450,000 from church funds in return for staying quiet. "I've been involved in a cover-up. I've accepted money to be silent about it," Marcoux told ABC News reporter Brian Ross.

It was Topczewski who had to stand outside the archdiocese office and read a statement by Weakland denying the abuse allegations while, crucially, not denying the relationship. Weakland later admitted he was gay and had been in love with Marcoux. Weakland also claimed that long after their consensual relationship ended, Marcoux approached him to fund a religious video project called Christodrama and the archbishop eventually gave his ex-lover $14,000 from his personal funds. Weakland said that Marcoux threatened him with a lawsuit, and so the archbishop gave Marcoux $450,000 from church funds on the understanding that Marcoux would hand over any documents pertaining to their relationship and never go public with his story. Topczewski first heard about this situation less than twenty-four hours before the revelations aired, and he was inundated with a seemingly endless stream of daily phone calls and interview requests for months.

The Milwaukee archdiocese had already been preparing itself for a new archbishop long before Dolan's appointment. Weakland had celebrated his seventy-fifth birthday in April and sent his letter of retirement to Vatican City, as per protocol. The replacement process had been set in motion, but the transition typically took time, often years. Marcoux's actions changed all that. The day after the news of his affair broke, Weakland faxed a note to the Holy See asking for his resignation to be expedited. A fax came back immediately. His request had been approved, with immediate effect. Suddenly, the Archdiocese of Milwaukee was without a leader.

Weakland had been head of the Milwaukee archdiocese for twenty-five years and was a liberal and oftentimes controversial churchman. He was one of Catholicism's most outspoken and respected advocates for change and was considered something of a hero to the theologically liberal wing of the church. He had never ingratiated himself to the Vatican, however, and was often frowned upon by traditionalists for failing to take a tough enough stance on issues like abortion and celibacy. The year prior to sending off his letter of retirement to the Holy See, Weakland had also received scorn for a $4.5 million cathedral renovation project. Critics even petitioned the Vatican to stop the work altogether, but the changes eventually went ahead and included moving the altar to a more central position, moving the tabernacle to a side chapel, and replacing pews with moveable chairs. In light of Weakland's reputation, many Milwaukee priests were already nervous the Vatican planned to replace him with a company man more firmly attached to conservative church ideology. They had visions of a right-wing doctrinarian arriving with a directive to remold the archdiocese. These new revelations about Weakland's love affair only served to heighten fears that a dramatic change was on the horizon.

In waltzed Dolan. "Hello, everybody, how you doing?" he said, as he plowed into the introductions ahead of his first press conference hours after his appointment was announced. "I'm Timothy Dolan." He addressed the media on June 25 at the Archbishop Cousins Catholic Center on Lake Michigan, beginning with the words: "Praised be Jesus

Christ," the same phrase Pope John Paul II used to greet the world the night of his papal election. Flanked by Archbishop Weakland and Bishop Sklba, who was acting as the placeholder leader of the archdiocese, the crowd of reporters tried to quiz him on what he thought the differences were between himself and his scandal-beset predecessor. Dolan deflected the question with ease. "About fifty pounds," he quipped disarmingly, refusing to be drawn in. Many priests across the archdiocese caught Dolan's interview on television and watched with as much scrutiny and suspicion as the press. Among themselves, some had started cynically referring to him as the "smiling streamroller," but many were suitably impressed with his debut. The majority of the priests in the archdiocese had been ordained by Weakland and held him in high regard. They appreciated that Dolan did not discredit his predecessor and seemed to be a natural in the spotlight. One pastor with a keen eye on the developments remarked that Dolan didn't just feel like a breath of fresh air but "a windstorm of fresh air."

Topczewski was also pleasantly surprised. By this stage, he had spent much of the year surviving on only a few hours' sleep each night, and he knew the church needed him more than he needed the job. Given the myriad colliding problems, he made it clear he had no intention of sugarcoating his words. This was exactly what Dolan craved. "Jerry, tell me the truth, even if it does cost you your job," the incoming archbishop jokingly told him, borrowing a line from Ronald Reagan. The two men quickly realized they were going to get along.

During the summer months, Dolan wrapped up his duties in St. Louis and made frequent trips to Milwaukee to begin to familiarize himself with the area ahead of his formal installation on August 28. During one visit he discovered a member of the Priests' Council, the associate vicar for clergy, Father William Kohler, was not at the offices one day because his mother had died. Dolan's driver said the church where the funeral was being held was near the airport, and Dolan asked if they could make a diversion before his flight. Kohler was standing in the aisle at the visitation prior to Mass when he looked up and saw the incoming archbishop bounding toward him. The pair had not met yet, so Dolan introduced himself, then turned his attention to the rest of Kohler's family. The heavy presence of Celtic crosses on various items in the room also immediately caught Dolan's eye, and Kohler explained his mother had been Irish. "I said to myself, I can't go back to St. Louis until I stop and give you my condolences," Dolan told the priest. Kohler was blown away by the compassion of the new man in charge. "He wasn't even here and he starts to relate pastorally to one of his," Kohler said. "That was the first impression." Some of Dolan's other skills and personality traits also shone through in those early days before his installation. Right before his new job began, vocations director Father Bob Stiefvater took Dolan to a recording studio for a few hours to tape a sixty-second radio commercial targeted at eighteen- to thirty-five-year-old male listeners. Stiefvater had pulled Dolan aside quickly to suggest the idea on his very first day in Milwaukee in June, and Dolan had instantly embraced the notion. Inside the studio, Dolan showed his aptitude for speaking in succinct, off-the-cuff sound bites. He disregarded the prepared script diligently crafted by staff in Stiefvater's office and masterfully gave his own personal flair to the message, encouraging listeners to think about whether they were being called to the service of the Lord. It was broadcast 140 times on five local radio stations.

One of Dolan's main priorities was finding a personal assistant. Father Jerry Herda was working half-time in a parish and half-time in a high school and came highly recommended, so Dolan invited him to his new residence while in town for Irish Fest in mid-August. He arrived for the appointment to find the archbishop dressed casually and smoking a cigar. In a back porch area, Dolan asked Herda a few questions about his previous assignments and experience, and it didn't take long for him to be convinced Herda was a good man for the job. He quickly put him to work, handing him a stack of invitations to various functions and asking him to sift through them. For the next five years, they spent hours together each day. Given his own Irish roots, Dolan was a willing participant at that year's Irish Fest. It is a big annual event on the Milwaukee archdiocese's calendar, and he was the principal celebrant at the outdoor Mass, which attracted a record crowd of 14,397. It was the incoming archbishop's first major public appearance since being named in June, and people were eager to get a glimpse of him with their own eyes. He looked out across the vast congregation. "This is a second collection audience," he joked. The sea of people started warming to him immediately.

Dolan's installation began on the evening of August 27 with a vespers ceremony inside the newly renovated Cathedral of St. John the Evangelist. New archbishops typically enter by knocking on the door to symbolically request entry into the archdiocese and the welcome of its people. The congregation sat quietly in the pews, listening carefully for the tapping noise. Suddenly three loud bangs reverberated through the cathedral. If it hadn't been evident before, there was now no mistaking there was a new man in town who was going to make a big impression. The service was filled with prayers, speeches, and songs. Weakland was also in attendance. "All I want to do is thank you for opening that door and letting me in when I knocked," Dolan said at the service where he thanked his family, friends, and church leaders for helping him make the transition to Milwaukee. "Then again, you've all been opening your hearts to me," he added. St. Louis archbishop Justin Rigali offered a few words to the congregation during the evening Mass, leaving no doubt of his admiration for Dolan's talents. "I know that you will all be attracted to the joy that he finds so difficult to conceal, and which is in fact so contagious to those around him," Rigali said. "His only ambition is to render humble, pastoral service to you from now on. You can't help but

love him," he continued. "St. Louis's loss is Milwaukee's gain. We hate
to lose him but he's yours now. Treat him well."

The following day, Dolan was formally installed as the tenth archbishop of Milwaukee and, at fifty-two years old, he became the youngest
archbishop in the country. He composed a special prayer for the moment, giving thanks for "the constant gift of a fresh start and new beginning." A few dozen of Dolan's former seminarians from his days as
rector at the North American College made the journey to witness the
occasion, presenting him with a binder full of personal letters. His family
was in the audience, as were Sisters Bosco and Rosario, 350 priests,
seventy bishops in long white robes, and eight red-clad cardinals. Incense
wafted through the air and flowers decorated the church. "What a tribute to this great archdiocese that eight princes of the church would honor
us this afternoon," Dolan said in his homily. "One more and we could
field a ball team, which considering how our Brewers are doing might not
be a bad idea," he added, unable to resist the opportunity to inject a bit of
levity into the two-hour service and take a dig at his new baseball team.
He also made it clear he did not plan to shy away from the difficulties the
church was grappling with. "We've heard so much in recent months about
the Catholic Church in crisis," Dolan told the congregation. "The antidote for this crisis . . . is fidelity. A fidelity that gives rise to holiness." As
the official new leader of the archdiocese, Dolan's first order of business
was to embark on a tour. He visited eight parishes for Mass in nearly as
many days, pausing only for Labor Day, and tried to get himself as geographically close to the sixteen districts the archdiocese was divided into
as possible. It was standing room only at every service. The final celebration ended with a huge outdoor Mass and picnic where he momentarily
swapped his miter for a Cheesehead in honor of the local Green Bay Pack-
ers. Some of those watching were wondering if this guy could be for real.

Once settled in Milwaukee, Dolan had to acquaint himself with a
whole new administrative team. The archdiocese was going through the

darkest time in recent memory and staff members were struggling to stay focused and optimistic, but Dolan had a steady hand and an easy manner. "It was like someone turned a light on," Susan Wawrzonek, one of the personal secretaries working in the Cousins Center, later recalled. He sought to surround himself with competent people whom he liked, trusted, and knew would work hard. His own approach to the job was tireless. He rose around five each morning and always dedicated the first part of his day to prayer, learning early in life that if he didn't set aside time as he woke up, other things would quickly get in the way. By seven A.M. he was ready to attack his packed agenda. Dolan had a housekeeper who took care of his meals and the basics around the house, but Herda took charge of his day-to-day affairs. He coordinated the archbishop's schedule, picked up his prescriptions, made dentist appointments, and kept his checkbook, but one thing Dolan was fastidious about going through personally was his mail. He marked the corners with initials to indicate who needed to attend to the correspondence but was obsessive about looking at it himself, even at Christmas when hundreds of cards arrived for him. He kept them all in a box and waited until Christmas Day to open them personally. Herda drove Dolan everywhere and his week often included visits to parishes, functions, and hospitals. There was no such thing as a typical or predictable week with Dolan, but he tended to spend part of his day in the office and always wanted to get out somewhere in the community at some point. Often Dolan realized he was in a neighborhood where someone he knew was in need and tried to convince Herda to redirect the car in that direction so he could let them know personally they were in his thoughts. If he had nothing in his schedule for a few hours, or a rare day entirely free of appointments, he called Herda and said simply, "Let's go!" Dolan would direct them to a hospital where he had heard of a child sick with cancer or to someone's home. Being in the presence of people energized him and he always kept his ear tuned for a tale of a person in the community who might appreciate a call or a visit. He routinely showed up at wakes or was on hand to comfort the parents of an ill child. "He never wanted to be behind a desk," Herda recalled.

The pair spent hours together in the car, and Dolan turned his long rides into a cell phone ministry. He would whip out his little black book and playfully turn to Herda and ask, "Okay, what letter should I start with today?" Dolan then flicked his address book open to whatever place in the alphabet Herda chose and started making calls. In an hour-long journey, he chatted to or left a message for as many as thirty people but never let the calls drag on for too long. "If somebody was sick and he went to visit them, he would call back the next day, a week later, and then a month later," Herda recalled. "He would continuously be checking in." At a Knights of Columbus dinner one evening, where Dolan was the guest of honor, the archbishop caught wind of a discussion about a married couple in the community who were in their sixties and both battling cancer. Dick and Elaine Jarvey had tickets for the evening's event but weren't in the mood for a party so stayed home. Later that same night, their phone rang.

When he first picked up the phone, Dick Jarvey thought he was being targeted by a telemarketer. Then, to his amazement, he realized he was talking to the archbishop of Milwaukee in the car on his way home from the function. "How's Elaine doing?" Dolan asked after inquiring about Dick's health. "Would you like to talk to her?" Dick replied. "Certainly," Dolan responded. Dick tried to hand the receiver to his wife, telling her Archbishop Dolan was on the phone, but she dismissed him at first. "Yeah, sure," she replied, until her husband eventually convinced her to listen for herself. The Jarveys lost count of how many times Dolan called them after that, never failing to leave a greeting on their answering machine if they weren't in. They took strength from hearing his voice and comfort from knowing they were in his prayers. When they finally met in person, he greeted them with bear hugs like old friends.

Some of the messages were never erased from their voice mail and continued to provide comfort for years to come. The couple considered him their spiritual physician and as much as they felt the attention bestowed on them was unique, they knew they were not alone because every time Dolan got in his car, out came the black book.

A practical joker at heart, Dolan could not resist the opportunity to tease those he worked with closely. When he was in his car with Herda, he sometimes called his personal secretary, Gwen Fastabend, to check in and feign that he couldn't hear her. "She's gonna hang up on me, she hangs up on me all the time," Dolan muttered playfully before the line clicked dead. "He didn't even want anything," Fastabend mused, but she appreciated her boss's attempts to make her laugh and lighten the mood in the office. Each evening, Fastabend stopped by Dolan's residence on her way home at about five-thirty to drop off the "diplomatic pouch," as they jokingly called it. Inside was correspondence Dolan needed to attend to. Fastabend knew that her boss wouldn't even have time to start looking through it for several more hours, but without fail, by seven the next morning he had dealt with the entire bundle and marked down any edits or changes he wanted made. He used every minute of his time productively and generated a tremendous amount of work, but on the ride home with Herda at the end of each long day, Dolan allowed himself to nod off briefly with the gentle motion of the car.

The day-to-day operation of the archdiocese was in relatively good order when Dolan arrived, but morale was desperately low among both clergy and laity. It was abundantly clear to Dolan that this needed to be the focus. One day he called Topczewski in for a meeting to ask if he would become his chief of staff, not just the media spokesman. "I need someone to keep things going administratively, tell me what to look at, tell me what I don't need to look at," Dolan explained. "I need someone to keep it going because I'm not going to be here, I need to be out." Dolan did not like to micromanage from behind a desk but preferred to look at big-picture issues and give his staff autonomy over their own jobs. They, in turn, encouraged him to play to his strengths and this enabled him to maintain a strong presence in the community, where he could let his pastoral skills shine.

Dolan was ideologically attuned to the more traditional, conservative wing of the Catholic Church and not a trailblazer by nature. He was loyal to Rome and obedient to any directive handed down from the Holy See. Arriving in Milwaukee, he was acutely aware of Weakland's legacy as a reformer and that priests in the archdiocese were considered by outsiders to be on the progressive end of the spectrum. Dolan did not appreciate such polarizing labels personally and sometimes remarked to staff, "They think I'm some right-wing conservative, anywhere else I'm moderate." Still, during his time in Milwaukee, he gently returned the church to a more mainstream position through his support for various groups and initiatives that fell in line with more traditional, back-to-basics values. Under Dolan's tenure, groups like the Men of Christ and Women of Christ started to gain more traction. They were not run by the diocese but held daylong events with speakers, debates, and break-out sessions that centered on conservative theology. Another local group organized youth rallies that were evangelical in nature. While other archbishops might not have encouraged these grassroots organizations so wholeheartedly, Dolan met with them and said Mass with them, and his quiet encouragement enabled them to get notice and followers.

To allay the anxiety among clergy about his arrival, Dolan didn't make drastic changes; he made it a priority to observe first and let situations unfold naturally while also working hard to establish good, trusting relationships. In that vein, he quickly got to know people's names. A couple of months after his arrival, Father Donald Hying, pastor of Our Lady of Good Hope on the north side of Milwaukee, randomly rang the doorbell of the archbishop's residence on the grounds of the Saint Francis de Sales Seminary to say hello. Dolan came to the door and immediately knew who Hying was and where he was assigned, and even had knowledge of a parish mission he had organized. "We had never met formally," Hying recalled. "We had shaken hands at his installation, but how could anybody remember that whole blur of events?" It was astounding to Hying, but the encounter was far from unique as Dolan continued to impress people with his incredible recall for names and faces. "I know you," he confidently told Father Curt Frederick from St. Dominic Parish, northwest of Milwaukee, the first time they met during his installation. Frederick told the archbishop he was mistaken—they had never actually met before—however, Dolan was convinced. "I wrote you a note to welcome you to Milwaukee," he suggested, hoping that might be what jogged the archbishop's memory and also fearful he had already done something wrong to attract the new archbishop's attention. "That's not it," Dolan said, perplexed, but wouldn't let it rest. "I know you," he reiterated. Frederick racked his brain and then suggested, "Would the name Bishop Harvey mean anything to you?" Harvey and Frederick were classmates, and Harvey had also been a year ahead of Dolan at the North American College. "That's it. That's how I know you," Dolan said. It was likely weeks, if not months, since Harvey had mentioned he knew a priest in Milwaukee, where Dolan was headed, but the information had stuck in his mind. Frederick was impressed.

In January 2004, a little more than a year after becoming archbishop, Dolan approached Frederick about becoming a vicar general for clergy. It was an important post acting as the liaison between Dolan and the priests and deacons around the archdiocese and, most crucially, acting as intermediary in any disputes. Frederick accepted. Anytime a clergy issue came across Dolan's desk, be it a complaint about a priest from a parishioner or a priest complaining about another priest, he would scrawl Frederick's initials, *C.F.*, on top and send it his way. Dolan

had to put a lot of trust in Frederick and relied on him to help make decisions. When a minor squabble arose that Dolan was inclined to inject
himself into, Frederick made it his responsibility to stop him. "You can't,
you're the archbishop," he told his boss. Dolan quickly nicknamed him
Dutch, because he was like a Dutch uncle who serves to give you frank,
sometimes harsh, but well-intentioned advice. "I was his truthsayer," Frederick explained. He also found support from Bishop Sklba in getting to
grips with the history of the diocese and challenges it faced, including the
looming issue of parish mergers. Sklba had grown up in the archdiocese,
so understood it intuitively and could explain how the various councils
and committees worked. He introduced Dolan to members of the Archdiocese Resource Development Council, laypeople with skills in profes-
sions like banking, marketing, public relations, and fund-raising who
volunteered their expertise to help the archdiocese, and Sklba also provided background on the major personalities Dolan would have to contend with and who could be relied on for advice.

Dolan absorbed it all but quickly discovered being responsible for a
flock of priests was unpredictable, and he faced his first head-to-head
confrontation just seven months after his installation. On March 25, he
learned a prayer service was taking place in a matter of hours presided
over by a woman who was advocating for female ordination, an issue
that went firmly against church tradition and law, not to mention Pope
John Paul II's teaching. It was annual World Day of Prayer for Women's
Ordination and the pastor of St. Matthias Parish, Father David Cooper,
had agreed to let the group use his church to pray. "What's wrong with
praying?" Cooper thought at the time. "Everyone can pray. Prayer is not
a bad thing." An announcement appeared in the *Milwaukee Journal
Sentinel* three days prior, and Cooper had informed people locally but
had neglected to call headquarters. "It turned out to be a little bit more
than a prayer meeting," he later confessed. Ginny Kiernan Dahlberg,
the woman who presided over the service, did not stand behind the

altar but did put on an alb and stole, which she later ceremoniously dropped on the floor, saying she was denied from wearing the clerical items simply because of her gender. She also held aloft a basket and chalice, giving the clear impression to those present that she was impersonating a priest. The press was present and cameras captured it all.

Even before the service began, Dolan's office started to get complaints. Cooper was not present at the service but exacerbated the situation by acknowledging to a reporter he supported the ordination of women. "I started getting letters from around the world," he explained. "It was 95% in support, 5% condemning my soul to hell." Dolan was not impressed and called Cooper in for a meeting. The new archbishop appeared highly agitated and upset as Cooper arrived, offering him coffee, water, soda, and finally even some nuts before they sat down to tackle the task at hand. "Would you like to eat some cashews?" Dolan asked the priest. "They calm you down." Dolan asked if Cooper had received any reaction to his statement and without waiting for an answer butted in: "Well, I have." It appeared the calls had been coming in thick and fast from bishops around the country, all wanting to know how Dolan was going to pull this wayward priest back in line. "Well, Archbishop, I anticipated the fact that probably this might happen," Cooper said, passing across a letter he had prepared, offering his resignation. Dolan read it carefully, grunting quietly to himself as he did until he got to the last line and looked up. "I don't want you to resign," he told Cooper. "I want to work with you." Dolan proposed a compromise. He asked the priest to write a letter retracting his previous statement and explaining he supported Pope John Paul II and believed the ordination of women was not a possibility. "He wanted me to continue to be a priest, he saw no reason to try to push me out of the priesthood but the only possible way then of repairing the damage, so to speak, was to rescind publicly everything I said," Cooper would later say. He agreed and returned to his parish to write. Within twelve hours his phone rang. It was the archbishop, wanting to know if the letter was ready yet. "I want that in my office immediately," Dolan urged. When it finally hit his desk, Dolan made additional tweaks before he was satisfied it could be published in Milwaukee's *Catholic Herald* and the drama could be put to rest. "I understood this wasn't a personal vendetta on his part, that everyone was breathing down his neck, that just as I had no choice in the matter, neither did he," Cooper explained. "There was no other possible road."

With one crisis averted, it was only five more months before Dolan had another hot-button issue to contend with. In August 2003, three Milwaukee pastors banded together to write a letter advocating for optional celibacy and debating whether priests should be able to marry. They sent copies to 442 active and retired priests across the archdiocese, asking for their signed signatures. One hundred sixty-three were returned and dispatched off to then-president of the United States Conference of Catholic Bishops, Bishop Wilton Gregory. The trio, Fathers Tom Suriano, Joseph Aufdermauer, and Steven Dunn, said their concerns were borne out of the severe priest shortage, which was afflicting all parishes and showed no sign of abating. They claimed many parishioners were being denied the chance to celebrate the Eucharist, among other sacraments, because there simply weren't enough priests to go around. They argued that giving priests a choice about celibacy would entice more to the vocation. Instead of replying directly to them, Gregory directed his response to Dolan and was unequivocal. Celibacy was, he wrote, "a powerful spiritual means to draw closer to Christ," adding that marriage and celibacy were each "a grace that enriches the Church." He dismissed the argument that there was any evidence to suggest seminary enrollment would increase if celibacy were optional. Again, Dolan had to call his priests into his office for a stern conversation. "He disagrees totally, and I do, too," Dolan told them. He explained he planned to publish Gregory's response in the *Catholic Herald,* as well as his own reasons for being pro-celibacy. However, unlike the subject of women's ordination, which went definitively against church teaching, celibacy is a discipline that could conceivably be changed, so Dolan adopted a different tactic for dealing with this priest conflict. "If you want to give an interview to the diocesan newspaper, go ahead, give it your best shot," he said. Dolan knew the Vatican was also on his side but did not want to stifle the priests' opportunity to have their say. In his newspaper column of September 4 he said he was celibate "not just because I'm 'supposed to,' or reluctantly 'have to,' but because I want to. . . . This is the time we priests need to be renewing our pledge to celibacy, not questioning it," Dolan wrote. "The recent sad scandal of clerical sexual abuse of minors, as the professionals have documented, has nothing to do with our celibate commitment."

"He was very clear . . . but he was not heavy-handed," Suriano recalled. "He didn't say: 'Okay, you guys, change your view,' . . . he said: 'I disagree with you completely and as you know the Vatican disagrees with you totally as well.' " "It was an adult discussion and it was fair," Suriano explained.

For the rank-and-file priests, it became clear the new archbishop was more faithful to Rome than Weakland had ever been, but they also realized he was less of an ideologue than they had feared. He did not plan to call priests out on every small divergence from liturgical rules, and he valued dialogue with them above all else. In an effort to develop a good rapport, he started to call every priest on his birthday and the anniversary of his ordination. "Just wanted to say happy anniversary to a classmate," he cheerfully told Father Thomas Eichenberger, who was sitting on the church patio in shorts, soaking up the sunshine one Memorial Day weekend when his cell phone rang unexpectedly. The archbishop remembered they had both been ordained in 1976, and the gesture made a lasting impression. Dolan also visited parishes so he could see how they were being run and got a chance to meet with the pastors face-to-face. He talked, he visited, and he paid attention. He regularly invited two priests for lunch, asking one to come slightly early so they could have a one-on-one discussion before the meal and telling the other to stay behind afterward for his own private chat. With the passage of time, the priests started to see an engaging pastoral shepherd in Dolan and after a couple of years, signs emerged that opinions were changing. Each year the priests in the archdiocese attended a three-day, two-night spring assembly with prayers and scheduled talks on particular topics. At Dolan's first as archbishop he was direct with them: "Here's the deal," he said. "I will talk for half an hour, please be quiet and listen. Then I want you to talk for half an hour and I will be quiet and listen." There were standing microphones in the hall and, sure enough, they kept to schedule and were able to have their say. By the end of the conference he had earned everyone's respect, but the applause had only been polite. When his third spring assembly came around in 2005, the priests rose to their feet at the end of Dolan's address and the applause was sustained and genuine. As vicar for clergy, Father Frederick looked on thinking, "We're home. We've made it." "The priests knew that he belonged with us, and we belonged with him, and we could get things done together," he explained. "He'd won them over."

Whatever conflict he had with various priests, Dolan was quick to move on and never gave the impression of holding a personal grudge. When he heard that Father Suriano, who had penned the letter questioning celibacy, and Father Cooper, who had spoken out in favor of the ordination of women, were in a book club together with a group of other priests it piqued his interest. Dolan came bounding up to Suriano one day and asked about it. "Guess what happened to me?" Suriano told the other men awhile later. "The archbishop wants to be in our book club." They were surprised at first but ultimately gave their approval on the condition the boss understood they were not going to alter their choice of titles or the way they spoke. Suriano relayed the message: "I am commissioned to officially invite you into our book club," he told the archbishop. "But we're not going to change, we're going to be exactly the same." "That's what I want," Dolan reassured him. Dolan became a welcome presence to the discussions. He would absorb the texts, retain them, and speak about them with intelligence and depth. "First of all, I realized that he was a very brilliant man," Cooper said. "And then second of all learned that he was a really good listener, so that you knew that even if he didn't agree with you, he would listen to you with not just his ears, but with his heart."

Not everyone would share that sentiment or get the same diplomatic treatment. A couple of years later, an outspoken and liberal theologian at Milwaukee's Marquette University wrote a letter to the United States Conference of Catholic Bishops, saying he believed church leaders were too caught up in "pelvic issues" to deal with core biblical concerns like poverty, justice, and peace. Dolan fired back a curtly worded letter. It was "preposterous and disingenuous" to infer there was any support for issues like abortion or same-sex marriage in Catholic moral teaching, he wrote to Professor Daniel Maguire. Dolan then went one step further by e-mailing his priests to say he could abide most people speaking at their parishes, regardless of their philosophical beliefs, but Maguire was "so radically outside church teaching that his appearance at any parish would be a grave scandal." The message was clear. Maguire was effectively banned from the Milwaukee archdiocese. There would be no love lost between the two and Maguire later branded Dolan a "backslapping autocrat" who, he believed, was "just a steely conservative behind that smiling face."

Having his middle brother, Bob, on tap in Milwaukee was a bonus to the post and the pair was able to spend valuable time together—more time than they had spent together consistently since Bob had visited Dolan in Rome when Dolan was a seminarian at the North American College. Bob, his wife, Beth, and their two girls often attended Dolan's Sunday

Mass at the cathedral, and they'd see each other several times a month for dinner at one of their homes, at a restaurant, or for a quick cup of coffee. The archbishop also appeared as an occasional guest on his brother's "Weber and Dolan" morning drive-time radio show during Lent, Advent, and at the death of Pope John Paul II, in April 2005, and for the subsequent conclave to elect Pope Benedict XVI. When Bob Dolan left the station to start his own video production company, one of his first projects was called *Living Our Faith,* a weekly half-hour program that aired from Advent through Easter Sunday for three years on Milwaukee's ABC affiliate, Channel 12. Bob was producer and host and Archbishop Dolan was cohost on the well-received show where audiences listened to Dolan tell stories and give instruction about issues facing Catholics.

The rest of the Dolan family also came to visit from St. Louis. Dolan's mom, Shirley; his younger brother, Patrick; Patrick's wife, Mary Theresa; their babies; and her parents, Bill and Jeannie Kelly from Little Flower, would all pile into the Honda Odyssey for a five-day visit. They crammed in the vehicle on top of one another, resembling something out of a Chevy Chase movie. Before one visit, Mary Theresa suggested they bring mattresses with them as well because she didn't like the beds at the residence but was quickly shot down. "I don't think that will look too good if we drive up with mattresses on top of the car," her mother warned. "They'll think: 'Who would ask that collage of people to your home?'" But Dolan took great pleasure from having his family in town, regardless of how they looked when they arrived. On other occasions his sisters, Lisa and Deb, came with their families. They had married brothers they knew from Holy Infant who owned a successful butcher business in Missouri and had eight daughters between them.

Ahead of their visits, Dolan got his home ready by buying a big blow-up pool for the kids to play in. During their stay, he always rose early for his morning prayers and often grabbed the kids so their parents could sleep in. When Patrick and Mary Theresa's youngest child and

Shirley's first male grandson was barely a toddler, Dolan took him down to the basement chapel with a box of cereal while he enjoyed some moments of quiet contemplation. Dolan was kneeling serenely at the altar while his little nephew, Patrick, crawled around in the background, leaving a trail of crumbs in his wake. Dolan never batted an eyelid or worried about the mess. By the time the rest of the house was awake, the smell of breakfast was wafting through from the kitchen, as Dolan had cooked up piles of bacon for the family to dive into. This was the kind of generous and effortless hospitality they always found when the siblings and their kids went to visit Uncle Tim.

Dolan's energy appeared to know no bounds to those around him, and he was never afraid to throw his hat into the ring, be it when he had donned a Cheesehead or at Mass celebrating the one hundredth anniversary of Milwaukee's Harley-Davidson motorcycle company. That event occurred in the beginning of September 2003, and he brought his family along for the spectacle. They could only look on in amazement as he was presented with a black leather jacket at the outdoor service on Holy Hill and the one-thousand-strong crowd of bikers treated him like a rock star. Dolan's love of baseball was as ardent as ever, and he never passed up an opportunity to meet the local sporting heroes. He threw the first pitch at a Milwaukee Brewers game wearing the local team's baseball cap, and when the St. Louis Cardinals came to town, he rallied together any friends and family he could to sit in the bleachers and cheer on his childhood hometown team. There were many common traits between the down-to-earth, meat-and-potatoes Catholics Dolan had grown up around in St. Louis and the people in the pews in Milwaukee, and locals took to him instantly. They shared a Midwestern outlook on life and it was evident he was just as enthralled presiding over a First Communion as he was attending a fish fry. He also always kept a special place in his heart for visiting a children's hospital, remembering back to when his own niece had cancer. And if he heard that a classmate or colleague's parent was sick, he made sure to send flowers or a gift, or to stop by to visit unannounced. His friends often felt like Dolan was more attentive and thoughtful to their mom or dad than they were, sometimes prompting them to up their own game. "He reacquainted me with generosity," one priest said. Every time Dolan served Mass, he was mobbed by throngs of people who wanted to meet him and Herda was always in charge of trying to keep him on schedule but typically failed. "I always had to be the bad guy," he said. "He would stay as long as he could until I came in and said: 'Okay, we have to go, Archbishop.'"

Despite Dolan's desire to be among the community, the administrative aspects of managing the Milwaukee archdiocese made constant demands on his time, but sitting around a boardroom table was not his strongest attribute. He fidgeted constantly in long meetings and if a discussion dragged on too long, he became distracted. He had a sharp mind and was a quick study, so he often subtly excused himself from the table once he felt he had grasped the issues or his contribution was complete, to resume other work in his own office, letting the remainder of the discussion continue without him. He rarely, if ever, used a computer and wrote notes in longhand on 8.5-x-11-inch yellow notepads. He was a fastidious note taker and list maker, constantly handing folded pieces of paper with scribbled messages to Topczewski for review, or stacks of yellow pads of paper with homilies, articles, or talks to his secretary to type. His handwriting was so illegible that Fastabend struggled to decipher his script at first but eventually developed the technique of looking at the page sideways to make the letters more legible. Priests in the archdiocese quickly learned that admin was not their boss's strong suit. When one priest arrived for an 8:30 A.M. meeting with a stack of letters for the archbishop to sign, Dolan came out of his office declaring, "If I have to sign another letter today, I'm leaving." He was clearly joking with his secretary, but it was common knowledge that the paperwork got to him. Priests could find themselves frustrated the archbishop wasn't tied to his desk more often. It could feel like a letter they had sent him for signing was taking forever to come back, and then they would flick on the television news or open the newspaper and see their boss hanging out at Miller Park with baseball hall of famer Hank Aaron. Despite their personal irritations, most soon came to the realization Dolan was maybe on to something. "He's an icon for the archdiocese," one priest explained. "The church should be where the people are . . . he did more good with that photo than signing one hundred letters would have been."

If he managed to schedule some downtime, Dolan devoured books. He always had at least one title on the go and loved reading books about American politics, mysteries, biographies of sports personalities and politicians, or the Brother Odd series. For vacation he headed up to Washington Island or rented a cabin in the woods and spent time walking, sometimes accompanied by some of his family or friends. Once a year Bob and his family planned a weekend away with Dolan on Elkhart Lake or in Door County, popular vacation spots around Wisconsin. He attended retreats with other priests and made frequent trips back to St. Louis, never missing a baptism or First Communion for one of his siblings' kids. Christmas was always a busy time of year with a multitude of obligations to his parishioners, so his family traveled to him if possible. If they could not, he made the rounds in Milwaukee on Christmas Day, stopping in on people who extended their hospitality and quickly settling into the festivities like one of the family, even wearing a pair of special festive Christmas shoes. He also made sure priests who didn't have families of their own were never without somewhere to go on holidays and offered up a place at his own dinner table if he had something planned.

For a man so disciplined when it came to his faith, Dolan continued to have little self-control with food. His weight had been an ongoing struggle since his youth, and during his time in Milwaukee, Dolan did his best to stay fit, but his waistline continued to expand. He found it hard to turn down a plate of wholesome, home-cooked food like meat loaf or macaroni and cheese and often joked that he wouldn't stay long at a function if the mashed potatoes weren't real. He was always trying something new to keep his weight in check—even the latest fad like cleansing shakes or the Atkins diet—but they usually ended in failure. His father's untimely death from a heart attack weighed on the minds of everyone in the family, and keeping fit was a priority. Topczewski sometimes arrived at Dolan's residence to go over notes only to be beckoned inside to talk while his boss worked up a sweat on the elliptical machine or the treadmill. Some old friends gave him an old Schwinn bicycle, which he used for long rides along Lake Michigan, right on the doorstep of his home, and he loved to take long walks at a brisk pace. If anyone ever accompanied him, they found themselves taking two steps for every one of his large strides, but he always carried a stick after once getting knocked over by a dog while in Mexico, an incident that left him slightly anxious around the animal.

Weakland's shock departure had greatly exacerbated the disillusionment already felt by clergy and laity as a result of the sex abuse crisis, and as the drama continued to unfold nationally, the scandal became an ever-pressing local concern. Before Dolan arrived in Milwaukee, the archdiocese removed all priests from ministry who were known to have substantiated allegations against them. The hope was, it would enable the incoming archbishop to start his tenure with a clean slate, but Dolan still inherited a community of victims who demanded answers and sought solace. Less than a month after his installation, he approved the recommendations of an advisory commission that had been looking into how the archdiocese should deal with the abuse of minors. The report laid out a zero-tolerance approach and the immediate reporting of any abuse allegations to authorities, officially bringing the archdiocese in line with the USCCB Dallas Charter's "one-strike" policy. The commission also asked religious orders, like the Jesuits and the Franciscans, to provide documents proving their priests had clean records before they could be assigned to work in Milwaukee. While Dolan's predecessor later acknowledged he had not fully grasped the gravity of the situation and admitted known offenders were not reported to authorities under his watch, Dolan quickly realized the crisis he was stepping into and took affirmative steps to address it. He said the protection of children was a priority to him and the new policies would be enforced "with vigor."

A few months after his installation, in the fall of 2002, Dolan found himself in Rome and requested a private audience with Pope John Paul II. They had met several times before, but it had never been more than a fleeting introduction. Given the myriad issues on his plate, he felt it prudent to meet face-to-face. The pontiff remembered Dolan from his time as rector and was intensely interested to know how he was coping with the challenging situation. "He'd say, 'Tell me how Milwaukee is? How are the priests? Tell me about the vocations? How was your reception?'" Dolan later recalled. "But most of the time he would let me talk." The pair spent about fifteen minutes together and Dolan left feeling great comfort and closeness from the exchange. "Anybody that met Pope John Paul II will tell you that he mostly listened," he said. "He enjoyed listening very much. You could see that he was very attentive. I think he knew that people liked to talk to the pope, and the greatest service he could provide was to listen to people, and he did it very well." The fondness appeared to be mutual, as John Paul II couldn't resist taking a playful stab at Dolan's fluctuating weight. "Holy Father, the archdiocese is growing," Dolan remembers telling the pontiff at one point in their discussion. "So is the archbishop," John Paul II replied in jest. "Holy Father, please assure me that is not an infallible statement," Dolan chimed back.

Back on home turf once again, Dolan was eager to work with the Survivors Network of those Abused by Priests (SNAP) from the outset.

As the most prominent and outspoken organization working on behalf of abuse survivors, cooperation between the Catholic Church hierarchy and the group was typically sporadic and fraught. Dolan acknowledged that some bishops might "bristle" at how the group chose to phrase some of its arguments, yet he felt strongly they needed a seat at the table. "We're talking 'big tent' here," he explained. "These people, they're my people. They're still Catholics, they're still believers. If they're hurting, we've got to respond." SNAP welcomed the spirit of collaboration, and Peter Isely, the head of the Milwaukee chapter, said the archdiocese's apparent openness since Dolan's arrival was a "terribly important first step." To open up dialogue further, Dolan took part in two "listening sessions" at the Midwest Express Center in downtown Milwaukee, where he came face-to-face with multiple victims, their families, and their friends. At the first meeting, which was open to the press, about two hundred people sat at long tables set with jugs of water, pencils, and an abundance of tissues. Microphones were positioned around the hall, where long lines of men and women of all ages waited their turn to recount their painful story. They spoke of being molested in a rectory, on a retreat, on the altar. One woman said her perpetrator was a nun. They came from all walks of life, and while some had spoken openly prior to that evening, this was the first time many had summoned the courage to talk about a past that continued to haunt them.

Dolan sat on the stage with Sklba and a panel of experts, including the Milwaukee district attorney, counselors, and Isely from SNAP. He listened with his head bowed for much of the time, rubbing his fingers across his forehead and occasionally removing his glasses to wipe tears from his eyes with a white handkerchief. "I cannot say 'I'm sorry' enough," he told the people. "The bishops did not respond with the conviction and compassion they should have exhibited." One middle-aged man sobbed, speaking about being abused while he was an altar boy and choir member. He wanted to believe in the church again, and knew other victims felt the same, but he seemed to lack conviction he could trust the institution that had so failed him. As the man concluded his speech, Dolan stepped off the stage and embraced him. "The psychological, emotional, and physical horror of what was done to you by people who dared to say they represented the Lord is beyond belief," he told the audience during the four-hour session. "I find myself speechless; I find myself helpless on knowing what to do."

Aside from the tears, there was also much anger and a demand for answers. Sklba—who had been Weakland's go-to guy on many issues, including sex abuse cases—incurred much of the scorn, including from one outraged mother who said the bishop had promised to phone her son, who had been victimized as a child, but the call never came. "Is this a compassionate way to treat people who have suffered so much?" she asked. Sklba said he had tried to reach out after learning of her child's story, but his calls rang unanswered. He could have left a voice mail, the woman shot back, evoking widespread applause from the crowd. Dolan defended Sklba at the end of the night. "He has my confidence," he explained. "I need him. I need him as part of the solution." But Dolan had also had his eyes opened to the depth of the issues he would be dealing with. "We can't do business as usual. That's sledgehammer-obvious to me this evening," he said. The candidness and sheer scale of these sessions were virtually unprecedented compared with how other dioceses were tackling the crisis, and Dolan continued to address the issue head-on. He scheduled three days of behind-closed-doors meetings with individual victims and his approach to the problem was held up as a model. Isely offered his praise. "I did, even against my own better judgment," he would later acknowledge. "Because I wanted to believe him, and I liked him."

In terms of providing financial compensation to victims of clergy abuse, the Archdiocese of Milwaukee was in the unique situation of being largely exempt from legal action because a pair of Wisconsin Supreme Court decisions in the 1990s ruled the church could not be held responsible for the negligent supervision of priests on its payroll and eliminated any liability for people with suppressed memories. The rulings left victims with little recourse to sue the archdiocese for failing to protect parishioners from a known child abuser. Despite this, there was still a desire within the church to provide financial and spiritual relief. Dolan expressed concerns about where that money should come from. He felt it was wrong for the average Catholic to suffer cuts to their services or be burdened with making additional financial sacrifices through their donations "to compensate for the sinful actions of a few in which they had no part and which they roundly condemn," he wrote in a column in Milwaukee's *Catholic Herald*. In an attempt to circumnavigate this problem while still providing help to victims, he announced the establishment of a $4 million settlement fund for victims created by the sale of church property. He also established an independent dispute resolution system for individual mediation. It dealt with victims on a one-by-one basis and went beyond offering mere financial compensation to providing therapy, too. SNAP requested to join the mediation as a group representing more than fifty victims, and the archdiocese said yes. The two sides had their first sit-down just before Christmas 2003. Marquette University Law School professors Daniel Blinka and Janine Geske, who was a former Wisconsin Supreme Court justice, served as mediators, and both parties left the first meeting feeling optimistic. However, by March 8, SNAP had walked away from the negotiations, claiming the archdiocese had made nonnegotiable demands. The process broke down with both sides blaming the other.

Dolan seemed disappointed by SNAP's withdrawal from proceedings, but the experience was an indication he was never going to be able to please everyone. Close confidants began to see his gradual transformation into a tougher decision maker. "He was trying to do whatever was asked of him," one recalled. "Finally, I think he said, 'I'm not going to ignore them, I want to always be listening, but I am going to do what

I think is right.'" Individual mediation continued, and Dolan met with many victims face-to-face, listening, expressing remorse, and giving them an outlet for their pain. He also participated in healing circles, including one that was filmed for an hour-long DVD aimed at letting victims and priests tell their firsthand stories of being caught in the middle of the chaos and accusations. Dolan spoke honestly about his positive experiences growing up Catholic and how devastating it now felt to realize what had been going on simultaneously in other parishes. Mediators found him easy to work with and able to bring a pastoral approach and inherent sensitivity to the discussions. He was in the habit of beginning his meetings with prayer but made sure to ask if that was appropriate in this circumstance, rather than assuming. "I need to talk to the survivor and see how they feel," Geske told him, and he intuitively understood. "He was sensitive to try not to revictimize the people he was listening to," she explained. "Many were rightfully angry at the church and the hierarchy. He never got defensive with them. He would listen to them." The meetings were often difficult and acrimonious. Survivors appreciated the church's willingness to listen but felt frustrated that Dolan's abundance of compassion did not translate into generous dollars and cents. The archdiocese did not have to provide any compensation, of course, but it still caused friction. Ultimately, the independent mediation process reached settlements with more than 190 victims for an undisclosed sum.

After nearly two years of weighing competing arguments, Dolan decided to release the names of forty-three diocesan priests who had credible accusations of sex abuse against them. The idea had first been floated long before his arrival in Milwaukee and was something SNAP had been calling for incessantly, but he had been conflicted about the idea. "Boy, I wouldn't hide the fact that it was a tough decision and that in my own mind I found myself going back and forth," Dolan said in a deposition hearing several years later. Members of victim-advocacy groups were nearly unanimously in favor of the move, seeing it as a measure that could protect other children and potentially encourage more victims to come forward. Opponents said it was misguided, arguing it risked reopening old wounds. Some victims even feared the release of priests' names could jeopardize their own anonymity. Dolan was also warned that no matter how many names were released, it would never be perceived as sufficient, and he could not avoid thinking about the impact on his clergy. "I was worried about priestly morale and the morale of the people," he said. "I thought, good God in heaven, all they do is every day hear bad news about the church. We are beginning to make some progress, we are beginning to make some healing here, and now I'm going to publish this list again and it's going to tear open the scab and priests are going to say that these Bishops are using—trying to regain their credibility by hanging priests out." Dolan listened, consulted, and took all the arguments on board. He continued to go back and forth until July 2004, when he finally decided the list should be published. In a letter to parishioners, Dolan acknowledged the minefield he was stepping into. "Some will see it as a vengeful act. Others will see it as too little, too late. Others will question why the names of religious order priests are excluded. Some will criticize me for not releasing information about every priest that has ever been accused, but whose alleged offense has never been substantiated," he wrote. Sure enough, there were calls for more. SNAP wanted Dolan to publicly identify priests from religious orders who posed a risk to children, but he resisted. The reason was that religious order priests such as Jesuits, Dominicans, or Franciscans belong to a religious community, not a diocese. They promise obedience to their religious superior at ordination, instead of a bishop, and that religious superior vows to take responsibility for them. Unlike diocesan priests, men from religious orders can also be sent anywhere geographically to serve, and the decision is entirely beyond a bishop's control. Dolan said he had encouraged each religious superior to release names, but since the archdiocese did not have jurisdiction over these men directly, he therefore could not be held accountable for them, or their actions.

Even though there was no threat of litigation locally, a court ruling in California came to have a damaging financial impact on the Milwaukee archdiocese's finances. In 2002, a local law passed there gave a one-year reprieve on the statute of limitations and, as a result, nearly one thousand cases were filed against the Catholic Church. Ten of these involved two priests from Milwaukee who had been temporarily assigned to California decades earlier. Father Siegfried Widera was involved in nine of them, resulting in forty-two counts of child molestation. He went on the run and in May 2003 jumped to his death from a hotel balcony in Mexico after being tracked down by federal authorities. The same month, Father Franklyn Becker was arrested in Wisconsin and charged with sex abuse of a minor in California many years earlier. Both had been removed from ministry prior to Dolan's arrival, but the California law meant their decades-old crimes were being revisited.

Becker's case was one of the more egregious in Milwaukee involving a living priest. His file had allegations of inappropriate relationships with teenage boys dating back to 1970 and, records show, he had been repeatedly moved from parish to parish where parishioners had little to zero knowledge of his past. Attempts at rehabilitation had failed, and he frequently reoffended, often while still receiving treatment. In 1983, a therapist said Becker was an "ego-centric, pedophile and homosexual," yet he was not placed on restricted ministry for another decade. In 2002, as the nationwide sex scandal erupted, Becker had been suspended from public ministry, but the church remained responsible for giving him a monthly stipend in addition to paying his health insurance and pension premiums. This was the case with all priests in Milwaukee in the same situation. Becker's arrest in 2003 changed the status quo, as his past had now been fully exposed. Mere removal from ministry was no longer adequate. Two weeks later, Dolan wrote to then-Cardinal Joseph Ratzinger, who was prefect of the Congregation for the Doctrine of the Faith and therefore responsible for investigating claims of clergy sex abuse. He requested Becker's immediate laicization. It would wash the archdiocese's hands of Becker entirely, both financially and spiritually, and strip him of his status as a priest.

"The public display that will now take place in the criminal trial in California, to say nothing of the civil lawsuits that could arise there, makes the potential for true scandal very real," Dolan wrote. Correspondence went back and forth. The Vatican asked if Becker would volunteer to be laicized as a "sign of his heartfelt contrition." If a priest went by choice, the process was typically much quicker, which greatly reduced the financial burden the church had to bear. Becker had refused when asked before but was reapproached with the request. Again, he doggedly said no. "While attempts to present a defense based on cooperation and need for sustenance, in interviews with him, there is little display of repentance," Dolan wrote to Ratzinger. "His sorrow is not over what effect his immoral and abusive behaviors had on others, so much as it is remorse that he has lost a sense of status." It took nearly a year and a half for the request to be approved and throughout the process, and beyond, Becker continued to complain dramatically about how he was expected to cover his medical expenses and support himself into old age. "I am in a state of depression and desperation and you know where that can lead," he wrote woefully to one priest, saying his letters to Archbishop Dolan had gone unanswered. He threatened to go to the *Milwaukee Journal Sentinel* with his story, adding, "I can barely perform the basic task of life."

Becker was not the only priest Dolan was asking to be laicized. He wrote to the Vatican regarding at least a dozen men during his years in Milwaukee. Some agreed to go voluntarily, but many did not, which often made the process drag on indeterminately, bringing conflicting pressures. Victims called for the swift removal of known abusers, but the process had to go through formal Vatican channels riddled with bureaucratic delays. There were huge time lags between letters crossing from Rome to Milwaukee, and the Congregation for the Doctrine of the Faith repeatedly urged Dolan to try to get these men to go of their own accord first. When the Holy See kept stalling on requests to laicize fifty-six-year-old Michael Benham, for example, asking if he could go by choice or remain performing limited ministry since so much time had lapsed since his crime, Dolan said neither was an option, but he did seek other alternatives. Benham's case involved an eleven-year-old boy he had abused for four years, beginning in 1976. Dolan visited the priest and found him genuinely remorseful so asked archdiocesan staff if he might be allowed to live out a "life of prayer and penance." There was great resistance. "I have not seen that remorse translate into action," Chancellor Barbara Ann Cusack wrote in reply. "How do I honestly look a victim-survivor in the face in mediation and say we are acting consistently with Pope John Paul II's statement that 'there is no place in the priesthood for those who would harm a child'?" Archdiocesan staff were already frustrated money was being used to support unassignable priests when it could be diverted to help victims or support other church services. They wanted priests removed from ministry altogether, and expeditiously. Dolan conceded he must go. "I write again in the matter of Reverend Michael C. Benham," he penned to the Vatican in February 2007, three years after submitting his first request for defrocking. "He remains reluctant to seek voluntary laicization despite his admission of long-term sexual abuse of a minor." When no action was taken, Dolan repeated his request in January 2008: "I write again in the matter of Reverend Michael C. Benham. You will recall that he has been asked to seek voluntary laicization multiple times. He refuses to do so and remains obstinate in that position." The priest was eventually defrocked in August 2008.

It was felt that some priests were resistant to sign laicization papers out of concern for how they would support themselves into old age. The financial security the church salary provided, not to mention the vital health insurance coverage, was not something to part with lightly. Since being forced out by the Vatican was a process that could take years, it was worth the priests' while to let it run its course rather than to go voluntarily. Why be forced to fend for yourself sooner than absolutely necessary? Archdiocese officials looked for a solution and offering accused priests a lump-sum payment as incentive to leave voluntarily was floated as an option. It would get the priest defrocked more quickly, which was what the victims were clamoring for. It could save the church money in the long term since the archdiocese would not have to pay for the man's upkeep while his case was being dealt with at a snail's pace in Rome. Finally, in keeping with core Catholic values of charity and forgiveness, it would help him get back on his feet more quickly.

The policy of using cash to aid the transition from clergy to layperson predated Dolan's arrival, and at a finance council meeting he attended in March 2003, the idea was tabled. Minutes show the idea of giving up to $20,000 to priests who agreed to laicization was discussed. This seemed a logical solution to many involved, but would not become public knowledge for many more years.

Several priests took the money, which was given in two stages: $10,000 if they accepted voluntary laicization and $10,000 when the request was approved. Sometimes they were also offered a stipend while their case was being resolved. Becker, however, continued to fight his laicization doggedly and complain he was sick and penniless and unable to cope. The Vatican finally defrocked him involuntarily in October 2004. Soon after, he was again asking for financial aid, this time for his health insurance costs, since he was too young to be eligible for Medicare. Though there was no obligation for the archdiocese to pay him a penny, in December Dolan agreed to give him $10,000 as a final act of goodwill.

The payment to Becker came to light before the others, in 2006.

Dolan immediately came under fire. SNAP had fresh ammunition to bolster their argument that the church looked after its own first, despite the harm it had caused to innocent parishioners. Isely likened the move to giving a pedophile a bonus and said no other institution would treat a child abuser this way. "The issue is that a payment was made to a sex offender with no strings attached," he said. "What fund did it come from? What other payments have been made for priests and clergy who have abused?"

Dolan hit back at critics with a firmly worded statement: "For anyone to assert that this money was a 'payoff' or occurred in exchange for Becker agreeing to leave the priesthood is completely false, preposterous and unjust. What this was, instead, was an act of charity, in line with Catholic social teaching, that allowed a person to obtain health insurance coverage he simply could not afford on his own. If people want to criticize me for that charity, so be it." He continued: "Since coming to the [archdiocese] in 2002, I have made my commitment to working with victims-survivors very clear in both word and action, and will continue to do so to ensure the healing occurs, the Church is strengthened, and trust is restored." It was not until 2012, when documents were released during bankruptcy proceedings, that it emerged Becker was not the only one to receive money. The archdiocese admitted "a handful" of unassignable priests had been paid as motivation for leaving.

Becker's criminal case in California was eventually dropped, but the archdiocese was still being sued in civil court for damages as a result of his and Widera's actions. Dolan flew to the West Coast in 2006 for a two-day, court-ordered mediation where the archdiocese settled for $16.65 million. It was a devastating financial blow. An insurer paid $9 million, but the church was left to foot the remainder of the bill. Belt-tightening had already been taking place, but more drastic cuts were now needed. Staff was laid off, and the Archbishop Cousins Catholic Center was put up for sale, along with other real estate assets, while some short- and long-term investments were liquidated to counteract the payout. Shortly after this payout, the Wisconsin Supreme Court ruled in favor of a case brought by lawyer Jeff Anderson, who had been handling the claims of hundreds of abuse victims, and allowed the archdiocese to be sued for fraud. It narrowly opened the window for legal action for the first time since the 1990s, and suddenly there were renewed concerns that yet more money would have to be paid out. The archdiocese's attorneys, executive staff, and finance council, all consultative to Dolan, began to discuss filing for bankruptcy.

It was around this time that Dolan made a decision to transfer just under $57 million set aside for the perpetual care of cemeteries into a trust, a move approved by the finance council. It ensured the funds could be used only for the upkeep of Catholic burial sites and was now protected from legal action. Dolan wrote to Rome to get permission, addressing a letter to the prefect for the Congregation for the Clergy, Cardinal Cláudio Hummes, on June 4, 2007. "By transferring these assets to the Trust, I foresee an improved protection of these funds from any legal claim and liability," he wrote. The Vatican responded in forty-four days. Meanwhile, it had taken well over a year for Becker's laicization to be approved and more than five years in the case of another Milwaukee priest. Victims were outraged.

These letters were not made public until 2013, when more than six thousand pages of documents were released as part of the long and protracted bankruptcy case, but victims' groups argued that it was proof they had been right all along: The Catholic hierarchy's priority was money, not people. Indeed, shortly after arriving in Milwaukee, Dolan had also moved $70 million from a parish deposit account into a trust. This was where leftover money from each parish's budget was placed. Every pastor had access to their particular pot of cash within the fund, but it was invested communally by the archdiocese. Again, the decision to place this lump sum in a trust protected it from legal claims.

Dolan branded claims the money was "hidden" from victims "malarkey," "baloney," and "groundless gossip." He had followed the advice of the archdiocese finance council, which argued it was money that had always been allocated for a very specific purpose and safeguarding it was not wrong. "Our committee made this recommendation to help ensure that the church honored the fundamental promise that all Catholic cemeteries make to our deceased loved ones and their families—that the church will preserve and maintain cemeteries as sacred places forever," said Mark Doll, who was chairman of the finance council at the time. "The families of those resting in the Catholic cemeteries should not become new victims in the cause of trying to fairly address abuse victims and help heal their pain."

The battle showed no sign of abating, however. Victims said Dolan's letter to the Vatican saying he sought to provide "improved protection" from legal action for the $57 million was a "smoking gun." They claimed it provided clear evidence Dolan sought to put the money definitively out of the reach of victims who might sue and was therefore a fraudulent transfer under U.S. bankruptcy law. "There was nothing innocent about it," Anderson said. "He moved the money to hide it from survivors," he continued. "His own words say that's what he was doing. He can call it whatever he wants to, but he's the one that made the decision." An editorial in *The New York Times* said it was "shocking," while the *Milwaukee Journal Sentinel* said the documents provided "validation for victims . . . and reveal a church hierarchy that seemed far more interested in protecting the institution—and themselves in some cases—than in serving victims. It's a textbook case of what to do wrong at almost every step." Dolan said these were "old and discredited attacks." Isely found the news upsetting on a more personal level, given how positive he had felt about Dolan when he had first arrived in Milwaukee. "In some ways, believing in him and having this result is even more devastating than having it happen from someone who you never bonded with and you didn't believe in," he said.

It would be delusional to think the sexual abuse of minors by trusted Catholic priests could be anything but hugely divisive. Now, more than a decade on from that first *Boston Globe* story, it remains a complex and highly emotional subject. As Dolan's prominence continued to rise, the issue followed him. SNAP became hardened in its dislike and distrust of him as a church leader, attributing his success to being a "company man." Meanwhile, Dolan became more vocal in doggedly justifying his actions and saying he felt questions about his handling of the matter had been answered.

Regarding the payments to known child abusers: As egregious as it is, Dolan was never going to leave priests high and dry. They were not just colleagues; they were spiritual brothers, and he felt responsible for them. His close confidants also still argue with total conviction that it was the quickest and cheapest way to achieve closure. "You want them out or not?" one said. "If we kept them in until we could get them out administratively, we'd be absorbing a ton of cost." But this was a bitter pill to swallow for those who had suffered most. Victims already felt betrayed and to discover years later that perpetrators were given money while their cases languished in court felt like a second blow.

As for moving the cemetery funds into a trust, again, there is un-equivocal certainty in Dolan's camp that the money had to be used for its intended purpose. Early during his tenure in Milwaukee, Dolan expressed concerns about everyday Catholics being made to suffer financially for the sins of a few. Terrible wrongs had been committed, but was this justification for bleeding the church dry? Right or wrong, it is clear there was a motivation to protect the money from lawsuits. The victims' lawyer "wasn't talking tens of thousands, he was talking tens of millions," one insider said. "Well, we don't have that kind of money."

One victim advocate who worked closely with the community on behalf of the archdiocese never questioned the depth of Dolan's concern but regretted not being given an opportunity to weigh in on these money matters. The worker pondered whether input from their group might have been able to give a "better perspective than finance" by showing the personal hurt these decisions could cause. After all, this was about so much more than just dollars. Sadly, it seems improbable this deep discord in how and why events unfolded will ever be resolved.

Those closest to Dolan noticed how heavily all these issues weighed on his mind. "You're not going to win this one," one of his aides commented after a particularly fraught meeting. "I'm not even going to tie," he lamented in reply. After a particularly challenging day he occasionally called his old dorm room neighbor from the North American College, Bob Busher, at night to talk through his experiences and express how tired he was. Still, he tried not to let it slow him down. He didn't try to whitewash the matter, but he wanted to deal with it and move forward. He liked to tell people there is no Easter Sunday without Good Friday, and wanted it to be a teachable moment for the church. His knowledge of church history helped him, as he was able to see the crisis in a wider context, and he kept reminding people that the church can, and would, endure.

The numbers of young men entering the priesthood was at an all-time low when Dolan arrived in 2002. Only one young man had been ordained in the Archdiocese of Milwaukee that year, and a five-year plan instituted by Weakland to manage the priest shortage had expired in July. The fallout from the sex abuse crisis became an aggravating factor, and vocations director Father Bob Stiefvater was all too aware of the challenge on his hands. As the abuse crisis continued to make headlines, he got threatening e-mails from panicked parents warning him not to even dare talk to their child about becoming a priest. He was also making frequent trips to Colombia and other Latin American countries with an excess of priests to see if the local parishes were willing to send men to be trained in Milwaukee, where the Spanish-speaking population was on the rise. Dolan had a natural interest in the formation of seminarians, and Stiefvater was eager to get an early sense for his new boss's management style, so Stiefvater phoned the St. Louis archdiocese's vocations office for some advice. "He's an ideas man, he always comes up with ideas," they told him. "And if he mentions it three times, then take it seriously." Stiefvater had no reason to fear Dolan would be constantly looking over his shoulder, though his methods for finding new recruits were unlike anything the vocations director had seen before. During one early interview, Dolan made it clear he had no intention of shying away from Catholicism in embarrassment despite the recent battering to its reputation. "I think now the big question that I and any Catholic leader face is, 'Are we going to retreat to the bunkers or are we going to go to the housetops?'" he said. "As for me, this is a time to go to the housetops. This is the time to be filled with all the energy and enthusiasm and creativity that we can get." He set about using the skills acquired in his days as vice rector in St. Louis and rector in Rome to get young men excited about the priesthood again. Dolan always tried to be an inviting presence. When he led Mass at youth events he paid extra attention to anyone he heard express an interest in the vocation. He sometimes asked a seminarian to accompany him to a confirmation or drive him to an evening parish function, hoping their presence would be a positive influence to others considering the same path. He returned from functions with the phone numbers of potential priests he wanted Stiefvater to call and, if a man came directly to his residence seeking advice, Dolan sent them over to the vocations office located a short walk from his own home within the grounds of the seminary campus. Stiefvater appreciated the steady flow of possible candidates but initially assumed the archbishop had vetted these men and deemed they were high caliber and arriving with the Dolan seal of approval. He quickly realized the boss was just sending over anyone who came his way. "I had never worked with a bishop who had recruited the way he did," he explained. "We hadn't had an extrovert in years."

Dolan's infectious joy for his calling became an inspiration to many of the aspiring priests who craved a positive and happy role model to look up to, and he was, above all, approachable. At the seminary he stopped by the student lounge to say hi and made sure the men knew his door was always open. With any who were still on the fence but displaying real seriousness about the priesthood, he invited them to informal barbecues at his home. These types of meetings had taken the form of small semiformal dinners under Archbishop Weakland and were attended by only a small group of people, including the young man's pastor. Dolan was a man from a different era with an altogether different disposition. He threw open his backyard, invited as many guys as he could, and told them to bring their parents. He made the afternoon a relaxed and joyful affair, circulating through the crowd laughing.

Jacob Strand had grown up in Milwaukee and was contemplating entering the seminary when he got an invitation to join Dolan for coffee one Saturday at nine A.M. The young man came from a strong Catholic family. One of his older brothers was already in the seminary, and another was very active in the Catholic community at Marquette University. Strand had first met Dolan fleetingly during his tour of the Milwaukee parishes in the weeks after his installation. Still in high school, Strand had been volunteering at the shrimp dinner when Dolan saw him, walked over, and introduced himself, an interaction that made a lasting impression. Dolan heard that Strand, now in his second year of college at the University of Wisconsin–La Crosse, was seriously considering following in his older brother's footsteps and wanted to see if he could be of help. "We just sat down and had a cup of coffee for an hour and chatted about life and how I sensed the Lord might be calling me to the priesthood," Strand recalled. "For me this casual meeting was very important. I realized that Archbishop Dolan, despite bearing the heavy burden of leading the Church of Milwaukee, truly cared about me and my vocation. I was never just a number." Strand received a few phone calls and a couple of notes from the archbishop after their sit-down, where he expressed an interest in the young man's decision and his continued support. "These were not meant to pressure me," Strand explained. "But just to show me that he cared about me and my vocation." Years later, Strand was ordained a priest after being sent to study at the North American College in Rome.

In 2005, Dolan asked Hying—who had knocked on his door to introduce himself in person several years before—to move to the seminary to take on a new position overseeing the formation of the seminarians beyond their academic life. The role involved taking charge of the men's social and leadership skills, and looking at how they were integrating what they learned in the classroom into their daily life. The job also involved ensuring they had adequate support accepting a life of celibacy. There was a growing trend within seminaries to have students taught by parish priests, rather than intellectuals, and Hying had been pastor at Our Lady of Good Hope and fit the bill. He accepted Dolan's request out of obligation but soon found the transition to a more administrative role difficult. He met with the archbishop monthly to discuss issues within the seminary and in the February of Hying's first academic year he verbalized his doubts. "Think and pray about it," Dolan told him. "If you sincerely do want to leave, I will get you out in June." Knowing he was not bound to the position ultimately made Hying conclude he wanted to continue and by 2007 he was named rector of the seminary as enrollment numbers continued to rise. "He gave me the freedom to leave and that was the trigger for helping me to discern to stay," Hying explained. In the year prior to Dolan's departure from Milwaukee in 2009, six priests were ordained.

When Dolan arrived in Milwaukee, the budget was balanced and parishes and schools were in decent shape administratively, but there were signs that changes still had to be made. During his tenure, more than twenty parishes and eight schools were forced to merge or close. Still, in an effort to combat the decline in funds and bring fresh money into the system, in 2007 he also instituted a highly ambitious capital campaign called Faith in Our Future, which had a three-year goal to raise $105 million. It was a parish-based initiative whereby every parish ran their own fund-raising drive; 60 percent of the money remained in the parishes and 40 percent went into a diocese-wide trust. Dolan brought together business leaders and members of the Catholic community to consult on the project and his enthusiasm for schools drew many people in. By the halfway point in the campaign, more than $57 million had already been pledged, although ultimately it fell $21 million short of its target after three years.

After Dolan had been in Milwaukee seven years, rumors circulated wildly that he might be on the move. Throughout his time in Milwaukee, whenever a prominent archdiocese became vacant, there was speculation about who would fill it. Dolan's name came up frequently. One by one, however, those spots were filled and Dolan remained in Milwaukee. Those closest to him found he never wanted to discuss the possibility of moving on. He knew that day might eventually come, but it was important for him to be in the moment and remain focused on the task at hand. Then, in February 2009, the rumors started swirling again with increased intensity. Herda, Dolan's former priest-secretary, got a call. "You want to come with me to New York?" Dolan said, tongue in cheek, without any introduction. "No, but I will come and visit," Herda replied. "You will stay in the room that I'm in," Dolan told him. Milwaukee's Catholic leader was calling from the guest room of the residence next to St. Patrick's Cathedral. He was in New York City and about to be officially named archbishop of the most influential pulpit in the United States. Or, as Pope John Paul II referred to the job, "Archbishop of the capital of the world."

Only a handful of people were privy to the news before the Vatican made the announcement on February 23. Dolan's brother Bob had been following blogs and articles by influential Catholic journalists for months and knew Dolan was widely tipped as the favorite to succeed Cardinal Edward Egan, who had turned seventy-five in 2007 and submitted his resignation letter to the Holy See. However, there was an unwritten rule in the family that it wasn't appropriate to ask, so they waited patiently to be told. The Thursday night before the news became public, Bob, his wife, and their oldest daughter arrived at Dolan's home at around six P.M. to go for dinner and the suspense was finally over. "Well, everyone, the rumors are true," he told them, explaining he had been officially informed he was heading to New York. There were hugs, congratulations, and a few teary eyes that Dolan's Milwaukee chapter was soon to be behind them. Dolan's childhood friend, Monsignor Dennis Delaney, was also in the room and simply looked on and smiled. Two days later, Bob drove his brother to the airport to catch a flight to New York, where the world was soon let in on the secret.

New York was a daunting proposition. Dolan was a Midwesterner to his core and Milwaukee, despite its challenges, had not been a huge transition culturally. People started to warn Dolan about the city—the media were fierce, they said; the people were rude; it was a Sodom and Gomorrah. But it was also an incredibly prestigious appointment that clearly acknowledged Dolan's talents as a Catholic leader as well as a skilled communicator of the church's message. "It's the bully pulpit, he's got the world at his feet in New York," explained Cardinal Edwin O'Brien, Dolan's predecessor as rector at the North American College in Rome, who had also been touted as a contender for the New York job. "It's the communication center of the world." Dolan spent the weekend before the news became public in meetings with Egan and a couple of key priests from the archdiocese. They gave him the lay of the land and en-sured he was up to speed on some of the challenges that lay ahead. On Monday morning, as word of the announcement spread, Dolan ap-peared beside Egan inside St. Patrick's Cathedral to concelebrate Mass, smiling widely. He received congratulatory phone calls from Mayor Michael Bloomberg, New York governor David Paterson, and President Barack Obama and addressed the media at a packed press conference before heading up to Saint Joseph's Seminary in Yonkers to meet the young men training for the priesthood. Recruiting more seminarians was a key challenge facing the incoming archbishop, and Egan joked that asking each man present to recruit four more priests could be the solution. "If you get four more, I'll ordain you early," Dolan quipped to applause from the seminarians. It was a whirlwind introduction to New York and only the beginning. The boy from Ballwin was about to be thrown into the glare of the media spotlight in a way he had never experi-enced before.

Dolan returned to Milwaukee and had less than two months to set about wrapping up his duties and saying his good-byes with conflicting emotions of excitement, sadness, and trepidation at what lay ahead. Catholics across Milwaukee wanted to bid him farewell, and he found himself receiving one standing ovation after another. During his final meeting with the Priests' Council, Father Tom Eichenberger, a district dean, couldn't let the session end without saying a few words about how much Dolan had come to mean to them all personally. "You've affected us all," he told him. "And we're going to miss you deeply." Everyone in the room nodded their heads in agreement and clapped. "We loved him," said Father Frederick, also at the meeting. "We'd learned to love Tim Dolan." The outgoing archbishop gathered with the priests on the grounds of the seminary, where they joined him in a prayer service followed by a lunch. Everyone wanted to wish Dolan well, and many of the priests, especially those who had feared his arrival, felt proud of how close they had become. As Suriano—one of the trio who had penned the letter questioning priestly celibacy—approached, Dolan told him honestly he had been anxious about coming to Milwaukee because as much as he was excited to be named an archbishop, he had heard tales about the priests in the archdiocese and wasn't sure what to expect. "I'm glad I didn't believe the book about you guys, and thank you for not believing the book about me," Dolan said. The majority of the priests had grown to respect and admire Dolan's human touch and believed that as much as he had shaped them, they had also shaped him. "It wasn't just a one-way street," Suriano would later say. Dolan told another priest, "I'm not the same bishop I was when I came. You formed me as much as I formed you." It also fell to Dolan's chief of staff, Jerry Topczewski, to phone the Archdiocese of New York's head of communications, Joseph Zwilling, and discuss the handover with him. Before signing off, Topczewski said he had some advice for Zwilling and shared the same words of wisdom he had received seven years earlier from the press spokesman in St. Louis: "Hold on to your hat. It's going to be quite a ride."

All that was left was Dolan's final Mass in the Milwaukee cathedral. He gave his secretary his homily to type up and as she took it, she asked him, "Are you ready for this?" He told her he had read it repeatedly until it no longer made him cry, and when he knew he could get through it without breaking down, he knew he was ready. It was standing room only inside the cathedral on Easter Sunday 2009 when Dolan delivered his final homily. "As excited as I am and as hopeful as I am, this is down-right sad," he told the congregation. "It's kind of a little dying and some rising, which is what Holy Week and Easter is all about." As he walked down the aisle greeting parishioners after Mass, he was met with warm words and embraces. "He's been a father to us," Deacon Mark Brandl remarked. "He's bigger than Milwaukee, so it's time." "He moves you like you never thought you could be moved," a woman told reporters from New York who had flown to Milwaukee for the occasion. "New York is so lucky to get him. He's warm; he's sincere; he means every-thing he says, you will feel that." On his way out of the church, Dolan came face-to-face with Isely from SNAP. "I really wish you the best of luck in New York," he told the archbishop. "Well, Peter, I'm going to need a lot of luck in New York, 'cause I sure didn't get much here." Be-fore Isely could say anything more, Dolan was swept up in a crowd of well-wishers.

9

NEW YORK

The huddle of photographers stood on Madison Avenue, at the back of St. Patrick's Cathedral, waiting. They had been assigned to get a picture of Archbishop Timothy Dolan as he arrived at his new home, so positioned themselves with a clear view of the entrance. Reporters had been dispatched to Milwaukee to attend his final Easter Sunday Mass, which ensured their counterparts in New York knew he was now on a plane and heading their way. The only thing left to do was to be patient. The local media didn't have a particularly warm view of Catholic leaders. Dolan's predecessor, Cardinal Edward Egan, had been regarded as an aloof and oftentimes stern archbishop who had never been at ease talking to the press. He was a gifted administrator with a stellar academic record, but his character had always seemed ill suited to the vibrancy of the city and the multifaceted demands of the job. As a result, the photographers waiting for a glimpse of the new man soon taking the helm at St. Patrick's Cathedral did not know what to expect. At best, they figured they'd have a few seconds to snap a couple of frames as he crossed the sidewalk and climbed the steps to the front door. When the two vehicles carrying Dolan and his family finally pulled up, the photographers were poised and ready. Dolan immediately spotted the waiting media and bounded over. "Hi, I'm Archbishop Timothy Dolan," he said jovially, calling over his niece, who had also hopped out of the car. He draped his arm around her shoulder, introduced her to the press pack, and posed for photos, smiling warmly. "This isn't what we're used to," one photographer remarked to Dolan's entourage, which included his brother Bob; Bob's wife, Beth; and their second daughter, who had all flown with him from Milwaukee on the private jet.

Dolan was suddenly in the spotlight in a way he had never been before. Statements he had made in Milwaukee appeared in the local news but rarely did they go national, let alone global. He quickly discovered that was all about to change dramatically. The front pages of the city's newspapers had already been emblazoned with Dolan's image and even late-night talk show host David Letterman was talking about him. The tabloids were filled with headlines such as "Heaven Sent" and "Dolan Out the Love." An editorial in the *New York Daily News* welcomed Dolan's arrival as a "blessing for the soul of New York" and said he was a "cheerful warrior of faith." In his own self-penned column in the newspaper, Dolan said his mission was "to be a happy bishop, sharing joys and laughs with you." Dozens of reporters' bylines appeared on stories covering every aspect of Dolan's arrival in the city, and Sister Bosco was even tracked down at her convent in Ireland and asked what she thought about the appointment. "I find it very humbling to think I helped in getting him there, as he claims," she said modestly. When one journalist asked how Dolan felt about joining an archdiocese with such a rich history of Irish-American archbishops, he wasted no time in crafting a reply. "That's a sign of the Holy Father's infallibility, don't you think?" His quick-witted responses ensured the multitude of column inches devoted to the archbishop's arrival were peppered with amusing quips and colorful anecdotes. In a city that thrives on its quirks and celebrates colorful characters, it took barely any time for the people of New York to feel Dolan was a natural fit.

The two-day installation ceremonies followed a pattern similar to those in Milwaukee, just on a far bigger and grander scale. A solemn vespers service took place on the evening of April 14, where, once again, Dolan entered last by knocking on the closed cathedral doors to symbolically request welcome from his flock. The traffic on Fifth Avenue had been stopped, and as he approached the twenty-thousand-pound bronze doors, he paused momentarily to wave to the cheering crowds who had gathered behind barricades across the street before being handed a simple wooden hammer. He took aim at a section of the door void of beautiful carvings of American saints and rapped six times. The doors did not move. So he knocked again three times. Quiet laughter rippled through the crowd inside as the second round of knocks rang out. Finally the doors swung open noiselessly and Dolan was inside St. Patrick's Cathedral, making his way down the long aisle as cameras flashed from all directions. "Allow me to assure you, that's the last time you're going to have to knock twice to get into St. Pat's," Cardinal Egan said to his successor during his opening remarks at the altar. Dolan's mother and family were in the first pews, along with Sister Bosco, who had flown from Ireland. She gave a reading from the First Letter of Saint Peter and soaked up the occasion with awe, marveling at how far her young student had come. When he took to the pulpit, Dolan made reference to the picture she had showed him in Holy Infant Grade School of Jesus knocking on a door without a knob, which she had explained symbolized the need for people to open their hearts to the church from the inside. As Bosco sat listening to her student use this same story to teach a lesson to the audience, she was overcome with pride.

His first homily to the New York congregation was vintage Dolan. There were baseball references and honest acknowledgment of his fears and trepidation at the assignment. "Go away, Lord! I'm not your man," Dolan said, describing his initial reaction to the news he was New York bound. "My Spanish is lousy and my English not much better. I'm still angry at New York for taking Favre and Sabathia from us in Wisconsin. The Yankees and the Mets over the Cardinals and the Brewers? Forget it!" The audience chuckled to hear such self-deprecating comments from a man who possessed so much skill. Then Dolan adopted a more serious tone and made reference to some of the challenges the church faced, including the clergy sex abuse crisis, showing he was not going to be afraid to tackle the tough issues. He kept his remarks that night relatively short as the real big-hitting speech was expected the following day.

The next morning, Dolan woke up early inside the residence attached to St. Patrick's Cathedral ready to face one of the biggest days of his life. He'd quipped he had crows, not simply butterflies, in his stomach at the thought of becoming New York's Catholic leader, but it was finally time to get this very big show on the road. "I hope at my core, I hear Jesus say, 'Timothy, be not afraid,'" he said. "Then I take a deep breath and say, 'Let's go,' and I'm going to enjoy it and I'm going to give it my best." In the morning, he gave a press conference at the private all-girls Cathedral High School on Manhattan's Upper East Side, where he arrived with arms outstretched and took time to shake the journalists' hands and ask them to introduce themselves so he could begin trying to remember their names. He thanked them for their presence, but any hopes for an easy introduction to New York life and politics were swiftly dashed. He was peppered with questions from reporters about the issues ahead, including the fact that the very next day the New York governor planned to introduce a same-sex marriage bill in Albany, the state capitol. "You can bet I'll be active and present on that," he said. When asked if he planned to take advantage of the bully pulpit he now commanded, Dolan took exception to the word *bully*, but conceded his new podium did have a "particular prominence." "We bishops aren't into politics, we're into principles, so you can expect that from me," he told the press.

A few hours later, the moment was finally upon him. St. Patrick's Cathedral was full to capacity for the two-hour installation ceremony, and a long procession of seven hundred cardinals, archbishops, bishops, and priests was wrapped around the building from Madison Avenue, along Fifty-first Street, and slowly filtering in through the main doors on Fifth Avenue. Dolan stood outside the entrance, greeting as many people as he could. He took time to walk over and chat to members of the NYPD assigned to provide security and waved incessantly at the crowds of people crammed behind barriers on the opposite side of the road. They could not get inside the cathedral but wanted to be part of the momentous occasion oozing with pageantry. "Look! He's waving!" one woman shouted excitedly to her friend. "Whooo-hoo!" her companion replied. This was the hottest ticket in town that day, and some spectators had arrived hours earlier to secure the best vantage point. "I need to see my shepherd," a hospital worker from the Bronx said of her reason for coming. Other well-wishers remarked how down-to-earth Dolan appeared. "There's a sense of new life, of everyone feeling renewed," Father Keith Fennessy of St. Margaret Mary Church in Staten Island said as he looked on. "I think he's giving everyone a shot in the arm." "Pray for me!" Dolan hollered at the people before entering the cathedral. "I'm staying until I see everything," exclaimed a Brooklyn woman standing outside. "I don't care if it rains. When you are Catholic, you make sacrifices."

As Dolan walked down the aisle, robed in white, he stretched both hands out in front of him, marveling at the sights of so many people from his time spent in St. Louis; Rome; Washington, D.C.; Kansas City; and Milwaukee. When he reached the front-row pew, he paused first to shake hands with some of the most influential politicians in the city, including Mayor Michael Bloomberg, Governor David Paterson, and Senators Chuck Schumer and Kirsten Gillibrand. He also greeted the beloved former New York mayor Ed Koch, an outspoken and brash city icon. Then he turned his attention to the pew across the aisle, where Shirley Dolan sat in a vibrant pink coat along with his siblings and their families. He whisked his two-year-old nephew, Patrick, up into his arms briefly before heading to the altar to get the formalities under way. Dozens of media outlets were crammed into nooks around the cavernous cathedral, jostling for spots and craning their necks to see and absorb everything that was happening. When the papal nuncio, Archbishop Pietro Sambi, read Pope Benedict's appointment letter, Dolan sat still with his head bowed and his hands clasped in prayer by his face, occasionally closing his eyes tightly to take in the gravity of the occasion. Then vibrant applause rang out as Dolan, led by Egan and Sambi, was invited to sit in the big carved wooden archbishop's chair. It was official; he was now the archbishop of New York.

Bishops, the heads of various clergy departments, and representatives from other Christian and non-Christian faiths were invited to greet Dolan one by one during the ceremony. As acting head of the Priests' Council, Father Joseph LaMorte was among them. He had been impressed by Dolan from the day his appointment had been announced back in February. LaMorte had been in his office at the Church of the Holy Trinity in Poughkeepsie, catching up on work when his secretary excitedly informed him Cardinal Egan was on the line. LaMorte picked up his phone and, sure enough, it wasn't a hoax. After exchanging some brief small talk, Egan said, "Archbishop Dolan wants to talk to you." The appointment had been made public only a few hours prior, at noon Rome time, six A.M. New York time, as is protocol for all official Holy See announcements. Their conversation lasted less than a minute, with Dolan simply wanting to convey how much he looked forward to working with the Priests' Council, but it set a tone. "The incoming archbishop of New York is a listener and a collaborator," LaMorte thought. "He left an impression on me right from the beginning that he would take time." As LaMorte approached Dolan at the altar of St. Patrick's Cathedral, he once again introduced himself and could see the flash of recognition in the archbishop's eyes.

The service followed a prescribed pattern, but there was room to inject some personal flair. At Dolan's request the Irish-born tenor Ronan Tynan, who frequently sang "God Bless America" at Yankee Stadium, entertained the congregation with Franz Schubert's "Avé Maria" and

Cesar Franck's "Panis Angelicus" during the Mass. Egan had requested opera singer Renée Fleming during his installation in 2000, an early indication of the different personalities the two possessed. In his homily, Dolan paid tribute to all the dignitaries and clergy present but then said perhaps he had been too quick to be thankful. "Maybe I shouldn't be so flattered or surprised that so many are here. After all, everybody wants to claim sanctuary on income tax day." As the laughs subsided, Dolan saved special thanks for his family. "Whatever God gives me in life, his greatest gift to me remains that I am Bob and Shirley Dolan's son," he said. "And I mean that very much, Mom," he added, looking down at her from the pulpit with unmistakable affection as the audience clapped. Then he looked out across the crowd and admitted, "I am really relieved to see Mom. We were a little afraid this morning that she might not make it. She found out there was a sale on at Macy's." The cathedral erupted in loud, sustained laughter, and Dolan couldn't hold back his own chuckles at successfully pulling off the quip. His siblings laughed among themselves. Shirley was well accustomed to this kind of playful teasing but not in front of such a dignified audience and would later scold her son lightly, telling him people did not yet know her well enough to realize he was only joking. The twenty-five-minute speech, likely one of the longest homilies Dolan had ever given, was listened to closely by an array of people, from rank-and-file Catholics to elected officials and the media. It was a crucial indicator of the politics and principles of the new archbishop and, similar to the night before, once the jokes were over, Dolan made his stance on core Catholic issues clear. The church "continues to embrace and protect the dignity of every human person, the sanctity of life, from the tiny baby in the womb up to the last moment of natural passing into eternal life," he said to sustained applause and a standing ovation lasting more than one minute. The pew of New York politicians also rose out of respect, but did not clap.

Dolan continued to hammer home his message using terms that

were more friendly than combative, tellingly choosing not to use the word *abortion* even once: "Yes, the Church is a loving mother who has a zest for life and serves life everywhere, but she can become a protective 'mamma bear' when the life of her innocent, helpless cubs is threatened. Everybody in this great mega-community is a somebody with an extraordinary destiny," he said. "That's why the Church reaches out to the unborn, the suffering, the poor, our elders, the physically and emotionally challenged or those caught in the web of addiction." Dolan touched on the "horrible" church scandals, calling them a "crime," and referenced how the church was "ridiculed for her teaching on the sanctity of marriage." However, he sought above all to make his speech a reminder to Catholics of what was great about their faith. "Does she have power and clout, property and prestige?" he said, personifying the church. "Forget it! Those days are gone, if they ever did exist at all. . . . The Church," he said, "really has no treasure but her faith in the Lord."

The *New York Post*'s headline the next morning exclaimed "Dolan's Mass Appeal," while its tabloid rival, the *New York Daily News,* tried to go one better with a classic tabloid stunt. It had dispatched a reporter to track down Dolan the previous morning, hours before his installation got under way, to deliver a framed copy of their front page, which was of Dolan's smiling face. The cover that next morning showed New York's freshly installed archbishop holding the gift beneath the headline: "It's his day!" And it was. "It's hard to get your arms around," Dolan's brother Bob explained. "When he moved to New York, that was when we realized that our brother was pretty special. Even though to us, he's still just a brother. That's when it hit home."

As in Milwaukee, Dolan's first order of business was familiarizing himself with his new staff and surroundings. That included the local baseball teams. He had tactfully remained on the fence when asked who he was now going to root for and received a personal invitation to watch

the Yankees home opener at their new stadium in the Bronx the day after his installation. His brothers, Bob and Patrick, joined him, along
with Dolan's two brother-in-laws, Jerry Topczewski, and a few other
close friends. They all hopped in a small minibus and, as they reached
the stadium, were met by a police escort to help navigate the congestion
around the gates. "Can you believe this?" Dolan remarked to the others.
This wasn't the sort of treatment any of them were used to. In Milwaukee
they drove themselves to the game. The invitation to Yankee Stadium
had come from Mindy Levine, a Milwaukee native and the wife of
Yankees president Randy Levine. They were welcomed into the Steinbrenner Suite, where they greeted Yankees owner George Steinbrenner
himself and the other invited guests, including business tycoon Donald
Trump, former secretary of state Henry Kissinger, and Elaine Kaufman,
who owned a legendary Upper East Side restaurant. Dolan's entourage was
also introduced to former New York mayor Rudy Giuliani, TV show host
Regis Philbin, and retired baseball stars Reggie Jackson and Yogi Berra. In
a week jam-packed with excitement, it was a standout moment and VIP
treatment Dolan could only have dreamed of as a kid. The following day,
he headed to the Citi Field stadium at the request of Mets owner Fred
Wilpon, where the home team was up against the Milwaukee Brewers.
He invited Egan and some of the New York bishops to the private box,
which was a less star-studded affair. Dolan appeared content to be able to
sit back and actually enjoy the game without having to socialize.

Dolan endeavored to make himself as visible as possible to the community and press in his initial days and weeks. He visited a food pantry
in the Bronx, attended an interfaith service in Manhattan for Holo-
caust Remembrance Day, prayed at the World Trade Center site, and
visited the Bedford Hills Correctional Facility to say Mass for 150 female inmates. With the formalities, jovial introductions, and first few
media appearances aside, it was time to get down to work and get to
know his Catholic community. There was a lot to take on board. Dolan

had never spent any significant time in New York and had to get to grips with the geographical boundaries of his archdiocese first and foremost. It spanned 4,683 square miles, encompassing the New York City boroughs of Staten Island, Manhattan, and the Bronx as well as seven counties farther north. It had more than 2.5 million Catholics, about 370 parishes, and roughly 630 archdiocesan priests. It was second in terms of population only to the Archdiocese of Los Angeles and far bigger, more complex, and more diverse than Milwaukee. Dolan immediately made trips to as many parishes as he could in different geographical areas. He would have dinner with the local clergy, attend a prayer service in the church, and stay after for a reception with the community. "You are as important to me as Saint Patrick's Cathedral on Fifth Avenue," he told the congregation of St. Joseph's Parish in Kingston, nearly one hundred miles north of Manhattan, at one such visit. His comments were met with a raucous round of applause. The church was filled to the brim by the time Dolan arrived, and he had made his way down the aisle slowly, smiling, shaking hands, and giving blessings. Everyone was eager to cast their eyes on this man who had been making so many headlines.

This was the first time the incoming archbishop of New York had a living predecessor to turn to for guidance. Dolan and Egan spent several days together ahead of the installation ceremony, and Egan continued to take time to impart whatever wisdom he could. Dolan happily discovered the archdiocese was in steady shape financially, thanks predominantly to Egan's stellar administrative skills. However, there were several looming issues that had to be dealt with. Vocations were down, a problem the Catholic Church faced nationwide, and plans had already been set in motion to merge the Archdiocese of New York's seminary with the two neighboring seminaries in the Dioceses of Brooklyn and Rockville Center. A handful of Catholic schools had been closed under Egan's tenure, but far more sweeping closures and mergers needed to take place to secure the education system into the future. Further down the road, a similar reorganization strategy had to be applied to parishes, too, to counteract declining numbers, geographical population shifts, and mounting costs. Of course, fund-raising was also always an issue. Egan had been a strong champion of Dolan throughout his rise up the Catholic hierarchy, and the Missouri native was hugely grateful for the support and confidence, even telling him, "If it weren't for you, I would still be in St. Louis." Yet it was apparent not everyone had such warm views of Egan, which Dolan found both mystifying and troubling. Egan had been in charge of the Archdiocese of New York for nine years but had inherited the top job at a difficult time when the city was mourning the death of Cardinal John O'Connor, a beloved New York figure. Egan had been an auxiliary bishop in New York for three years prior to his appointment, so priests in the archdiocese knew him, but it did not take long before he was thought of as distant, even bad tempered. Where O'Connor held press conferences at St. Patrick's after Sunday morning Mass and publicly took on Catholic politicians who championed legislation not in line with their religious beliefs, Egan was uncomfortable in the limelight. In 2006, a group of rank-and-file priests penned an anonymous letter accusing Egan of having a "severely vindictive nature" and saying his relationship with priests had been "defined by dishonesty, deception, disinterest and disregard." The missive called for a vote of no confidence and was signed by "a committee of concerned clergy." Though their identities were never revealed, the episode did little to help Egan's public image. Dolan found these opinions of his predecessor confounding, and the inevitable good-guy, bad-guy comparisons that arose between himself and this man who had done so much to help him were unsettling. "He's anything but this unfriendly, stern, reclusive, crabby guy," Dolan told *National Catholic* reporter John Allen. "He's just the opposite. You never want your compliment to be at somebody else's expense."

There was no denying that Dolan had more of O'Connor's gregarious style about him than Egan's composure, and in an effort to get to know his priests, he hosted a barbecue at Saint Joseph's Seminary in Yonkers, just north of the city. Decked out in pants, a sports shirt, and a baseball cap, he mingled among the crowd. "Father, help me with your name, have we met?" he inquired when he came across a face he couldn't recall. He needed to be introduced only once, and he wouldn't forget again. Despite New York City's reputation for being one of the most open and liberal areas in the United States, many of the priests were not accustomed to this informal, laid-back approach. When O'Connor wanted to be casual, he put on a blue sweater; Egan was the first archbishop most of them had seen in a sports shirt. Dolan joked and laughed and had no qualms about taking off his clerical collar and dressing down or lighting up a cigar. "Other dioceses that are less formal, not in the spotlight, not the media capital of the world probably have experienced that kind of folksy relationship with their bishop," LaMorte explained. "Not in New York."

Another way to get to know his priests well and understand the issues they were concerned about was through the Priests' Council. LaMorte was vice president when Dolan first arrived but had assumed the role of president since the chair was vacant; he would be formally elected to the position within months. Dolan invited LaMorte to meet with him in his twentieth-floor office at the archdiocese's Catholic Center during his first weeks, along with Monsignor Gregory Mustaciuolo, who had served as secretary to both Egan and O'Connor, and Monsignor William Belford, who was then chancellor. Dolan was keen to hear from all three men and especially took time to hear how the Priests' Council functioned and how he hoped to function within it. LaMorte explained that the thirty-five-member board met monthly and was composed mostly of priests who were elected to serve on the council in addition to a handful of ex-officio and appointed representatives. It served an important function as an intermediary between the archbishop and pastors in any diocese, but somewhere as large as New York, it was vital. In addition to core cabinet members, bishops, and department heads that Dolan would inevitably rely on, it provided one of his main lines of communication to the rank-and-file and an important source of counsel. The Priests' Council had to be technically reconstituted when Dolan arrived, but once those formalities were out of the way the members gathered for their first meeting with the new boss. It took place at Saint Joseph's Seminary and everyone was promptly seated at the start time, eager to make a good first impression. Many of those present had caught only a brief glimpse of Dolan inside St. Patrick's Cathedral prior to this moment and few knew him personally. He entered the room to a standing ovation and took his time working his way through the people, shaking hands, smiling, and thanking everyone for coming. Dolan told LaMorte early on he preferred to keep his comments to the end of the meetings, unless a commitment required him to leave early. He liked hearing what everyone else had to say first, before giving his feedback. Typically, LaMorte gave an opening report, the heads of various committees presented their reports, and after about an hour and forty-five minutes of discussion, Dolan got his turn. Everyone was thrilled to have a new archbishop who was young and vibrant and there was a honeymoon period in those early months. Dolan chose to listen and observe rather than make any sudden drastic decisions, although changes would inevitably come and with them, the first rumblings of discord. From the outset, however, New York's priests were charmed by their new archbishop.

Dolan was already highly regarded within church circles and in demand at Catholic conferences, but he now had a far broader appeal encompassing Catholics and non-Catholics alike. Everything he said also had wider ramifications. As he made time to meet one-on-one with major department heads, he turned to his director of communications, Joseph Zwilling, for advice on how to handle the media. The two men already knew each other vaguely since Zwilling's brother-in-law,

Archbishop Charles Balvo, had been a classmate of Dolan's at the North American College. They had met a few times over the years, the first time when Dolan was a rector in Rome. A few years later their paths crossed again at a bishops' conference where Zwilling was unsure if Dolan would remember him. He made the connection instantly. "How's Moose?" he asked, using the nickname he'd given Balvo. "How's your father-in-law?" he quizzed, recalling that he was a widower. "That was the first time I encountered the memory and the connection and the friendliness, and the asking personal details," Zwilling would later say. When it came to understanding and dealing with the New York press, Zwilling was a veteran. He had been in the job for nearly three decades, arriving for the final year of Cardinal Terence Cooke's time at the helm and serving throughout Cardinal O'Connor's and Cardinal Egan's tenures. Zwilling explained to Dolan that there were many people out there who could teach about Catholicism, and many people who could help deepen a person's faith if they desired, but Dolan's real strength was evangelization, and he hoped to use that to their advantage. "You've got to show the joy of what being a Catholic is all about," Zwilling explained. Dolan concurred, saying he knew no one wanted to join a grumpy, sour, mean-spirited group of people, a sentiment he came to use repeatedly. Zwilling knew his boss was already a natural with the media and that alone was a sea change from Egan, who preferred not to give interviews if it could be avoided. However, Zwilling also warned it was important they not overexpose him. There would be times when they would have to say no, even to major networks, to avoid people getting fatigued of seeing Dolan's face every time they turned on the television or opened up a newspaper. "I will rely on you," Dolan said. "If you think it's something I should do, tell me; if you think it's something I shouldn't do, tell me."

Zwilling suggested that one way for him to connect directly with people and get his message to a broader audience was to start a blog. Dolan had never had a real need for a computer and wasn't well versed in technol-

ogy beyond a cell phone, but once Zwilling explained what a blog actually was, he embraced the idea. It was soon put to good use in a heated
confrontation with *The New York Times*. The Catholic Church had long
felt the newspaper had an anti-Catholic bias, and when a series of articles
appeared that Dolan felt exemplified that prejudice, he felt compelled to
speak up. Dolan penned a response and did not hold back. He accused
The New York Times of "selective outrage," citing each recent story he
took objection to, including one that revealed child sex abuse within
Brooklyn's Orthodox Jewish community. Dolan questioned why *The
New York Times* did not call for the same transparency or accountability from this community that it demanded constantly of the Catholic
Church. A column by Maureen Dowd, one of the paper's most divisive
writers, attacking what she saw as the mistreatment of women by the
church drew the most ire. He branded it "intemperate and scurrilous"
and a "diatribe" that would never have made it to print had it been
equally critical of a religious issue affecting Muslims, Jews, or African
Americans. Dolan offered his retort to the op-ed pages, but the editor
responded that was not how they handled complaints and it was more
appropriate as a letter to the editor. Fearing his response would be con-
densed and fail to get his point across adequately on the letters page,
Dolan ultimately posted it to his blog. "The Catholic Church is not
above criticism," he wrote in conclusion. "We Catholics do a fair amount
of it ourselves. We welcome and expect it. All we ask is that such critique be fair, rational, and accurate, what we would expect for anybody.
The suspicion and bias against the Church is a national pastime that
should be 'rained out' for good." *The New York Times* did not let the
issue rest, either. The national religion correspondent wrote to Dolan
personally, standing her ground. The public editor published a lengthy
justification of the articles and column, expressing clear surprise at such
a sharp tone from a man who had been welcomed into the city only six
months prior and widely lauded as a conciliator.

The matter was temporarily put to rest, and Dolan headed back to Missouri for Thanksgiving to spend time with his mom and siblings, yet within months he found himself at loggerheads with the media again, this time defending Pope Benedict's track record as prefect of the Congregation for the Doctrine of the Faith, where he had dealt with clergy abuse cases. Dolan reiterated his pleas for fairness and accuracy, arguing the church had done more to tackle this problem than any other institution and that the abuse of children by people in positions of power and responsibility was not an issue confined to the Catholic Church. He once again turned to his blog and said this had the look of a "well-oiled campaign" against the Holy Father, fueling further debate. Former mayor Koch weighed in on the side of Dolan; *The New York Times* continued to defend its stance and even questioned whether the archbishop took such exception to these stories because he did not like the way the paper had historically shined the spotlight on the church's handling of sex abuse. Within the Catholic community there was also division. Many supported Dolan's firm stance addressing a bias that had long irked them, while some felt it was simply unbecoming and unfruitful. The arguments continued back and forth via the media and Dolan's blog for seven months. Confidants urged him to get used to it, explaining the Catholic Church had long been the subject of disproportionate scrutiny and held to a different standard. Eventually, he let it lie and thanked his community for having patience with him. "I guess I'm still new enough here in New York City that the insults of *The New York Times* against the Church still bother me," he wrote. "I know I should get over it. As we say in Missouri, it's like 'spitting into a tornado.'"

In the midst of this, Dolan continued to deal with the everyday demands of the job, including responsibilities emanating from outside the archdiocese. In January 2010 he jetted to Haiti for forty-eight hours in his capacity as chairman of the Catholic Relief Services to assess the damage, offer the church's support, and discuss ways to help. While there, he attended the funeral of the archbishop of Port-au-Prince, Joseph Serge Miot. Miot had died in the earthquake that claimed approximately two hundred thousand lives and brought the small, impoverished nation to its knees. It was a quick in-and-out where Dolan spent the first night sleeping outside the papal nuncio's residence, as the building itself had been nearly destroyed, and the second night in a tent at a refugee camp on a former eighteen-hole golf course. He was also invited to pray outside the St. Françoise de Sales Hospital amid the ruins of incubators, beds crushed under piles of rocks, and weeping mothers. More than forty babies had died in the neonatal unit, and the pile of rubble in front of him was now their grave. It was a sobering and intense experience. In May he was appointed by Pope Benedict to serve on an apostolic visitation to Ireland to help heal their own sex abuse crisis, look at the way it had been handled, and assess if adequate safeguards were in place to prevent its recurrence. Dolan was one of a nine-member panel and assigned specifically to attend to the Irish seminaries, a nod to his aptitude for being able to relate to younger generations of priests. He spent one week at the Pontifical Irish College in Rome, their equivalent of the North American College, before heading to Ireland to speak to seminarians directly. These responsibilities further cemented his standing as a key voice of the Catholic Church, but on November 16, his status took another huge leap forward. To the surprise of many, Dolan was voted president of the United States Conference of Catholic Bishops (USCCB), winning 128–111 in a third-ballot runoff with Bishop Gerald Kicanas of Tucson, Arizona, the sitting vice president. This marked the first time the deputy had stood for the president's spot and not been appointed. Dolan had narrowly missed being voted vice president over Kicanas back in 2007, while still in Milwaukee, and had been nominated as president twice prior, but confessed to being shocked at the appointment. It signaled a shift on many levels. Kicanas was widely seen as more left of center than Dolan, and Dolan's election gave a clear indication the bishops were looking to guide the church in a more conservative direction. Kicanas's record on the sex abuse scandal was also tarnished, and some felt it was simply time to end the predictability of the vice president getting the job. All the same, the USCCB had typically veered away from electing a president who already had a prominent pulpit to preach from, meaning the decision was a massive endorsement of Dolan's attributes and the skills he could bring to the table. During his time in New York, he had already more than proved himself as an outspoken, well-liked, and media-savvy voice for the church who could handle tough issues with tact and grace. The election was a sign the bishops felt he was the best man to champion their cause nationally also. Dolan said he was humbled by the decision. "The posture of the bishops, of course, is you don't really run for office, you run from it," he added with a laugh.

Since Dolan's first day in the city, one big political issue had been on his radar, the first of many he would have to contend with both as archbishop of New York and now as president of the USCCB: same-sex marriage. Four states had already given gay and lesbian couples the right to wed, and Governor David Paterson was hopeful New York could be next. Legislation had been introduced the day after Dolan's installation, and it was a battle the church needed to face head-on. Dolan was well versed in the arguments. He had been embroiled in the issue in Milwaukee, where he had been attacked by both sides. Proponents had taken objection to the church defining marriage as exclusively between a man and a woman, while opponents criticized the church for decrying homosexual acts but not the people themselves. "A person's dignity is not dependent on their sexual orientation," Dolan had said in response. He argued he was not going to turn his back on a human being simply because of his sexual orientation, even if he could never condone homosexual activity. In 2006, Dolan threw his weight behind a Wisconsin state constitutional amendment defining marriage as "between one man and one woman," and it had been passed by popular vote. The battle over the issue in New York promised to be far tougher. The first bill, introduced by Paterson, was defeated by the state senate in December 2009, buying the Catholic Church some breathing space, but at the end of 2010, Paterson decided not to run for re-election and was replaced by Democrat Andrew Cuomo, the former New York attorney general. He posed an altogether different challenge. Not only was he a shrewd political operator and intensely well connected, but despite being Catholic, he did not adhere to many of the church's dictates. For one, he was divorced and living with his girlfriend, Food Network host Sandra Lee. He also supported same-sex marriage and abortion rights. The Archdiocese of New York was no stranger to the Cuomo family. The new governor's father, Mario, held the same position from 1983 to 1994 and had been embroiled in constant confrontations over abortion rights with Cardinal O'Connor. It had never been a warm, friendly relationship, with some even calling for Mario Cuomo's excommunication, which O'Connor did not discourage. The church had to be prepped for a battle once again, but it soon became evident the younger Cuomo was a force to be reckoned with and determined to get his way.

Cuomo had campaigned on the gay marriage issue in his run for governor and was voted in by an overwhelming majority, giving him a huge popular mandate. He felt it was a piece of legislation that could define his early time in office, and he framed it as a civil rights issue, not a political one. He told his father that seeing the same-sex marriage law change in New York was "at the heart of leadership and progressive government," and he was also under pressure at home, as his girlfriend's brother was openly gay and she felt strongly the time for change had come. Dolan made no secret of his stance on the issue during a face-to-face talk with Cuomo in Albany on March 8, 2011. Over a lunch of salmon and cheesecake in the executive mansion, Dolan and other bishops from the state were afforded an opportunity to discuss items on the political agenda and their clashes of conscience. The meeting was part of an annual day of lobbying by the New York State Catholic Conference, which brought close to one thousand Catholics to the state capitol. Regarding same-sex marriage, Cuomo made it clear he understood the bishops' viewpoint and had no intention of harming the church, but he reiterated this was something he felt personally compelled to do. The very next day the governor invited same-sex marriage advocates to the capitol for a closed-door meeting, where he assured them of not only his full support, but also his intention to take a leading role on the issue, using the full weight of his electoral popularity.

For the first four or five months of the legislative session, Cuomo did not appear to have the requisite number of votes to make the bill pass, so there was little cause for alarm among Catholic lobbyists. When same-sex marriage had been defeated in 2009 under Paterson, a number of Democrats had voted against it. Now, two years on, three of them were still in office and they committed privately to voting the same way again. But "assurances in politics are as good as the day they were given," one insider explained. The tide of public opinion had changed rapidly in those intervening years, and Senate Majority Leader Dean Skelos, a Republican, did not want this to become a partisan issue. He said he would allow a conscience vote on the measure from members of his party. As the legislative sessions barreled toward a vote in June, millions of dollars started to pour into the pro–gay marriage campaign from both inside and outside the state. Dolan reiterated that he was not anti-anybody but pro-marriage as defined by God, and again used his blog as a mouth-piece for a tersely worded statement. "The stampede is on," he wrote in the weeks before the vote was put to the Senate chamber after it passed the state assembly. "Last time I consulted an atlas, it is clear we are living in New York, in the United States of America—not in China or North Korea. In those countries, government presumes daily to 'redefine' rights, relationships, values, and natural law. There, communiqués from the government can dictate the size of families, who lives and who dies, and what the very definition of 'family' and 'marriage' means. But, please, not here!" Catholic bishops, Dolan included, had been enlisted to make phone calls to legislators thought to be on the fence to shore up votes, and the Catholic community was mobilized to flood legislators' in-boxes with e-mails imploring them to vote no. However, political negotiations were also going on with fervor behind closed doors.

As the vote neared, Dolan headed to Seattle, Washington, to attend the annual spring meeting of the USCCB, his first as president. Meanwhile in Albany, Cuomo saw success within his grasp. He appeared at a news conference with the three Democrats who had previously been no votes—Senators Carl Kruger, Shirley Huntley, and Joseph Addabbo—where they announced they were now in the yes camp. In Kruger's case, her position had changed partly due to mounting pressure at home. The woman he lived with had a gay nephew who was so angered by Kruger's no vote two years prior he had severed all contact. With their names in the bag, the governor turned his attention to the Republicans, and some started talking openly about flipping to support same-sex marriage, too. The Catholic camp sensed trouble. From Seattle, Dolan phoned in to the popular radio show hosted by the *New York Post*'s Fred Dicker, which is well listened to in political circles, saying he felt this law would be "detrimental for the common good," but Cuomo had won over four key Republicans, in part by promising substantial financial and political backing during their future reelection campaigns for voting against the will of many Republican voters.

Senator James Alesi was the first to publicly switch allegiance after finding he felt tormented and anguished at having had to vote no previously. "You can't have equality unless you treat others equally," he said of his decision. Senator Roy McDonald took a more blunt approach in explaining his actions: "You get to the point where you evolve in your life where everything isn't black and white, good and bad, and you try to do the right thing," he told reporters. "You might not like that. You might be very cynical about that. Well, fuck it, I don't care what you think. I'm trying to do the right thing. I'm tired of Republican-Democrat politics. They can take the job and shove it. I come from a blue-collar background. I'm trying to do the right thing, and that's where I'm going with this." Two more Republicans also ultimately said yes—Senators Stephen Saland and Mark Grisanti. Saland's wife had supported gay marriage for years, and he said he ultimately came around to her way of thinking after a "long deliberative process." With the three Democrats in his corner, too, the deal was done. "[Cuomo] threw money at candidates to vote their way," a member of Dolan's camp explained. "He rammed it through despite assurances from individuals that it was not going to happen."

Cuomo ultimately secured thirty-three votes in the sixty-two-seat Senate chamber. Catholics were deflated and there were jubilant celebrations in the streets outside the Stonewall Inn in Manhattan's Greenwich Village, a gay bar where violent clashes with police in 1969 became a pivotal turning point in the modern-day gay rights movement. Criticism was leveled at Dolan for failing to take a tough enough stance and for being absent in the final days and hours of the debate. "There's a certain sense among some people, questioning, did we cave at the last minute?" one New York priest said. "Could he have really spearheaded something in Albany by his presence there?" Catholic lobbyists were doubtful Dolan could have done any more. They had been outgunned financially, and the popular mood had changed. There was now widespread support for same-sex marriage, even among many Catholics, so the image of Dolan marching into the state capitol to throw his weight around could have been hugely counterproductive, though that did little to stem the disappointment. It was over. Cuomo had achieved what many had thought was unachievable. "We have been bloodied, and bruised, and, yes, for the moment, we have been defeated," Dolan said. "But, we're used to that. So was the Founder of the Church."

When questioned about the bill several months later as the next year's legislative session got under way, he confessed to feeling "burned" by Senate Republicans who had claimed at the time that the measure did not have a chance. "Our Senate leaders, we highly appreciated them being with us all along. When they kind of assured us it didn't have much of a chance—not that we let up, but we probably would have been much more vigorous and even more physically present if we knew there was a chance," he told reporters. "We got a little stung," he added. "It could be as much our fault as anyone else's." At the same time, despite whatever political assurances Cuomo had given the four Republicans who joined his ranks, only one was sworn back into office two years later.

Locally, things were going more smoothly, but tough decisions were now being made and changes being implemented. One of the most difficult was dealing with the long-term sustainability of Catholic schools. Dolan inherited a system riddled with challenges. As parish populations shifted, demographics altered, and church membership declined, it no longer made financial sense to have parish-based schools like the one he had grown up with in Ballwin, Missouri. The schools were not failing academically, but there were too few students in too many buildings and subsidizing tuition to make the schools affordable for low-income families was bleeding the system dry. In 2010, the first full year after Dolan's arrival, the 279 Catholic schools in the archdiocese reported a $20.5 million deficit, according to published financial reports. It had to be stemmed. It was an emotional subject and required some serious leadership.

Dr. Timothy NcNiff, superintendent of the archdiocese's schools, had been brought on board by Egan to address the problem, but as he was getting to grips with the job, Dolan took over as archbishop and implementation would now take place under his leadership. Just as Dolan was working to establish credibility and likeability in his new community, McNiff presented him with his strategic plan, called

Pathways to Excellence, and explained there were close to sixty schools in serious difficulty that might have to close. It was a colossal number and the closings would undeniably be unpopular. "Most people said yes you have to close schools," McNiff explained. "But—not my school." Dolan decided the closures needed to go ahead. He said he refused to treat the schools like they were "on hospice," merely keeping them comfortable until the money died off. However, he wanted closures to take place in two waves. McNiff was asked first to highlight those schools considered unsalvageable. A list was drawn up and after more debates and discussions it was decided twenty-six elementary schools and four high schools would shutter at the end of the 2011 academic year. Parents, teachers, and students were dismayed, but placement counselors were brought in, and each child had the opportunity to be accommodated in another Catholic school, if desired. This bought the archdiocese some financial breathing space, but the next round of closures still had to be addressed.

The plan to merge seminaries was also moving ahead as planned. Although Egan had laid some of the groundwork, implementation ultimately came down to negotiations between Dolan and his two neighboring bishops: Nicholas DiMarzio of the Brooklyn diocese and William Murphy from the Diocese of Rockville Center. The idea made sound economic sense, but Murphy in particular was reticent. No bishop wanted to be presiding over the closure of a local seminary. Dolan put his diplomacy skills to work to get everyone on board. He was able to draw on the skills he garnered as a student at the North American College and as a vice rector and rector to explain why it was necessary, what worked during seminary formation, and which pitfalls must be avoided. A decision was finally announced in November 2011.

Changes were also being implemented via the Priests' Council. A committee had been established to look into an array of personnel issues, including how long a priest should remain in a parish and what the retirement age should be. The archdiocese rules stated pastors should be assigned to a parish for a six-year term with the option for having their stay renewed only once. That was no longer being enforced, and there was a handful of pastors who had been in their parishes for eighteen years or more. The committee's recommendation came back that the existing six-year rule be enforced. Dolan gave it his stamp of approval. "However difficult this can be for our priests and people, in the long run, it's good for both," he said in a column in *Catholic New York,* the archdiocesan newspaper. The news was met with discontent among several priests who were comfortable where they were. Some had looming parish anniversaries and wanted to stay for the culmination of the celebrations; others were of the attitude that if they were happy and the parishioners were happy, there was no reason to change the status quo. Despite a desire to be sensitive to his flock, Dolan was adamant. "If we're gonna do it, we're gonna stick by the rules" became the approach, a member of the Priests' Council explained. In the discussion over retirement age, it was decided eighty years old should be the universal cut-off regardless of the priest's desire or ability to continue. Once again, there were some pastors and parishioners who lamented the decision. One elderly priest who had been in his parish for eighteen years wrote to Dolan to see if a special exception could be made since, despite being eighty years old, he was still as eager and able to work as ever before. Dolan invited him to meet in person and received a rather unconventional request. "I told him I could dye my hair and challenged him to an arm wrestle," Monsignor Joseph Martin said. Dolan explained Martin was the perfect exception, but if he made one exception, he would be asked to make others. "I can understand where he's coming from," Martin later conceded. "That's his job. He's looking to the future."

In the midst of all the political wranglings, pastoral issues, and media appearances, the Dolan family always found time to visit. If he could take a week off during the summer, Dolan invited his mother or his sisters and their families to join him on a vacation. Or one of his brothers would head to New York with his wife and kids for a long weekend exploring the city. One Easter it was the turn of Patrick, Mary Theresa, and their three children. In the morning, Dolan grabbed the youngsters and beckoned them to come with him so their parents could relax. "Come downstairs, let Mom and Dad get dressed and showered, you guys come with me," he told them. When Patrick came downstairs a short while later, he panicked. There was his son Patrick, nearly three years old, sitting in the beautiful white papal chair ornamentally positioned on a platform in the dining room munching a bowl of Coco Pops. Meanwhile, his two girls were exploring every corner of the ornate reception room, touching anything they could get their hands on and scribbling in their coloring books on all the tables. Patrick immediately thought of how much everything must cost and the damage his kids could cause. "What are you worried about?" Dolan asked his youngest brother casually. "It will clean up." The kids loved being with Uncle Tim. Sometimes he took them out for early morning hot dogs or stopped past a firehouse. He especially doted on Patrick Jr., the only nephew in the family, and sat with him on the steps outside the front door of the rectory looking over Madison Avenue to watch the trucks go by. "Patrick's feet have never hit the floors of New York because he's always carrying him," Mary Theresa would tell friends. Having his family around was an antidote to the endless boardroom meetings and responsibilities of the job, but they were always mindful of not getting in his way or being an added burden to his already hectic life. They had no cause to worry. "He is in the best mood I've seen him in in three weeks because you are here," his priest-secretary, Father Jim Cruz, reassured them. Dolan loved having the people who meant the most to him in his life visit, and he always made a point of remembering important dates in their lives. When Sister Bosco was staying in his residence one time, it happened to be the anniversary of her entering the convent. She woke in the morning to find a gift at her door with a little card: "This was a great day for you, for the church and, for me," it said. "That touched me very much," Bosco said. "Those are the things that I remember about him."

Old friends and familiar faces from Dolan's life back in the Midwest randomly stopped past St. Patrick's Cathedral if they were in New York. Milwaukee attorney Matt Linn and his wife brought their son to the city to check out St. John's University and decided to attend an eight A.M. Friday Mass. They immediately spotted Dolan concluding the earlier seven A.M. service and he instantly recognized them and waved them over. "Matt, how's Oli?" Dolan said, using a nickname for his mother, Olive. "How's Paul doing?" he asked, remembering that Linn's brother had been sick. Linn told Dolan his son was considering enrolling in St. John's University, and the archbishop beckoned the teenager up to the altar and threw his arms around him, making the young man squirm slightly with embarrassment. Dolan urged him to please get in touch if he moved to New York. "I get tickets to Yankees and Mets games," he said. "I'll take you to a game." Linn's son enrolled in the actuarial science program in summer 2010. He never reached out to the archbishop and just before Thanksgiving, received an e-mail: "If you don't go back to Milwaukee for Thanksgiving, you're welcome to have it with us at the rectory," it read. The family had no idea how Dolan had tracked down the e-mail address, but Linn especially was grateful. "He's got nothing to gain from it, other than the satisfaction of being kind to someone who probably feels lonely in a city of fifteen million," he said. "He's not a perfect man but he is a tremendous example of a man of faith who wants to lead people to Christ. I don't think there's a phony bone in this guy's body."

Dolan continued to use any free time to pick up the phone and check in on old friends, call priests on their birthdays and ordination dates, or let the sick and those in need across the community know he was thinking of them, especially during car rides. He told his staff that if they ever met someone who asked if the archbishop could pray for them or a family member, to be sure to get their contact details. Without fail, he found time to phone and added their name to the index cards he flicked through during his early morning prayers. He also put them in his ever-expanding contacts book and continued to touch base regularly. During a meeting with some members of the Bronx community in his twentieth-floor office at the Catholic Center in September 2011, one of the women pulled Dolan aside quietly afterward. "Could you please pray for my son?" she asked. "He's in the hospital and having a lot of problems." Dolan had recognized the lady when she first arrived. They had met only once, a couple of months after his installation two years prior, but he recalled the encounter and their chat about where her husband's family was from in Ireland. His attention to detail was impressive and flattering. Without going into specifics, the woman said her name was Ann and her family had been going through a very difficult time. Dolan promised he would keep her son, Michael, in his prayers.

Two days later, Ann's cell phone rang shortly after seven A.M. "This is Archbishop Dolan. How's Michael?" the voice down the line asked. The woman had no idea how Dolan got her number, but the timing was impeccable, as the family had had a particularly horrific twenty-four hours. Michael had been battling drug and alcohol problems for many years and had been homeless and recently hospitalized over fears he was suicidal. Dolan listened patiently as she offloaded the full story and some of her worries and fears. "Tomorrow is the Feast of Saint Michael," he told her reassuringly. "He'll be in my prayers." Two days later, Dolan called to check in once again. And then again two weeks after that. He called the day after Christmas and the day before Easter. When Ann told her son the archbishop of New York was praying for him, he struggled to believe her until one of the phone calls arrived while they were together. Michael was finally convinced his mother was not fabricating stories and was clearly moved by the gesture. "This is one of the busiest people in the world," Ann said. "I wasn't seeking him out. This was something he did on his own. I'm just a Catholic, I'm just a Catholic mom. I'm not anybody." On January 5, 2013, Dolan called for an update once again. She told him how grateful she was for his concern and compassion, and how surprised she was he had not forgotten about her. "It's very hard to get off my prayer list," he replied. The phone calls provided immense spiritual support to Ann and her family during a deeply challenging time, strengthening her faith and commitment to Catholicism. "When you're in these situations as parents you pray, but you're so exhausted it's hard to pray. You don't know how to pray, you're just in the storm," she explained. "It's always reassuring to know there are other people praying for you so for someone of that stature to take his time . . . to reach out to offer that spiritual support, it just meant the absolute world to me."

Dolan frequently placed calls to all his family also, especially his mother, whom he touched base with at least once a week. On the evening of January 5, 2012, Shirley Dolan was inside her small two-bedroom bungalow in Washington, Missouri, when the phone rang. She picked up the receiver to hear her oldest son's voice on the line. Dolan had just been home for Christmas, his first in Missouri since moving to New York, where he'd stayed in her spare room and cooked her scrambled eggs in the morning. He had also spent time with his two sisters, who live a few streets away from their mom's house, and a couple of doors away from each other. Bob had flown in from Milwaukee with his wife and two daughters, and Patrick was only a short drive away in St. Louis, near Little Flower Church, where Dolan had spent some of his happiest years as an associate pastor. The entire family came together to celebrate, an increasingly rare occurrence given Dolan's increasingly demanding schedule. Now, just a few days after the new year, he was phoning again. Their conversation that evening began like so many others. "Hi, Mom, how you doing?" he asked, plowing straight in before moving on to ask about every other member of the family. It took ten minutes of casual banter for Shirley to realize there was a far more important reason for her son's phone call that night. A few hours earlier Dolan had received a phone call from the papal nuncio in Washington, D.C., saying Pope Benedict XVI was naming twenty-two new cardinals, and her firstborn was among them. Shirley told her son how proud he made her. "I'm proud of you, too, Mom," he replied.

The next day, the rest of the world found out the news and it was plastered across news Web sites, TV screens, and the front pages of the newspapers. Being named a cardinal was not a surprise to Dolan—it had become an inevitability as soon as he was appointed to New York— but the timing was unquestionably unexpected. Egan was still two months shy of turning eighty, the age at which he became ineligible to vote in the conclave, and it was virtually unprecedented for a successor to be elevated before the preceding cardinal in the archdiocese was aged out. But Dolan was developing an aptitude for being an exception to the rule. He had promised NBC anchor Matt Lauer he would go on the *Today* show when he heard he was getting his red hat. They had spent time together in Rome when NBC aired a feature on Dolan, and he kept his word. The show's producers were phoned the night before and, without revealing why, asked if they could make space for Dolan the next morning. They agreed and as soon as the Holy See issued the news, he made his way to the studios at Rockefeller Center to appear on air. Sitting on the sofa next to cohost Al Roker, Dolan looked ecstatic. "Are you allowed to high-five a new cardinal?" Lauer asked, and he reached his palm out to meet Dolan's. The new title also meant Dolan would be appointed to various congregations in Rome, which would require him to journey there more frequently, but the biggest honor was that it made him eligible to vote in a conclave to elect the next pope. "God willing I'm not going to have to do that for a while," Dolan said. "That's the heaviest responsibility a cardinal has." Lauer offered his congratulations and reminded viewers Dolan was a Missouri native and Cardinals fan, as they presented him with a pennant. "The only cardinal I ever really wanted to be is Stan Musial," Dolan joked. Two cherished gifts also arrived for Dolan from none other than Musial himself. One was a signed red Cardinals baseball cap with a note: "Here's a real red hat." The other, a signed baseball with the words "one cardinal to another." It was proudly placed in a cube-shaped Perspex box and positioned on a side table inside his residence for all to see.

As the news spread, the phone in Shirley's home started to ring off the hook. She received at least one hundred congratulatory calls and had to start keeping a list so she didn't forget whom to thank. Even the furnace man knew about her famous son, and when the bill arrived a little note was attached: "No charge, enjoy Rome." Nearly two dozen of Dolan's family members excitedly booked their plane tickets to Italy and began to plan their wardrobe. It would be Shirley's tenth visit to Vatican City, and she saw it as her grand finale. She was now eighty-three years old and the journey was getting to be a lot, but this was an occasion she could not miss. Like any proud mother, Shirley could also not avoid letting her mind wander to her son's chances of getting the ultimate top job one day, since cardinals who enter the conclave choose a successor from among themselves. "Anything's possible but it would be very far-fetched, I believe," she explained. "We've never had an American pope and I just can't see that happening." Then, with a twinkle in her eyes, she added mischievously, "But, they'd be wise if they did." Meanwhile, Dolan was interviewed by every New York media outlet and his appearances were burned onto a DVD and sent to his mom. He said he was "honored, humbled, and grateful" at the appointment. Excitement aside, Dolan's family also wondered how often they would now see their loved one, given the extra responsibilities, and they worried what impact the hectic new schedule could have on his health. Bob

Dolan's untimely death still played on all their minds. Dolan had been watching his weight, too. He had a nutritionist in New York who was successfully helping him shed some pounds and he had an exercise bike and elliptical machine in his home. However, the temptation of lots of good pasta in Rome was always a challenge.

As plans were set in motion for Dolan to head to Italy, there was another looming political confrontation to attend to, this time with the president of the United States. Two months earlier, Dolan had been invited to meet President Barack Obama in the White House. The sit-down had been facilitated by Vice President Joseph Biden, who was Catholic, as an opportunity for the church to air its concerns about what it perceived as attacks on religious liberty as a result of universal health care reform. For decades, the Catholic Church had been calling for sweeping legislation that would ensure everyone in the country had access to medical benefits. Now, finally, here was a president willing to champion it, but there was a major glitch. The Affordable Care Act, col-loquially known as Obamacare, called for employers to provide women access to contraception, which went against Catholic principles. Inside the Oval Office on November 8, the issue was frankly discussed. Dolan was grateful for the opportunity to air their differences, always prefer-ring to meet with his detractors and work out common ground rather than be combative. Despite being awestruck at having such a privileged audience with the president, he was firm. As head of the USCCB, Dolan explained the Catholic Church objected to a provision in the bill that said only religious institutions such as churches were exempt from pro-viding contraception to their female employees. It failed to extend that exemption to other Catholic-affiliated institutions such as schools, uni-versities, charities, or hospitals because they did not employ and serve mostly Catholics and espouse Catholic teaching to all who used their services. Dolan took exception to the government defining what consti-tuted a religious organization and asked for the exemption to be extended significantly. Obama appeared to take the concerns on board. He had worked in Catholic parishes on Chicago's South Side during his days as a community organizer and knew the valuable contribution they made to society. He said his administration did not want to jeopardize the work of the church and he took the protection of rights of conscience seriously. Dolan left the forty-five-minute meeting with no assurances but confident the president was sympathetic, if not fully supportive, of their viewpoint and they could work together. He headed to a meeting of U.S. bishops, where he relayed the details of their conversation.

Some senior White House officials had not even been aware the face-to-face was taking place, and Dolan's statements about his positive meeting with the president immediately caused upset among supporters of the current religious mandate. "It caused great confusion," one senior Obama administration official explained. "Proponents [of the HHS mandate] hadn't really weighed in politically and they came right in after the Dolan meeting." Some advisers felt the meeting was an ill-conceived idea that caused more harm than good. "I didn't think we were ready for it," an Obama insider said. "There was confusion about where we were going." There was significant pushback and political maneuvering in the proceeding weeks and the issue became a cause célèbre for women's rights groups, activists, and lobbyists. They vehemently opposed making any concessions to the Catholic Church and pressured Obama to go back on whatever assurances he had given to Dolan.

On the morning of January 20, a few weeks after Dolan had received word of his elevation to cardinal, the president got in contact again. Obama explained the so-called Health and Human Services (HHS) mandate was being announced later that day and the contraception exemption had not been extended. It would still apply only to organizations employing Catholics, serving Catholics, and espousing Catholic teaching. But nonprofit religious employers had one year to enforce the contraception coverage rule, a small concession that bought them time to adjust. "Sir, are you asking me my thoughts on this? Are you floating this to see if this will work? Or are you telling me this is your decision?" Dolan asked the president during the phone call. Obama said his mind was made up. It was deeply disappointing.

The backlash was fierce. It was an election year and Republicans were quick to brand the decision a betrayal of Catholics, a key voting block. Dolan released a statement through the USCCB saying, "In effect, the president is saying we have a year to figure out how to violate our consciences," a pithy sound bite that was picked up widely. He also went on TV to express his dismay publicly. "I left with high hopes that nothing that his administration would do would impede the good work that he admitted and acknowledged in the church and, I'm afraid I don't have those sentiments of hope now," he explained to CBS's Charlie Rose. He also admitted candidly he was skeptical to meet the president again, given how gravely he felt let down. Dolan sounded measured and open to dialogue, but unequivocal in seeing this as a battle over religious liberty, not simply contraception, and hopeful this might make the issue a rallying cry for others even if they did not share his views on birth control. "We can't have a government bureaucracy invading the privacy and the independence and autonomy and integrity that our Constitution gives to religion," he explained. As the interview ended, Rose congratulated Dolan on his imminent elevation to cardinal. "I'm kinda glad to get out of town with all this going on," Dolan quipped. He did not have to wait long for that to become a reality, as he soon embarked on a long-planned trip to the Holy Land with fifty priests from the New York archdiocese. During the eight-day pilgrimage Dolan visited some of the holiest sites in Christianity and celebrated Mass at the Church of the Holy Sepulchre, where Jesus was crucified and buried. It was a time for reflection, rejuvenation, and plenty of prayer before spending a few days back in New York, celebrating his sixty-second birthday and preparing to receive his red hat in Rome.

The day before Dolan's flight, Obama called again. In an attempt at compromise, the president explained he was now proposing that the burden of providing birth control coverage shift from employers to insurers so payments did not have to come directly from religious organizations that opposed it. The president hoped this might prevent religious organizations from feeling their morals were being compromised while still ensuring women had access to what many saw as a basic health care right. Again Dolan asked if Obama was seeking his opinion or merely informing him of the outcome, and again the president said it was the latter. The accommodation did satisfy some discontented Catholics, including Sister Carol Keehan, an Obama ally who had been closely involved in the developments as president of the Catholic Health Association. Initially Dolan said it was a good first step in the right direction, but after a few hours of more careful analysis, the United States Conference of Catholic Bishops released a strongly worded statement saying it raised "serious moral concerns." The mandate defining which religious organizations were exempt still remained far too constricting and many religious organizations were self-insured or obtained their coverage through Catholic insurance companies. Merely shifting the burden away from employers solved little. The issue was far from resolved.

Dolan landed in Rome and settled into his room at the North American College, attempting to shift his focus to the festivities ahead. Hundreds of well-wishers from the United States were ready to greet him at lunches, dinners, special Masses, and parties held in his honor. If being elevated to cardinal were a popularity contest, New York's archbishop won with ease. The Archdiocese of New York had organized a pilgrimage tour, costing about two thousand dollars per person, and 425 people signed up. There were hundreds more supporters who made independent travel arrangements, bringing his entire entourage to about one thousand people. They reflected the array of lives Dolan had touched throughout his rise up the Catholic hierarchy, from his close family to friends from high school and college. Former teachers, priests, and parishioners from St. Louis, Milwaukee, and New York also traveled to Rome. Dolan worked the crowd at each gathering oozing charisma, letting out hearty belly laughs, drawing people close to offer an embrace, and thanking them all for coming. He donned an NYPD baseball cap at one dinner and at another some of his childhood friends from Ballwin presented him with a St. Louis Cardinals jersey personalized with his name on the back. In the midst of the whirlwind of events, Sister Bosco turned to Shirley Dolan. They brought their heads together until their noses touched. "Shirley, did you ever think you'd see the day?" Bosco whispered. "Thank you for helping me bring him where he is today," Shirley responded to the second most important woman in her oldest son's life. The day before the consistory, the formal name for the ceremony elevating Dolan to cardinal, he was bestowed yet another honor. Dolan had been asked to deliver the keynote address on New Evangelization to the entire College of Cardinals, an unequivocal sign of the Holy Father's admiration and an invitation normally bestowed on only the most senior members of the Curia. It was unquestionably a privilege, but undeniably daunting. He had joked to the media he might need to put grappa in his water glass to give him the courage to get through it, and during dinner a few evenings before, he also admitted to his brother Bob his trepidation about the task ahead. First, it had to be delivered in Italian, and although Dolan was adept, his vocabulary was significantly more colloquial than the formal language typically used on these occasions. The speech was also to be followed by a question-and-answer session. "What if the pope asks a question for which I have no response?" he asked Bob. "I can hardly tell him, 'Hey, can I get back to you on that?'" He need not have worried. Positioned to the right of the pope inside New Synod Hall, Dolan delivered a rousing speech about the need to spread the church's message through joy. "The New Evangelization is accomplished with a smile, not a frown," he told the cardinals, outlining a seven-point strategy for bringing lapsed Catholics back to the church. He took the opportunity to defend the reputation of New York, refuting perceptions it is the bastion of secularism and describing it as "a very religious city," and he finished on the most sobering point of all: that receiving the cardinal's red hat was also a symbol of a willingness to shed blood as martyrs to spread the church's message. "Sorry to bring it up," he said, bringing a flash of levity to the serious topic. Dolan could not avoid apologizing for his primitive Italian, either. "When Cardinal Bertone asked me to give this address in Italian, I worried, because I speak Italian like a child," he told his audience. Then he recounted how the pastor at his first assignment after ordination at the Church of the Immacolata taught him the importance of speaking about the faith like an infant: in simple, comprehensible terms. It was a lesson that had remained relevant to him all these years, even now inside Vatican City, speaking to the most senior members of the Roman Catholic Church in the world.

The speech was a resounding success. Cardinal Egan caught Dolan's eye at the end and formed a circle with his forefinger and thumb to signify it was perfect. The Vatican press spokesman told journalists that those present had appreciated Dolan's "lively" remarks. However, the most important seal of approval came from Pope Benedict himself, who called the address "stimulating, joyful and profound." It was a turning point and propelled Dolan into the spotlight. The Italian media and influential Catholic journalists labeled him the star of the consistory and nicknamed his contagious exuberance and positivity the "Dolan effect." Whispered conversations took place among Vatican insiders that this man could be a *papabile* at the next conclave. He was undeniably one to keep an eye on.

The following morning, seated inside Saint Peter's Basilica alongside the twenty-one other archbishops also about to be elevated, Dolan looked enraptured. He was dressed in his new vibrant red choir robes and had a schoolboy beam on his face, marking him out from the rest of the pack, who looked older, some more frail and certainly more serious. He leaned back and crossed his legs in front of him, and when his time finally came, he virtually bounded up the ramp leading to Pope Benedict with a joy it was impossible to suppress. "Wow, it's official," Dolan thought to himself as his heart raced. It also flashed through his mind that he better not trip. As Benedict presented Dolan with his red hat and gold ring, designed specially for the occasion, the pontiff gave a look of genuine affection, cracked a smile, and thanked him for his New Evangelization speech. "Thank you for this," New York's newest cardinal replied. "I'm the one who is grateful." Seated in the pews, members of Dolan's family had to suppress the urge to break into loud applause. Dolan's loved ones were the first to celebrate with him back at the North American College after the ceremony. Shirley said she was simply numb after the morning's events and his brother Patrick felt speechless. The line of well-wishers looking to greet Dolan winded through the corridors of the North American College and the wait was more than an hour. He also found time for a quick word with the media, many of whom had flown over from New York for the occasion. "This hat is really for New York," he said. "I want to put it on the Empire State Building and the Statue of Liberty and the Brooklyn Bridge." When one reporter tried to ask him about the notice he'd been getting and if it was a sign he could succeed Pope Benedict one day, Dolan became suddenly uncharacteristically quiet: *"Non parlo Inglese,"* he quipped, meaning: I don't speak English.

Back in New York and down off the consistory high, Dolan was named one of the one hundred most influential people in the world in 2012 by

Time magazine, and the health care conflict raged on. The New York archdiocese became one of forty-three Catholic institutions to file a lawsuit in twelve federal courts against the HHS mandate, vehemently objecting to having to provide contraception coverage to employees and again explaining it as a worrisome attack on religious liberty. Dolan continued to protest that the mandate defining which religious organizations were exempt was so limiting it was "choking," "handcuffing," and "straight-jacketing." "When did the government get into the business of defining for us the extent of our ministry?" Dolan said on a visit back to the CBS studios, addressing host Charlie Rose. "I worry, Charlie, that members of his administration might not particularly understand our horror at the restrictive nature of this exemption that they're giving us," he continued. "That for the first time that we can remember, a bureau of the federal government seems to be radically intruding into the internal definition of what a church is. We can't seem to get that across." Attempts at negotiation continued, as did the legal proceedings.

The 2012 election campaign was reaching fever pitch across the country, and Obama was being challenged by Republican contender Mitt Romney in a contest fast becoming bitter and spiteful. The Archdiocese of New York had historically brought the two candidates together a few weeks before polling day as guests of honor at the Alfred E. Smith white-tie charity dinner, an important annual Catholic fundraiser held at the Waldorf Astoria. Barring a few exceptions, the invitation had been extended to both presidential hopefuls in an election year since 1960 and it was a night where the rivals attempted to put their differences aside and give quick-witted speeches poking fun at themselves, roasting their opponents, and mocking the political system. It was also usually the last time they shared a stage before voting began. Given the uproar over the health care bill, loud voices called for Obama to be denied a seat at this year's table. These arguments were further bolstered when the president went public with his support of same-sex marriage. Exhibiting his best diplomatic skills, Dolan explained why he was inviting Obama to the gala and laid out in detail why it was important to open up dialogue with his opponents, not shut them out. "It's better to invite than to ignore, more effective to talk together than to yell from a distance, more productive to open a door than to shut one," he wrote in a lengthy blog post two months before the dinner, directly addressing those who saw the invitation as scandalous. "That charge weighs on me, as it would on any person of faith, but especially a pastor, who longs to give good example, never bad," Dolan admitted. "So, I apologize if I have given such scandal." He asked for people's prayers for his decision and concluded with a strong appeal for some reason from detractors. "In the end, I'm encouraged by the example of Jesus, who was blistered by his critics for dining with those some considered sinners; and by the recognition that, if I only sat down with people who agreed with me, and I with them, or with those who were saints, I'd be taking all my meals alone." Not everyone was won over. The comments section of the blog had to be closed down due to the excessive volume of traffic, and Dolan said letters were flooding in by mail. Parishioners in parts of the archdiocese shared their discontent with their pastors. First Cuomo, a Catholic politician, had pushed through same-sex marriage with little resistance, and now it felt like Obama was being pandered to when he was spearheading a health care bill that ran counter to core Catholic principles. "There's a segment of the laity, probably priests too, who would say you've got to get tough with these guys," one priest from the archdiocese explained.

The recent consistory had only further heightened Dolan's profile, and he found himself constantly in high demand. Soon after Dolan arrived back from Rome, Governor Romney, a Mormon, began to court him and was granted a private meeting as part of a mission to improve his party's outreach to Catholics. The Republican Party also asked the cardinal to deliver the closing benediction prayer at their national convention in Tampa, Florida. Dolan agreed but made it clear it was a prayer, not an endorsement, and in an effort to not appear partisan or be used as a political pawn he informed the Democrats he would happily do the same at theirs. The Democratic Party extended the invitation, and Dolan accepted. Dolan was also invited back home to St. Louis by Archbishop Robert Carlson to celebrate becoming a cardinal with his hometown crowd inside the Cathedral Basilica. While there, he stopped past the wake for Lil Musial, the wife of his childhood baseball hero, Stan, who was now in his nineties. The couple had been married seventy-one years and Dolan had become good friends with the entire family. He could not help noticing how frail the man he had idolized his entire life had become. Dolan also appeared alongside comedian Stephen Colbert on the stage at Fordham University for a night discussing "humor, joy and the spiritual life." It was one of the rare times the political satirist and TV personality spoke publicly out of character about his Catholic faith. Dolan joked his way through the event, delivering impressive witty retorts to equal those of Colbert, who makes his living from comedy. He also joined Twitter in the hope of reaching a different, younger audience and used his first 140-character message to make a sporting jibe. "Hey, everybody. It's Timothy Cardinal Tebow. I mean Dolan. I'm on Twitter. And I'm live on Town Hall on SiriusXM's The Catholic Channel 129." Tebow is the NFL's popular Christian quarterback.

When the Al Smith dinner arrived in October, Dolan was in Rome attending the Synod of Bishops. To ensure he did not miss the event, he flew into New York for just a few hours, arriving on a chartered flight and leaving on the private jet belonging to Mort Zuckerman, a billionaire real estate tycoon and the owner of one of the city's two tabloid newspapers. The high-end dinner, where tables were set with silver cutlery, white tablecloths, and floral centerpieces, was a sellout that generated more than $5 million for the archdiocese. Dolan sat front and center at a long table on a stage looking out at the multitude of guests.

Obama was on his right, and Romney on his left, making the cardinal a buffer between two men who had a clear disdain for each other. He looked relaxed and waved at people he spotted in the crowd. He held his own with the two political powerhouses as he delivered his closing remarks peppered with jokes, including several that took a jab at his own waistline, one of his favorite and most reliable quips. He even playfully took aim at the pope. "Just before I left Rome this morning, Pope Benedict XVI pulled me aside and asked me to deliver a personal special message to both candidates," Dolan said. "Mr. President and Governor Romney, do you know what the Holy Father asked me to tell the two of you? Well, neither do I 'cause he said it in Latin and I don't understand a word of it." Laughs aside, Dolan's seven-minute speech ended with a more serious message alluding to the fights the church was embroiled in. He praised the United States as a country "which considers religious liberty our first and most cherished freedom," and went on to praise the founder of the evening's event, Alfred E. Smith, who looked out for the "uns" of the world. "The unemployed, the uninsured, the unwanted, the unwed mother, the innocent fragile unborn baby in her womb, the undocumented, the un-housed, the unhealthy, the unfed, the under-educated. Government, Al Smith believed, should be on the side of these uns." The room filled with applause. "But a government, he also believed, partnering with family, church, parish, neighborhood, organizations and community, never intruding or opposing since, when all is said and done, it's In God We Trust not ultimately in government or politics." Dolan's family and buddies back in St. Louis caught a recording of the night and watched in amazement, thinking: "There's the guy we grew up with." "You see so many people in his position have a different air about them or carry themselves differently," Monsignor Mike Turek, one of Dolan's oldest friends, would later recall. "He just doesn't put on those airs."

•   •   •

Now settled back into the routine of his daily New York life once again, Dolan faced the next pressing concern on the pastoral agenda: the second round of school closures. Dolan had insisted this wave be decided on a local level, with input from pastors and laypeople, as opposed to a directive from the superintendent's office. Committees were formed to give the community a say in the discussions, and they looked into the viability of different buildings. Principals of at-risk schools were told that if they could prove they were sustainable, they had the chance of a reprieve, and parents banded together to start campaigns and fund-raisers. Even when closures appeared inevitable, some fought the decision, including one school in the Bronx whose pastor deliberately ignored a whole slew of instructions designed to inform and prepare parents about how to enroll their children in a new Catholic school. "They just kind of said we're not doing that, almost like we're not going to close the school, or even acknowledge that the school is closing," one archdiocese official said. Dolan had to call the pastor in for a meeting and did not mince his words. "You're defying me, if you defy him," he said, pointing to McNiff, then laid out what the pastor needed to do to fall into line. It struck an uncharacteristically harsh tone but had the desired effect.

When the final list of the twenty-four schools to close was announced, Dolan weathered the media storm with surprising ease and without an abundance of inflammatory headlines. "We may have fewer schools, unfortunately, but the ones we got are gonna be fuller, more alive, more promising and more stable," he told reporters. When *The Wall Street Journal* asked for an op-ed on the issue, he proudly extolled the virtues of Catholic education; he reasoned this was a difficult decision but part of a national struggle, and Catholic schools still produced some of the best and brightest students, employers were always eager to hire. It was impossible to avoid upset, however. There were some in the community who felt that Dolan's skill as a leader was that he gave the impression of being open to dialogue but ultimately merely convinced people to come around to his way of thinking. McNiff was forever grateful that Dolan was able to be such a positive influence during a trying time tackling a sensitive issue. "The thing I most appreciate about Cardinal Dolan is that he's brought a smile on the face of the Catholic Church," he explained. "And in my work, going out there, that's what's needed more than anything." Dolan had given McNiff the freedom to do his job to the best of his ability, but when McNiff received criticism for bringing down the ax on a particular school, he always felt Dolan had his back. "I've caught a lot of bullets and I felt like he was there for me. People will say I'm the reason the schools closed, they say bad things about me in the press, and he will always step up and say no, you've got it wrong. That's kind of nice to know."

To secure the long-term vitality of Catholic schools, Dolan had also approved some vital reorganization of the way the system operated. It was decided schools would be divided into nine regions, doing away with the concept of parish-based schools for the first time—a hallmark of Catholic education. Each school was now answerable to a two-tier board within their geographic area that dealt with governance and fiscal management. The board was ultimately answerable to the superintendent's office but operated as its own nonprofit. The closures could not eliminate every school in the archdiocese with an annual deficit, so to stabilize funding further, each parish was also now subject to a sliding-scale tax. The majority of the cash stayed within the region but could be redistributed to areas that were harder off. The only money-generating idea Dolan resisted was the widespread sale of valuable church property. He felt it could set a dangerous precedent; these buildings were a commodity that, once lost, could never be bought back. He did, however, agree to the creation of a $40 million endowment fund that would be funded through the sale, lease, and rent generated by unused or shuttered buildings around the archdiocese. All these changes were implemented in September 2013.

• • •

Shortly after New Year's in 2013, Dolan said good-bye to a piece of his childhood when he received word Stan Musial had passed away. The Musial family invited him to St. Louis to preside over the funeral, which was to be celebrated by St. Louis archbishop Carlson. Dolan agreed without hesitation. Beautiful eulogies inside the Cathedral Basilica paid tribute to a hardworking sportsman, husband, father, and devoted Catholic, a man Dolan had admired as much for his skill on the field as for his devotion to his family and faith. Back at his pulpit in St. Patrick's Cathedral the next day, New York's cardinal could not help paying personal tribute to Musial and relayed his favorite story of spending time together. It was twelve years prior, when Dolan was still in St. Louis, and Musial had suggested they go out for breakfast together one day after Mass. "We started talking about baseball," Dolan recounted. "And I said: 'Stan, if you were playing today, what do you think you'd bat?' Remember his lifetime batting average was .331," he told the congregation. "Ahh," Musial replied. "If I were playing today with everything—with a juiced-up ball and bat and AstroTurf, I might hit .275." Dolan looked confused, and told him he was selling himself short. The Hall of Famer had shrugged: "Well, I'm eighty." "I gratefully remember Stan," Dolan said.

By now Dolan was no stranger to political battles and a second one was rearing its head against Governor Cuomo, only this time the Catholic Church intended to be better prepared. No longer would anyone assume a bill had no legislative traction the way they had during the first few months of the same-sex marriage bill, especially as the new measure being proposed posed a far greater moral threat. In his State of the State address, Cuomo outlined the Reproductive Health Act he hoped to put into effect in Albany, which sought to expand a woman's abortion rights in New York State. Catholic leaders had been given a heads-up about the contents of his speech but had no idea how prominently this issue would feature. Many felt his delivery was way over the top. "Because it's her body, it's her choice," Cuomo reiterated three times in succession in a battle cry of sorts. The bill, Cuomo and supporters argued, sought only to codify the existing *Roe v. Wade* legislation, but opponents said it expanded access to abortions and therefore served only to increase the statewide rate, which was already double the national average. Dolan wrote an open letter to Cuomo, instructing it be released to the press the minute Cuomo's address was over. In it, he came out swinging. "I am hard pressed to think of a piece of legislation that is less needed or more harmful than this one," Dolan said, expressing his great disappointment in Cuomo for pursuing the abortion bill while praising elements of his speech where they were in agreement, such as a call for gun law reforms. The Catholic lobby felt buoyed by Dolan's decisive leadership as, two years on from Cuomo's election to governor, they now knew exactly how talented a politician he was. It was imperative to dominate the dialogue from the onset. "More than ever, we got our work cut out for us in this state with the dramatically radical nature of the Reproductive Health Act," Dolan told a meeting of the Pro-Life Commission, where he welcomed hearing strategies to campaign against the bill. "We're now in a philosophical shift," he explained. "We're from a pro-choice mentality to a pro-abortion mentality. . . . Now abortion is a virtue, it's good, it's expected, it's a duty. Any restriction upon it is looked upon as evil, autocratic, oppressive, unenlightened. Any civil discussion about alternatives is looked upon as perilous." Abortion was no longer about being safe, legal, and rare, it was now "dangerous, legal, frequent," Dolan said. During the hour-and-a-half-long meeting, members of the commission presented their reports and views on how to tackle the bill, including calls for a tougher attack on Cuomo himself. "Is it possible, for example, to vote for someone who endorses infanticide? I think that's a question that has to be asked," one person present asked. "Can someone remain a Catholic in good standing and support this?" posited another. After delivering his opening remarks Dolan remained quiet, taking all the views on board. One attendee recounted frequently hearing people complain about the lack of public statement from the church regarding the legislation Cuomo championed: "The guy is Catholic, he's pushing it through. People feel like there's a silence so it gives the impression it's not serious enough." "*You* hear it a lot?" Dolan said as the room quietly chuckled. His intonation made it clear it was a complaint he listened to in abundance. There remained nearly six months before the bill faced a vote as part of the wider Women's Equality Act, but plans were well under way within the archdiocese to work out a strategy to ensure Cuomo's vision did not go according to plan this time.

Shortly before six A.M. on February 11—almost exactly one year since Dolan's consistory appointing him cardinal—the regular morning broadcasts were interrupted with a breaking news alert: There were unconfirmed reports coming from the Vatican that Pope Benedict had resigned. Zwilling was at home shaving when he heard the announcement on the radio and initially dismissed it as a false alarm. This was not the first time a rumor of this nature had circulated only to be quickly quashed. Nevertheless, he thought it prudent to phone the boss and let him know in case someone asked him about it later in the day. Dolan agreed it was most likely nothing, so after a brief chat the two men decided to give it little further thought. As Zwilling continued to get ready for work, the news reports kept coming. Then his phone start to ring. He was soon deluged by calls from journalists trying to confirm the story and it quickly became clear this was not another false alarm. The pope really had announced his resignation, an event that had not happened in nearly six hundred years.

Within the hour, Dolan was inside the *Today* show studios talking to NBC's Matt Lauer. "I find myself eager for some news. I find myself itching to read the statement," he said, clearly still processing the shocking announcement. "And I find myself kind of somber." Dolan explained he felt a special bond with Benedict. The ring on his right hand was from the pontiff, as was the large cross hanging around his neck. Of course, Benedict had also named him a cardinal and, he explained, "He's the one that appointed me to all of you as archbishop of New York." Talking in long, uninterrupted sentences, Dolan tried to wrap his head around the enormity of the situation and the fact that this meant he would shortly be voting in his very first conclave. "Boy, I've never been through this before," he said. "I'm still unpacking the red socks from a year ago when I was made a cardinal." The cameramen in the studio laughed loudly in the background. "So I'm gonna need some coaching here . . . except for prayer, I don't know what else to do. I'll await instructions with everybody else." "As a cardinal, are you allowed to vote for yourself?" Lauer asked. "No, only crazy people cannot enter the conclave," Dolan replied in jest. He ended the interview expressing his love for Benedict and the respect he had for what he saw as the ultimate act of humility. "He's winsome in his humble acknowledgment of his frailty and weakness. I think that's touched all of our hearts."

Dolan returned to his residence beside St. Patrick's Cathedral, where a cluster of reporters had now arrived also eager to hear his insights. "I don't have any insider information," he told them. "But I would presume that his esteem for the office as the successor of Saint Peter and the chief pastor of the church universal, that esteem is so high that, in all humility, he simply said I can't do it anymore." For the next two weeks, the questions were endless. There were inquiries about when the conclave would start and what the church was looking for in the next pope, as well as reports in the Italian press that Benedict's resignation was linked to a secret dossier that revealed a gay sex scandal in the Vatican. Dolan was asked to weigh in on it all, repeatedly. Of course, not a day could go by without someone asking what he thought about his own chances of becoming the first American pope, a question he always deflected with a laugh or a joke. He was finally booked on the overnight flight to Rome, which departed February 26, touching down just in time to attend the pontiff's final general audience with the people in Saint Peter's Square. It was a trip across the Atlantic Dolan had made countless times before, though this time the visit was very different. He was about to enter the Sistine Chapel to vote in a conclave. In the Catholic world, there was no bigger honor.

10

WHITE SMOKE

Inside the Sistine Chapel it was quiet. The heavy wooden doors were closed and a somber and prayerful mood had descended. After weeks of meetings, dinners, lunches, and discussions, not to mention rampant questioning by the media and endless speculation, barely a word was now being uttered. A calm, liturgical-like atmosphere consumed the 115 men in the room and the emotional energy and spiritual intensity of the moment was palpable.

Slowly, carefully, purposefully, each cardinal approached the altar to cast his vote. There, right under Michelangelo's *The Last Judgment,* the men filled out a white ballot card, trying to mask their handwriting to preserve anonymity, before holding the white paper aloft so everyone could see they were voting just once. Dolan patiently waited his turn and, finally, the moment was upon him. He was conscious of his humble Ballwin beginnings, his childhood dreams of playing ball for the St. Louis Cardinals, and when that dream slipped away, his hopes of becoming a simple parish priest. "And here I am, doing one of the most sacred awesome things that a Catholic could ever even think of doing," he thought. "Actually casting a ballot for the successor of Peter."

In Latin, Dolan pledged this was his one true vote. "I call Jesus as a witness, and he will judge me that I have elected according to my conscience," he said aloud, and dropped his vote in the beautiful copper urn. Then he turned and walked back to his seat to pray and wait. The same process was repeated 115 times that first evening inside the Sistine Chapel, with each cardinal-elector calling on the Holy Spirit to guide him as they set about picking the next pope. Back in his seat, Dolan let his mind drift to his family and loved ones: his father, who had passed away thirty-six years before; his mother in Missouri, anxiously keeping track of the conclave; his grandparents, also long deceased. "What are they thinking now, to see Tim here in the papal conclave?" he wondered. He was also filled with thoughts of the Sisters of Mercy, who taught him in grade school at Holy Infant; his neighbors in Ballwin; his classmates from Prep South and Cardinal Glennon College, who were now pastors in their own parishes. "That was with me," he would say.

Each round of voting lasted about an hour and a half. Once complete, the ballots were counted by three cardinals preassigned to act as adjudicators. The names on the cards were read aloud so everyone in the room could keep tabs and the final tally was announced. "All the time you're thinking, you're pondering, and you're watching and you're praying," Dolan said. A two-thirds majority, or seventy-seven votes, was needed to be declared pope, and after the first round of voting that first evening, the votes were far too scattered. The ballot papers were tied together with needle and thread and cast into a furnace at the far end of the room. Black smoke shot into the sky around 7:41 P.M., and the watchful crowd outside in Saint Peter's Square cheered and then quickly filtered away. Nobody expected white smoke that evening.

The cardinals returned to Casa Santa Marta for the night, where they had dinner, prayed together, and stayed up late talking about the way the afternoon had played out. That initial vote was the first time all the cardinals had showed their hand, and it was insightful to see which way the votes fell. It was later widely reported that Dolan had received a handful of votes in that first ballot, but the names were spread among far too many candidates for this to be any clear indicator of how the next day would unfold. That evening Dolan also thought about his niece Kelly. She was due to give birth that day, but he had no way of knowing if there was a new baby in the Dolan clan whom he would soon be asked to baptize. He was void of communication with the outside world and could not even hope for some fresh air: The windows of his room were nailed shut.

The following morning the voting resumed inside the Sistine Chapel. Each session started with a prayer, followed by roll call. This time there were two ballots in the morning and two ballots in the afternoon, a pattern that could continue day after day until a two-thirds majority was achieved. If a pope was chosen after any of the four rounds of voting per day, white smoke would immediately be sent up the chimney as the papers were burned. Failing that, the cardinals would wait until the end of the morning or afternoon session and burn the two ballots together.

At lunchtime black smoke again shot into the sky. Still there was no new pope. The crowd in Saint Peter's Square was now several thousand strong and lively debates were taking place about how long the voting would take. The cardinals returned to Casa Santa Marta for lunch and more discussions, but a pattern was starting to emerge. With each round, they could see the votes starting to converge.

The overriding feeling among the masses in Saint Peter's Square was that the conclave would not be decided that evening. Of course, the only people in the world who could know that with any authority were the 115 men locked inside the Sistine Chapel. However, the throngs milling around outside felt that with such an open playing field, and such an unprecedented resignation, it was surely going to take more than two days of voting to choose Pope Benedict's successor. Cardinal Joseph Ratzinger had been a clear front-runner going into the 2005 conclave and had secured enough votes on the fourth ballot, the equivalent of the first vote after lunch on the second day. This time, eight years later, it was anyone's guess. Surely this would take some time. Then suddenly, at 7:05 P.M., plumes of white smoke shot into the air. There were cheers, there were gasps, and the crowd surged forward. *"Viva il papa! Viva il papa!"* a man cried above the loud toll of the bells from Saint Peter's Basilica. "We have a pope!" another shouted. "Praise the Lord."

At that exact moment, right in the middle of Saint Peter's Square, in the company of thousands of strangers, Cardinal Dolan's youngest brother, Patrick, broke down into uncontrollable sobs. The anxiety of the past few days culminated in one moment when his world felt like it was caving in. The TV crew from St. Louis who had flown him over for the conclave was at his side. "Why are you crying?" the reporter asked. "I'm worried that my brother just became the pope," he answered. "Why does that worry you?" the reporter probed further. "Because I think I'll lose a brother."

In Milwaukee, Bob Dolan was with his family, glued to the television screen. "Am starting to freak out honestly," he replied to a text asking how he was holding up. "Hard to be so far away." In Washington, Missouri, Dolan's older sister, Debbie, walked out of Saint Francis Borgia Regional High School, where she worked as a secretary, as soon as she heard the conclave was concluding. "I have to go," she told her boss without further explanation. She called her sister, Lisa, who was on her way to the hospital to visit her daughter, Kelly, and her new baby grandson. Lisa had also just heard the news on the radio. They agreed they both needed to be with their mother instead.

Shirley Dolan had been waiting out the day with her granddaughter Shaila's family, who lived a couple of blocks from her home. The TV was tuned to the news, and their stomachs were in knots. By the time Debbie arrived, Lisa was already there with her husband and they all sat on the edge of their seats or paced the floor. Lisa cracked open a beer to calm her nerves. Four of Dolan's nieces had gathered together in St.

Louis; a fifth niece who was at college was on the phone, pining to be with the rest of her family. Kelly, in the hospital with her newborn, had been joined by her sister, Shannon, and a gaggle of nurses to watch events unfold. Dolan's four siblings were continuously texting one another. "The emotions were very high," Lisa later recalled. "Who would ever even imagine waiting to see if your brother was gonna be the pope."

The night before, Dolan's North American College pal, Father Bob Busher, had phoned Shirley to make sure she was holding up under the stress. A few hours earlier, Dolan's Prep South friend Monsignor Rich Hanneke had also phoned the family and asked if they had sorted out any security. "Security? No," they replied. They hadn't even contemplated it. He explained they might want to consider moving Shirley from the area "just in case" because of fears she would be bombarded by the media. He also suggested that they appoint a family spokesperson. A short while later, Hanneke called again. He had spoken to Archbishop Robert Carlson, who said the archdiocese would hold a press conference if Dolan was elected, and the family were invited to be part of it. Otherwise he recommended they avoid talking to the media.

If the thought of becoming pope was truly never a viable possibility in Dolan's mind, it had unquestionably suddenly become very real for his family. Even Zwilling, who had positioned himself to the side of Saint Peter's Square so he could easily get to the North American College as soon it was over, surprised himself at how nervous he felt. "My knees were shaking. My legs felt weak," he recalled. "I knew rationally it was a tremendous long shot, but there was just something. . . ."

The wait was agonizing. All eyes were on the balcony and, more precisely, the long red curtains that framed the ceiling-to-floor doors that the new pope would soon step through. Around the world, people livestreamed the news on their computers at work or were transfixed by the television screens at home broadcasting a minute-by-minute play of the unfolding events. In the square, it felt like every nation in the world was represented. Flags were being waved, camera flashes went off incessantly, and *"Viva il papa!"* continued to ring out. Occasionally someone started singing the soothing melodic hymn "Salve Regina," a prayer at the end of the rosary, and anyone who knew the words sang along in unison.

"The rain stopped. Just throwing that out there," remarked Christian Irdi, an Australian seminarian studying at the North American College. "It's been raining *all* afternoon." He was right. The weather had been horrendous all day—nonstop heavy rain of intense proportions—but as soon as the white smoke went up, the rain stopped and the umbrellas came down. Irdi was with half a dozen classmates, all buzzing from the excitement of being in Rome for a conclave. They were wide-eyed and beaming, backslapping each other, posing for pictures, and waving their giant American flag proudly in the air. *Imagine* seemed to be the word of the moment as the minutes ticked away. Imagine the celebrations at the North American College this evening if an American pope steps onto that balcony. Imagine the message it would send to the world. Imagine what was right now going through the mind of whoever it was that had been chosen as the 266th pontiff.

At approximately half past the hour, there was a sound of drums. The Swiss guards marched into view wearing blue cloaks, white ruffled collars, and helmets in a gallant display of pageantry. The Vatican and Italian national anthems played, and the crowd sang along. Still, the waiting continued and was becoming intolerable for the Dolans in their respective parts of the world. Finally, an hour after the white smoke appeared, the lights flicked on inside the room leading onto the balcony. Cheers rang out, but it still took nearly ten more agonizingly slow minutes before the curtains started to twitch, the doors opened, and French cardinal Jean-Louis Tauran, the cardinal protodeacon, stood at the lectern to announce, in Latin, *"Habemus papam."* We have a pope.

Most couldn't even catch what was being said above the chatter, cheers, and shuffling of the crowd, but those who caught the name Jorge

Bergoglio quickly relayed the news to those around them. "He's the archbishop of Buenos Aires," explained Christopher Kerzich, a third-year seminarian from Chicago studying at the North American College. "This is huge." "Obviously he's the first Latin American pope," he added, and started to reel off an impressively accurate biography of the next pope. "He's a very simple man, he's loved by the people but very intellectual. . . . I think we are in for a wild ride." As the newly named Pope Francis emerged into the night air, the crowd erupted and Dolan's family collapsed with relief. "It was the longest, most nerve-wracking couple hours of our lives," his sister Debbie said.

All the cardinals emerged in the windows to either side of Francis and looked down at the scene. Cardinal Dolan stared at nearly two hundred thousand people crammed into the square and surrounding streets. He couldn't hear what Francis was saying, he couldn't really see anything but flashes of thousands of cameras stretching all the way down Via della Conciliazione, but he soaked up the image. All those people were staring at one balcony, all celebrating the appointment of one man. And not just any man: the one Dolan and his fellow cardinals had just elected as the new spiritual father of the Catholic world.

"They don't know who the new pope is, they don't know where he's from, they don't know what language he speaks, they don't know what his theology is," Dolan said when asked to rationalize the crowd's reaction to seeing plumes of billowing white smoke. "All they know is we have a pope, and Catholics want that. He's our Holy Father. The Italians call him 'Il Papa,' which is the derivative of dad. So we all like being a family with our Holy Father and they didn't care who he was, they just knew we got a pope. And whoever walks out there, we're gonna love him and accept him."

Dolan returned to the North American College shortly after eleven P.M. to a hero's welcome. From the moment he stepped back into the college, his old home from his days as a seminarian and rector, he was eager to get upstairs to see the students. He knew the press was waiting to chat to him, and he wanted to answer their questions, but he cut a deal. "I'm gonna go up and see them? Are they up there? Then I'll come back and see ya, okay?" he told the reporters, photographers, and camera crews.

As soon as he came into view, the seminarians went wild. Several dozen of them had formed a human corridor and erupted into chants of "Car-dinal Do-lan, Car-dinal Do-lan" as he walked down their makeshift aisle, cheering like they were in the bleachers at a football game, not at one of the most respected seminary schools in the world. He beamed at the scene, genuinely touched by the spontaneous display of adoration, and disappeared briefly into the Red Room, reserved for staff and visiting cardinals. The ruckus died down outside, only to erupt again the instant the door was flung back open and Dolan came to stand in their midst once more. "This is better than the rector's conference," he laughed, his voice hoarse from the events of the past few days. He told the men he'd received word Pope Francis's installation Mass would take place at 9:30 A.M. the following Tuesday, on the Feast of Saint Joseph. "A free night in the lounge on me on Saint Joseph's night," he said, and more chants of "Do-lan, Do-lan, Do-lan" reverberated off the walls.

As promised, Dolan then headed down to the auditorium to greet the press and immediately started peppering them with questions. "Have you been up here? Or were you down in the square?" he said, looking out at the couple dozen reporters and cameramen. "I heard it rained all day?" There were some nods. "Tell me this," he said, before becoming suddenly self-aware this was not the way press conferences usually worked. "I'm asking you questions. What's going on?" He chuckled but plowed on: "Did the smoke work this time? It did work? Because that was fascinating, the furnace was in a corner of the Sistine Chapel, and we would see them put all the ballots in, but we didn't know if it was working or not because obviously we're closed off from everybody else. So it did work, it was pretty clear then, huh? The black and the white? Excellent." The crowd of tired and amused journalists nodded again, unable to get a word in sideways, but soaking up every sentence that came from his mouth.

With a raspy voice, Dolan spoke as candidly as he was able to about how it felt being a boy from Ballwin inside the Sistine Chapel. "Obviously it's my first time and I had listened to some of the veterans, some of the patriarchs, the cardinals that had participated in the past," he said. "I consider myself kind of a hard-boiled guy, but they said once you get in there you will feel the gentle breeze of the Holy Spirit, and you'll see God's grace very much at work. Not that there was thunder and lighting, or not that anybody was knocked off his horse. But you feel a beautiful sense of resignation and direction as you see things unfolding . . . and it really happened."

Dolan was back to his old self, back in his stride and eager to share everything he was able to about his time shut off from the world. The conclave had only been twenty-eight hours, but for a man who thrives on interacting with people, he gave the distinct impression that to him it had felt like many more. "And you know the great news? My niece Kelly had a baby, Charlie," he announced unprompted, his voice oozing pride as the journalists applauded. "And I didn't know it! I knew she was probably going to go in Tuesday so [it was] the first thing I asked when I got out. Father Jim was here with a picture of Charlie. That's another reason to say, if I could, 'Hallelujah.' But I can't—because it's Lent." He let out a hearty laugh once again.

Dolan described how inside the conclave, applause rang out three times that evening. Once when Cardinal Jorge Bergoglio reached seventy-seven votes and it was clear the new pontiff had been chosen. Again when the final votes were counted. And finally when he said he accepted the role and responsibility to lead the world's 1.2 billion Catholics. "You could just see a sense that this was in God's hands, even though that didn't absolve us of the responsibility and the hard work that we needed to do on a human level." Clutching a microphone in his right hand and continuously fidgeting with the thick gold cross and chain around his neck with his left, Dolan gave more fascinating insights into this most secret, age-old tradition.

He explained the pope had decided to take the name Francis as a nod to the world's poor and then entered the Room of Tears, directly off the Sistine Chapel, to robe in white vestments specially made by Gammarelli tailors, a family-run business in downtown Rome that has dressed every pope in the last century except Pius XXII. When he reentered, the attendants had brought in a special white chair and set it up on a podium where the 114 cardinals were supposed to approach him one by one to pledge their allegiance. As they tried to help Bergoglio to the seat, he looked at them. "I'll stay down here," he said. "He met each of us on our own level, which is what I want to do with you this evening." As Dolan had entered the auditorium, his staff had encouraged him to stand up on the stage to address the reporters, but he said he'd rather address them from the ground. "We just had a beautiful fraternal meal at Doma Santa Marta, where we've been staying," Dolan continued, saying the pope had jumped on the buses with the rest of them to go back to the residence instead of riding in a waiting chauffeur-driven car. And, when they went to toast their new pope at dinner, he had replied, "May God forgive you." "In other words, 'I hope you don't regret this later,'" Dolan explained, clearly already amused and impressed by the new man in white robes.

Finally, a question addressed how Dolan had captured the hearts of many Italians in the run-up to the conclave, and the fact that some of them appeared to be rooting for him for the top job. Now that it was over, did he feel a sense of relief? "I wouldn't say there's a sense of relief because, I didn't take those things seriously," he said. "I'd like to say this, especially to the New York press: I told you so!"

If there really was no sense of relief for Dolan personally, there was more than enough to go around on the part of his family. As Patrick watched the presser proudly from the side of the room, the color was back in his cheeks and the tension was gone from his shoulders. "I haven't cried that much since my dad died," he said, revealing he hadn't been able to eat for days due to a constant feeling of nausea. "Every time they listed the qualities they were looking for in the next pope, my brother ticked every box. . . . Every time I watched TV and they mentioned the front-runners his name would appear," he said.

Dolan was drained by the conclave. "It was tremendous emotional energy," he explained. "This was emotionally and spiritually very intense." Still, he spent twenty minutes talking to the reporters before peeling away for some more TV interviews and then headed up to his room to phone his mom and congratulate his niece on her baby boy. He did not get to sleep until about 2:30 A.M. "I was amazed, and I mean that, I was flabbergasted at how they had believed the rumors," Dolan said the following day. "And see I never say or said anything about it because I found them so preposterous. I said, 'Who's taking those seriously?' But, apparently they did. And they were all worried, so they were relieved, I guess. But I sure didn't take them seriously."

After a good night's sleep there was also time to think about all that had happened in the past week. He'd had some time to digest the events and was proud of their choice and hopeful for what Pope Francis's appointment would bring to the church. "He's a wonderfully simple man," Dolan said. "You heard him, he kind of comes across as shy and reserved. His voice is kind of conversational. He didn't have a big booming voice, but he's a man of confidence and poise, but that's blended with a beautiful sincerity and simplicity and humility." And amid all this excitement, Dolan was also very eager to get back to New York.

Four days later he would be back there. A few days after that he would stand again at the pulpit of St. Patrick's Cathedral, where the crowd were spilling out the rear doors and jostling for space to hear his homily. "You're gonna have to get used to me telling lots of stories about the conclave, everybody," he said before relaying a short tale about the very first day of the General Congregations. He was back to his board-room meetings and strategizing how to combat Governor Cuomo's state law seeking to amend abortion rights, which would be put to a vote in June. The Supreme Court was also deliberating the constitution-ality of the Defense of Marriage Act (DOMA), which denied same-sex couples legally married under state laws the right to claim any federal benefits. On July 1, the Archdiocese of Milwaukee was releasing nearly six thousand pages of documents about the sex abuse crisis as part of the ongoing legal proceedings in bankruptcy court. They included corre-spondence detailing Dolan's handling of the scandal and documenta-tion he sought to protect church assets from sex abuse victims seeking compensation by moving $57 million set aside for the upkeep of ceme-teries into a trust. Locally, difficult decisions lay ahead about plans to merge and close parishes. Finally, there was a new baby in the Dolan family that needed to be baptized.

For now, Easter Sunday was around the corner, marking exactly four years since Dolan's final Mass in Milwaukee. Four years that had thrown him into the media spotlight, made him a nationwide and, ar-guably, global name, a cardinal, a *papabile,* and one of an elite small group of men forever bonded together through a unique oath of secrecy about what went on inside the conclave.

EPILOGUE

Pope Francis's papacy began with the simplest of greetings to the crowds packed shoulder to shoulder in Saint Peter's Square: *"Buona sera."* It could not have been a more fitting indication of the down-to-earth style he would adopt as the world's new Catholic leader.

Within days, Francis had captured people's imaginations and affections with his humble acts, such as heading to the guesthouse where he had stayed pre-conclave to pick up his bags and pay his own bill, or personally calling his newspaper vendor in Buenos Aires to cancel his subscription. As he continued to reject many of the trappings associated with being clad in white, including choosing not to move into the papal apartments or spend his summer in the luxurious Castel Gandolfo, the world became increasingly enchanted by him.

Since his election on March 13, 2013, Francis's profile has continued to soar. By year-end he was named *Time* magazine's person of the year, and in those nine and a half months, more than 6.6 million people attended his events at the Vatican. By comparison, his predecessor, Pope Benedict XVI, attracted only 2.3 million visitors during all of 2012.

Francis has made headlines because of more than just his humility. He has adopted a less judgmental, condemning tone about contentious moral issues, such as the church's attitude to homosexuality. In addition, he has urged priests and bishops to refocus their attention away from so-called "pelvic issues" and more toward the poor. "If a person is gay and seeks God and has good will, who am I to judge?" he told reporters on a flight back from Brazil after World Youth Day in July. The quote made news around the world, and some pundits questioned whether the former archbishop of Buenos Aires was taking Catholicism in a fresh direction.

Dolan rejects the idea that the church's fundamental teachings have changed under Francis. The pontiff retains a deeply conservative stance on these core issues of conscience, and he is not calling for a reexamination of any fundamental Catholic values. What has changed, however, is the church's tone and approach. And, crucially, the wider world's willingness to listen. "What he's done is successfully broken the caricature that the church is this naysaying, crabby, negative, Thou-Shalt-Not type of church," Dolan said. "I've known, and I would like to think most Catholics know, that caricature was inaccurate. And Lord knows our recent popes haven't been that way, but the caricature was still there."

Still, it begs the question of how Cardinal Dolan now sees his future in the Catholic Church. Pelvic issues have, after all, dominated much of the latter part of his career, especially since arriving at St. Patrick's Cathedral. He fought same-sex marriage in New York and Milwaukee, stood up to President Obama about contraception provisions in his Affordable Care Act, and continues to oppose abortion vehemently. Dolan will argue it's the media and wider world that is hung up on these topics, not him or the church. "The people will say to me: 'Do you think Francis is right that you've been obsessed with sex and all?'" he said. "No, I think *you* are. I never talk about it. The only time I talk about it is when you ask me. . . . You didn't ask me on the program and we spoke about Syria." But is this change in emphasis from Francis a sign the United States bishops have been tackling these cultural wars the wrong way?

Dolan does not believe he would be expected to take a different stance on social issues under Francis, but he is in favor of U.S. bishops taking a look at their style and strategy. In November, he was quoted as saying he felt the church was "out-marketed" by the same-sex marriage lobby. So he welcomes Francis's shift in focus. "We start by showing the people our heart, we start by extending love and mercy and invitation and welcome to people. That's where you start," Dolan said. "Once they get captivated then they'll say what did [Jesus Christ] teach? What are his expectations? What changes in my life would he expect me to make?" Dolan said the church will continue to preach that couples should not live together before marriage or have sex out of wedlock, that abortion is a sin, that homosexual acts are immoral, and that marriage should be reserved for a man and woman. "But what [Pope Francis is] saying is don't start there," he explained. "Make sure you put first things first. Make sure you start with the heart and go to the soul and then you can go to the mind as to what we believe. And then you can go to the way we act."

Dolan has long tried to make the point that he is not "anti anybody" but rather pro traditional marriage; he's against homosexual acts rather than homosexual people. He now seems to hold out hope that Francis could help ensure that message gets through with a positive, rather than a negative, spin. During our interview, he recounted a recent encounter with a man who asked him, " 'Why do you pre-judge us gays, and why do you dislike us?' I said, 'Well, why are you prejudging me and why do you dislike me?' I'm not doing that to you, and if you think I am, I'm sure sorry. But now you're doing it to me. And he just sort of said, 'Oh, I hadn't thought of it that way.' We ended up having a decent conversation. . . . I've done that even before Pope Francis," Dolan added. "But he's almost said: 'Good strategy, good way to go.' "

Dolan believes Francis's real skill is that people see him as someone approachable, loveable, gracious, and nonjudgmental. He has become the world's parish priest, and as that reputation grows, he will be able to build trust. "What they're really saying is this man is like Christ," Dolan said. "And I found Benedict and John Paul to be that way, too, but how successful that he's shattered caricatures, and I'm saying, 'Thank you,' 'cause we've been trying to do that for a long, long time."

Every pope leaves a fingerprint on the church. To Dolan, John Paul II's was his emphasis on the soul. As pontiff he showed the importance of being deeply in love with Jesus Christ and talking to him every day in prayer. Benedict XVI's was an emphasis on the mind. He taught Dolan that thinking is good, reflection is good, study is good. "And now Francis is saying the heart, the heart, the heart," Dolan explained. "Lead with the heart as Jesus did. And don't be afraid to make a mistake, even if it results in getting hurt."

Dolan now wakes up every morning with a sense of awe and restlessness. "I'm thinking, I wonder what he said today that will cause me to think?" he explained. The new pope has prompted Dolan to examine his conscience and his actions in a way he never did under the previous two pontiffs. "That would be new," Dolan explained. "Although I learned so much from John Paul and Benedict, they would [teach me] more as I would read what they wrote. With Francis, it's almost as I watch him. . . . It's little practical things."

Dolan said he sees how Francis knows his duty is to be available. "His own schedule, his own convenience, his own needs always come second," he said. That example has made Dolan linger around even longer at functions to meet people, even if he's exhausted at the end of a long day and his aides have quietly pointed out the direction of the exit. He now gives more consideration to whether he should accept an invitation from a group he might previously have been at moral loggerheads with. Plus, he now thinks twice about letting his priest-secretary Father Cruz grab his briefcase for him as he exits his car. "I'd like to think that he has only affirmed some of the things that I consider important in my own pastorate," Dolan added. "Being with people, especially showing solicitude for the sick and the poor, wanting to welcome people and meet them and listen to them and talk to them. So one thing he's affirmed some of the values that I've tried to pursue as a priest, and as a bishop, but he serves as a good examination of conscience."

There were early indications this was the kind of man they had elected inside the Sistine Chapel. Francis did not step onto the podium to greet the cardinals but wanted to meet them on their own level. He did not climb into the chauffeur-driven limo to return to Casa Santa Marta but hopped on the bus instead. During the General Congregations before the conclave, the cardinals spoke incessantly about the need for a pope with a heart. "[We were looking for] an extraordinary compassionate, tender, and pastoral man who had great experience in governing and who himself was just a good pastor and a good bishop, and he obviously listened to that," Dolan said. He says Pope Francis has proven to be "even better than I thought."

"I think our hunch that this kind of pope would be very effective for the spread of the gospel has come true because it's working, isn't it? All of a sudden the world is very interested and very attentive." The beauty, Dolan says, is it's all genuine and unprompted with Francis. "None of those things that people are favorably commenting upon he would have had to think twice about, or paused and say, 'Oh, I know, I'll do that.' He just does it naturally and spontaneously. He doesn't need any marketer, he's just so spontaneous."

For Dolan's part, he feels the so-called "Francis Effect" is a vindication of the type of priest he has always tried to be. He's never been one for airs and graces, he preaches in plain terms, he tries to make himself accessible and open to dialogue, and he exudes a natural joy. "It is affirming a pastoral strategy that I think most priests and bishops have said for a long time, this is the way it should be, and this is the way it should work," Dolan explained. "Francis is almost putting the Good

Housekeeping Seal of approval on it. He says, 'You bet that's my strategy,' as well, and now it does not become risky or avant-garde to do that."

"There's a simplicity now, there's a sincerity, I like it very much," he added. "It's hard for me to say 'cause it sounds like I'm bragging, which I have no right to. It's almost saying to me, 'Hey, your gut has been right about all this.' . . . I think most priests and bishops have done that. We're all smiling and saying this is a great big atta boy."

As perceptions of the man at the top of the church have altered, there has been a noticeable trickle-down positive effect. Every time Dolan takes a walk he's now thanked for his role in voting for Francis. "You did a good job," people tell him. "We're glad you didn't win 'cause we like the guy we got," others have said. Looking into the future, Dolan feels Francis's real asset will be as an effective teacher. Once he has earned people's respect and trust, Dolan hopes he will be able to tackle some of the harder issues and bring people back to the gospel.

"You know how when you look back at teachers that you had, you know the teachers that were good and effective were not only those who knew their stuff, but a teacher who first intrigued you, and captivated you, and got you so interested, and built up such a bond of trust that you wanted to learn lest you disappoint the teacher. And you began to say, 'I like him.' Then, once a good teacher has got that, they begin to challenge you.

"So I think Pope Francis is shrewd," Dolan said. "And a good teacher who knows: I want to love people, I want to show them my heart, I want to embrace them. And when the trust is there, when the caricature is gone, when the perceptions have shattered, then I can speak to them. And I think he will be very good that way."

BIBLIOGRAPHY

Allen, John L. Jr. *A People of Hope: Archbishop Timothy Dolan in Conversation with John L. Allen Jr.* New York: Image Books, 2011.

Berry, Jason. *Lead Us Not into Temptation: Catholic Priests and the Sexual Abuse of Children.* Champaign: University of Illinois Press, 2000.

D'Antonio, Michael. *Mortal Sins: Sex, Crime, and the Era of Catholic Scandal.* New York: St. Martin's Press, 2013.

Dolan, Bob. *Life Lessons, From My Life with My Brother Timothy Cardinal Dolan.* Phoenix, AZ: Tau Publishing, 2012.

Dolan, Timothy Michael. *Some Seed Fell on Good Ground: The Life of Edwin V. O'Hara.* Washington, D.C.: The Catholic University of America Press; reprint edition 2012.

Dolan, Timothy Michael. *Priests for the Third Millenium.* Huntington, IN: Our Sunday Visitor, 2009.

The Investigative Staff of *The Boston Globe*. *Betrayal: The Crisis in the Catholic Church*. Boston: Back Bay Books, 2003.

Murphy, Brian. *The New Men*. New York: Riverhead Books, 1998.

Vecsey, George. *Stan Musial: An American Life*. ESPN Books, reprint edition 2012.

Weakland, O.S.B., Rembert G. *A Pilgrim in a Pilgrim Church: Memoirs of a Catholic Archbishop*. Grand Rapids, MI: Wm B. Eerdmans Publishing Co., 2009.

ACKNOWLEDGMENTS

My friends have always been one of my great sources of joy, and through-out this project they were also a truly invaluable source of support—and sanity. I was fortunate to be able to turn to an array of incredibly talented people for advice, and cannot thank you all enough. Even though I will now attempt to do exactly that.

First and foremost, my unfailing thanks must go to Cardinal Timothy Dolan himself for his openness and accessibility. This book would be a fraction of what is without him. I will always be grateful for the time he set aside to meet with me despite an incredibly demanding schedule, and I feel honored to have been given access and insight into the world of such a towering and influential figure. Also huge thanks to his director of communications, Joe Zwilling. He answered my calls and e-mails, helped me fact-check, and surely fielded countless inquiries from people wondering who I was, and if they should respond to my interview requests. My sincere thanks to the entire Dolan family also. I am well aware that having a well-known son, brother, uncle, or nephew was not their choosing, so I truly appreciate their generosity of time and willingness to talk. Bob Dolan especially fielded a colossal number of my questions with incredible patience, and Patrick and his wife, Mary T, were always an e-mail or phone call away and willing to point me in the right direction. That sentiment truly extends to the dozens and dozens of Cardinal Dolan's friends and fellow priests who shared their recollections, especially Sister Bosco in Ireland, Sister Rosario in Missouri, Jerry Topczewski at the Archdiocese of Milwaukee, and Monsignor Mike Turek in St. Louis, Missouri. Thank you all so much.

Now to my own friends and family. First, my mother for being the first person I trusted to read an early draft and for understanding when I fell off the radar for the best part of a year. Also my brother for picking up the slack on sibling responsibilities. Carrie Melago for casting her astute editor's eye over the manuscript, which helped me to focus my writing and make key improvements as the deadline approached. Also Larianna Evania for her thoughtful and insightful critique, not to mention her patience in rereading edits of passages I was grappling with. And Rich Schapiro, for being the kind of life coach no money can buy. They encouraged me, listened to me, but most of all provided criticism and advice that I trusted explicitly.

My gratitude also to Michael Daly, who helped me immeasurably by introducing me to his agent when this was no more than a kernel of an idea. And Katie Nelson for proofreading my book proposal when this all felt like a pipe dream. Also David Pexton and Julia Xanthos for their expert photo skills; Craig Warga, Rob Bennett, Sam Peters, and Tim Kelly for some fabulous pep talks; and of course Isaiah King, Christine Miller, and Joshua Watson, who always had absolute faith in my ability to complete this project. My life would be so less rich without you all.

Last but of crucial importance, thanks to my editor at St. Martin's Press, Michael Flamini, whose guidance helped turn this manuscript into something I can be proud of, and associate editor Vicki Lame. Also, my agent, Robert Guinsler at Sterling Lord, who helped me turn a nugget of an idea into a real, tangible book on store shelves. I'm still not quite sure how all this happened, but am so incredibly grateful that it did.

Thank you all.

INDEX